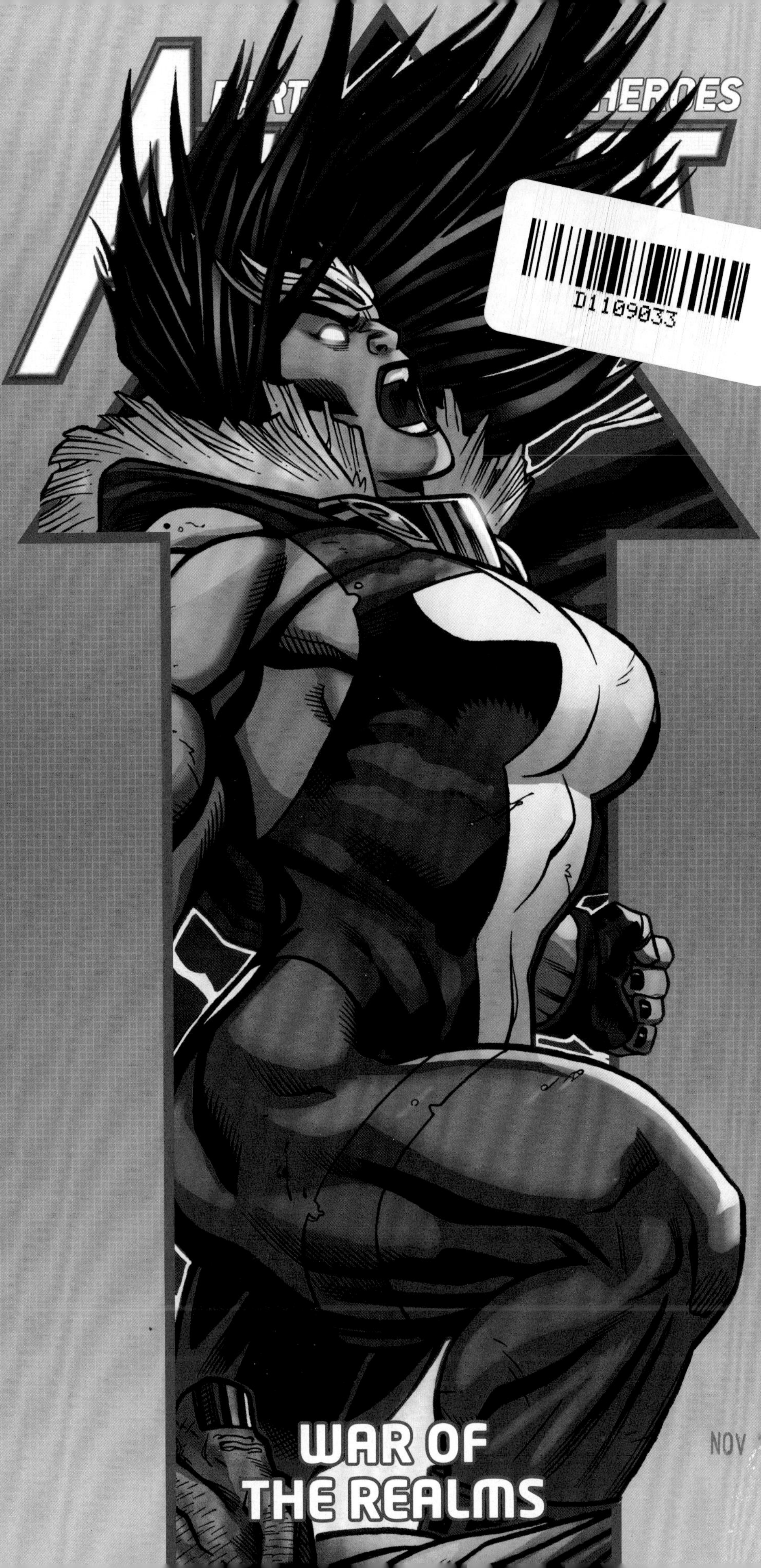
HEROES
WAR OF
THE REALMS

ON A DAY UNLIKE ANY OTHER, A DARK CELESTIAL INVASION LED IRON MAN,
THOR AND CAPTAIN AMERICA TO RE-FORM THE AVENGERS, ADDING BLACK PANTHER,
CAPTAIN MARVEL, SHE-HULK AND GHOST RIDER TO THEIR RANKS.

THE AVENGERS HAVE BEEN STRUGGLING TO KEEP THE PEACE BETWEEN
SEVERAL AGGRESSIVE FACTIONS, INCLUDING RUSSIA'S WINTER GUARD AND NAMOR'S
DEFENDERS OF THE DEEP. BUT THE U.S. GOVERNMENT'S RESPONSE TO AN AVENGERS
TEAM THAT WON'T FALL IN LINE MAY BE ABOUT TO UPSET THAT DELICATE BALANCE.
ENTER AGENT COULSON'S SQUADRON SUPREME OF AMERICA, JUST IN TIME
FOR THE TEN REALMS TO BREAK INTO ALL-OUT WAR!

AVENGERS BY JASON AARON VOL. 4: WAR OF THE REALMS. Contains material originally published in magazine form as AVENGERS (2018) #18-21 and FREE COMIC BOOK DAY 2019 (AVENGERS/SAVAGE AVENGERS) #1. First printing 2019. ISBN 978-1-302-91462-2. Published by MARVEL WORLDWIDE, INC., a subsidiary of MARVEL ENTERTAINMENT, LLC. OFFICE OF PUBLICATION: 135 West 50th Street, New York, NY 10020. © 2019 MARVEL No similarity between any of the names, characters, persons, and/or institutions in this magazine with those of any living or dead person or institution is intended, and any such similarity which may exist is purely coincidental. **Printed in Canada.** DAN BUCKLEY, President, Marvel Entertainment; JOHN NEE, Publisher; JOE QUESADA, Chief Creative Officer; TOM BREVOORT, SVP of Publishing; DAVID BOGART, Associate Publisher & SVP of Talent Affairs; DAVID GABRIEL, VP of Print & Digital Publishing; JEFF YOUNGQUIST, VP of Production & Special Projects; DAN CARR, Executive Director of Publishing Technology; ALEX MORALES, Director of Publishing Operations; DAN EDINGTON, Managing Editor; SUSAN CRESPI, Production Manager; STAN LEE, Chairman Emeritus. For information regarding advertising in Marvel Comics or on Marvel.com, please contact Vit DeBellis, Custom Solutions & Integrated Advertising Manager, at vdebellis@marvel.com. For Marvel subscription inquiries, please call 888-511-5480. **Manufactured between 10/4/2019 and 11/5/2019 by SOLISCO PRINTERS, SCOTT, QC, CANADA.**

10 9 8 7 6 5 4 3 2 1

EARTH'S MIGHTIEST HEROES
THE AVENGERS
WAR OF THE REALMS

JASON AARON
WRITER

AVENGERS #18-20

ED McGUINNESS
ARTIST

MARK MORALES WITH **ED McGUINNES** (#20)
INKERS

JUSTIN PONSOR (#18-19), **ERICK ARCINIEGA** (#19) & **JASON KEITH** (#20)
COLOR ARTISTS

VC's CORY PETIT
LETTERER

ED McGUINNESS & **VAL STAPLES**
COVER ART

AVENGERS #21

JASON MASTERS
ARTIST

JASON KEITH
COLOR ARTIST

VC's JOE CARAMAGNA
LETTERER

STEFANO CASELLI & **FRANK MARTIN**
COVER ART

FREE COMIC BOOK DAY 2019

STEFANO CASELLI
ARTIST

ERICK ARCINIEGA
COLOR ARTIST

VC's CORY PETIT
LETTERER

ED McGUINNESS & **VAL STAPLES**
COVER ART

SHANNON ANDREWS BALLESTEROS
ASSISTANT EDITOR

ALANNA SMITH
ASSOCIATE EDITOR

TOM BREVOORT
EDITOR

AVENGERS CREATED BY **STAN LEE** & **JACK KIRBY**

COLLECTION EDITOR **JENNIFER GRÜNWALD**
ASSISTANT EDITOR **CAITLIN O'CONNELL**
ASSOCIATE MANAGING EDITOR **KATERI WOODY**
EDITOR, SPECIAL PROJECTS **MARK D. BEAZLEY**
VP PRODUCTION & SPECIAL PROJECTS **JEFF YOUNGQUIST**
BOOK DESIGNERS **ADAM DEL RE**

SVP PRINT, SALES & MARKETING **DAVID GABRIEL**
DIRECTOR, LICENSED PUBLISHING **SVEN LARSEN**
EDITOR IN CHIEF **C.B. CEBULSKI**
CHIEF CREATIVE OFFICER **JOE QUESADA**
PRESIDENT **DAN BUCKLEY**
EXECUTIVE PRODUCER **ALAN FINE**

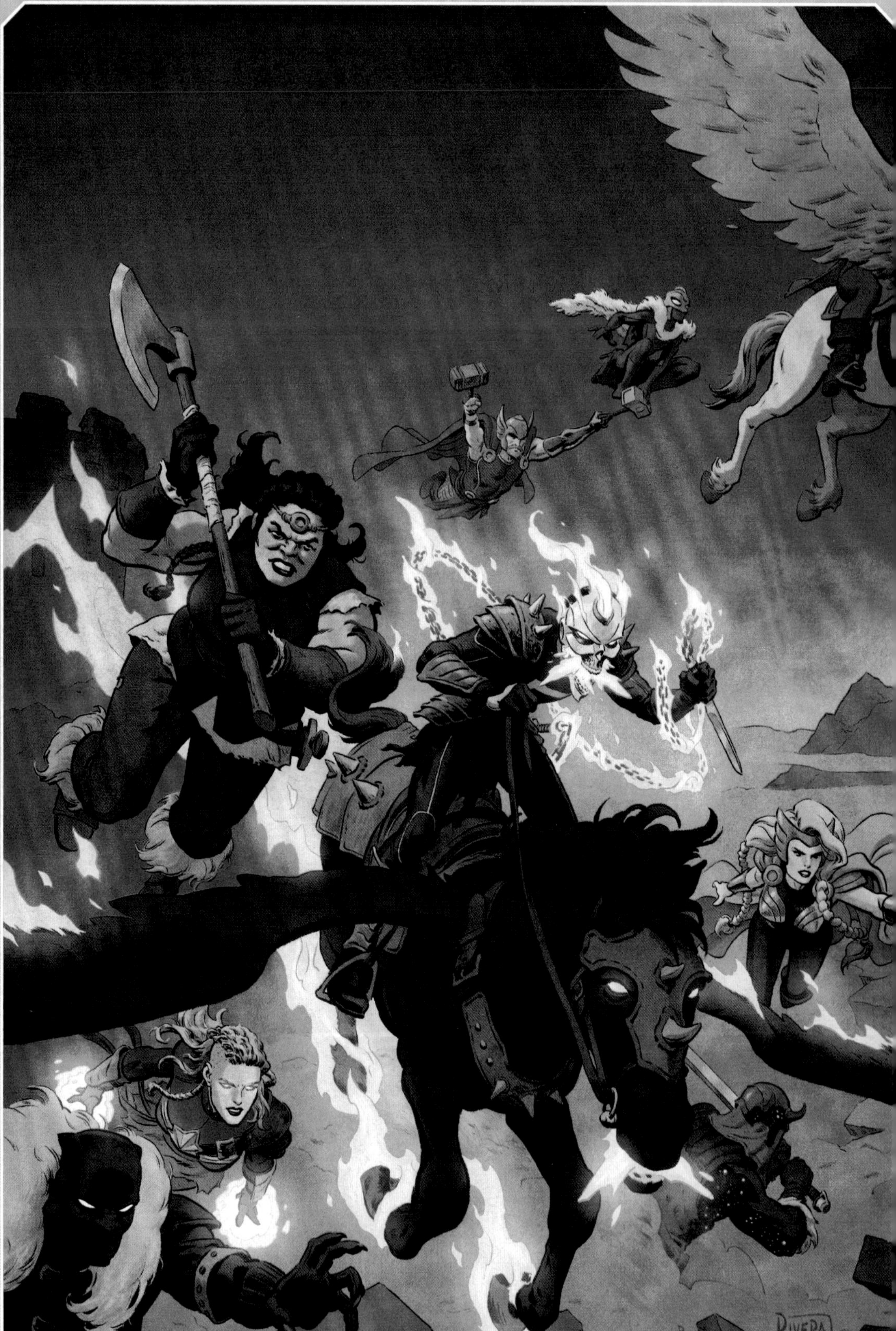
RIVERA

PAOLO RIVERA
18 ASGARDIAN VARIANT

18 CRISIS ON TEN REALMS

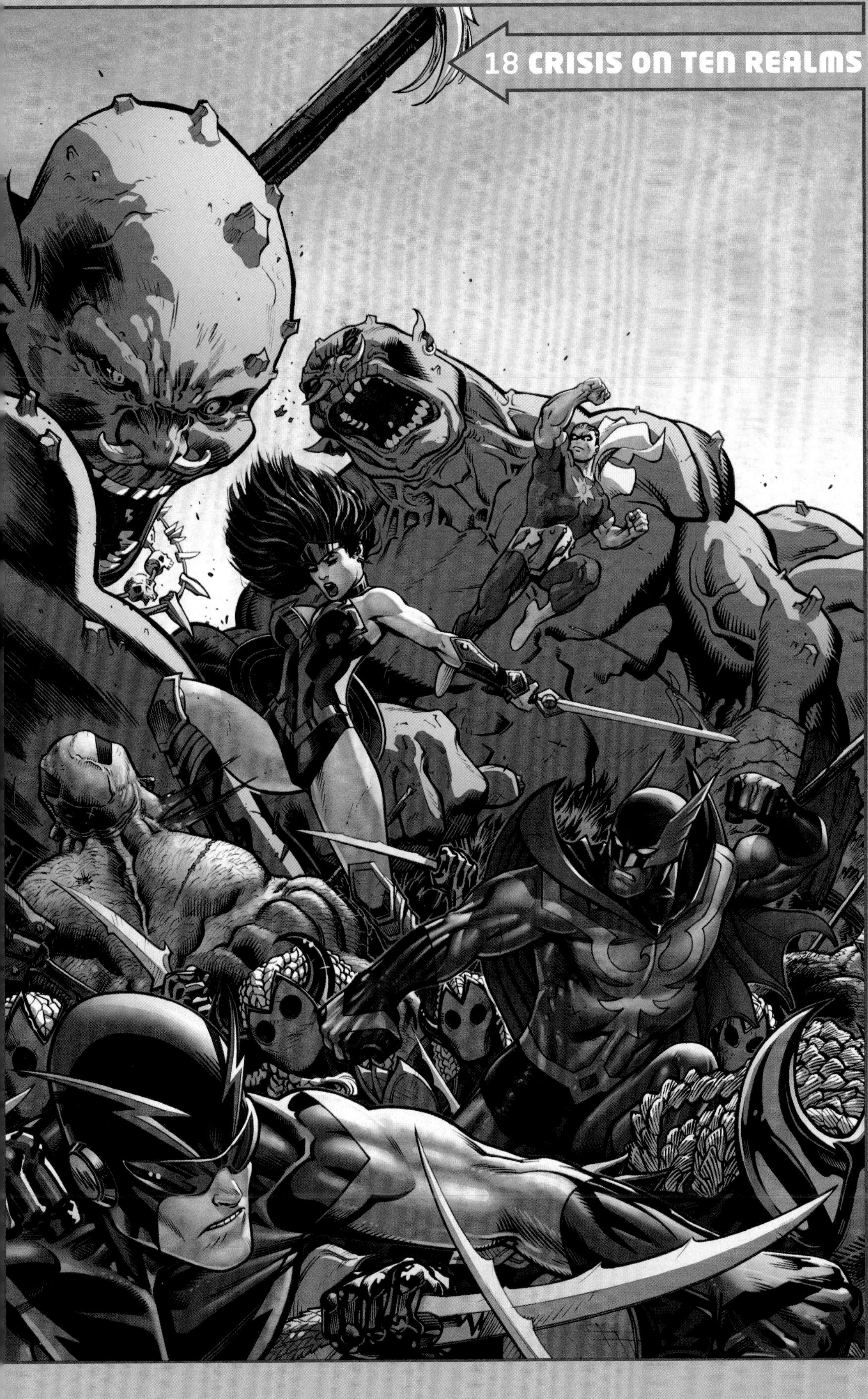

KENSINGTON, MARYLAND.

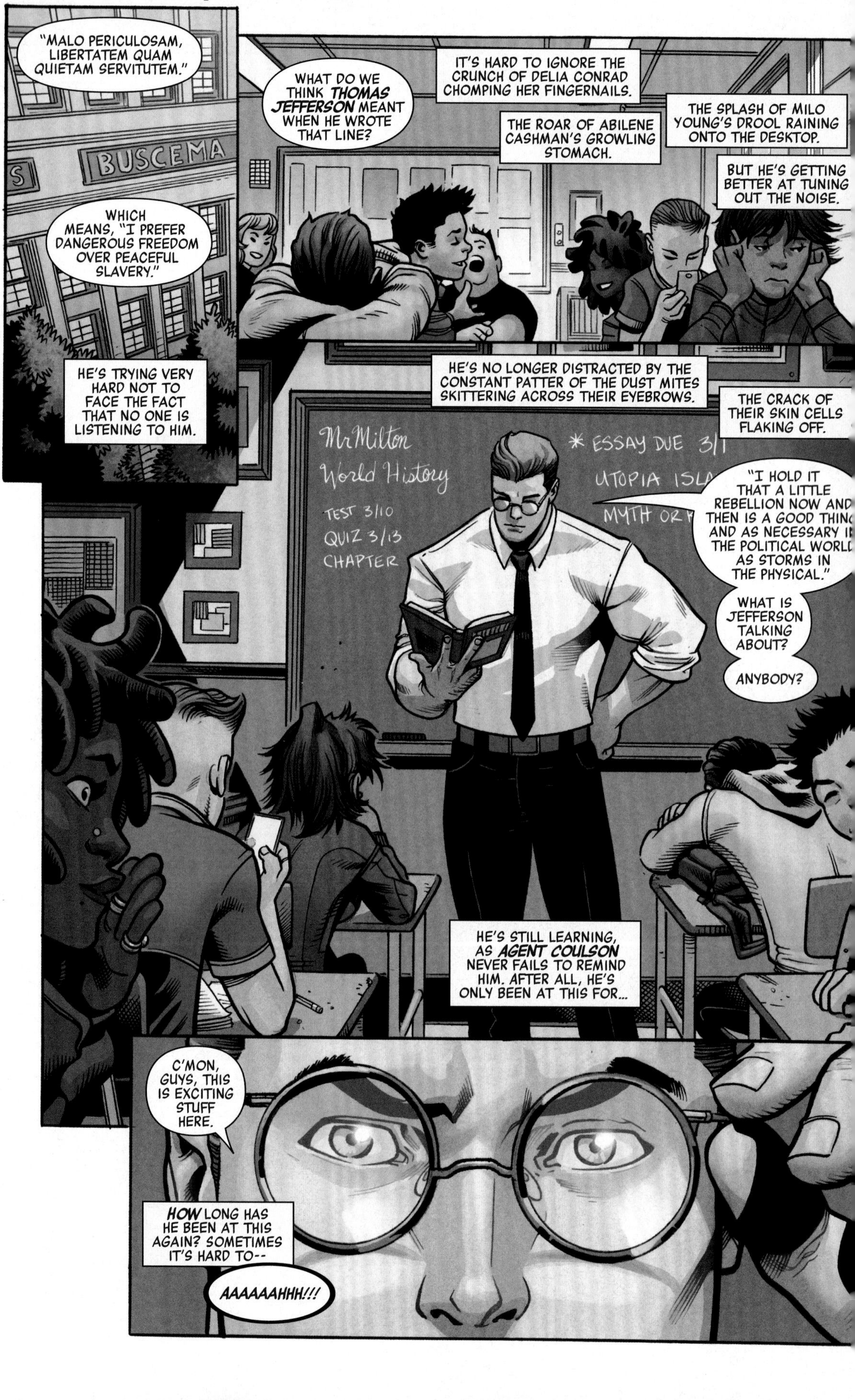

"MALO PERICULOSAM, LIBERTATEM QUAM QUIETAM SERVITUTEM."
BUSCEMA
WHICH MEANS, "I PREFER DANGEROUS FREEDOM OVER PEACEFUL SLAVERY."
HE'S TRYING VERY HARD NOT TO FACE THE FACT THAT NO ONE IS LISTENING TO HIM.
WHAT DO WE THINK THOMAS JEFFERSON MEANT WHEN HE WROTE THAT LINE?
IT'S HARD TO IGNORE THE CRUNCH OF DELIA CONRAD CHOMPING HER FINGERNAILS.
THE ROAR OF ABILENE CASHMAN'S GROWLING STOMACH.
THE SPLASH OF MILO YOUNG'S DROOL RAINING ONTO THE DESKTOP.
BUT HE'S GETTING BETTER AT TUNING OUT THE NOISE.
HE'S NO LONGER DISTRACTED BY THE CONSTANT PATTER OF THE DUST MITES SKITTERING ACROSS THEIR EYEBROWS.
THE CRACK OF THEIR SKIN CELLS FLAKING OFF.
Mr Milton
World History
TEST 3/10
QUIZ 3/13
CHAPTER
* ESSAY DUE 3/1
"I HOLD IT THAT A LITTLE REBELLION NOW AND THEN IS A GOOD THIN AND AS NECESSARY I THE POLITICAL WORLD AS STORMS IN THE PHYSICAL."
WHAT IS JEFFERSON TALKING ABOUT?
ANYBODY?
HE'S STILL LEARNING, AS AGENT COULSON NEVER FAILS TO REMIND HIM. AFTER ALL, HE'S ONLY BEEN AT THIS FOR...
C'MON, GUYS, THIS IS EXCITING STUFF HERE.
HOW LONG HAS HE BEEN AT THIS AGAIN? SOMETIMES IT'S HARD TO--
AAAAAAHHH!!!

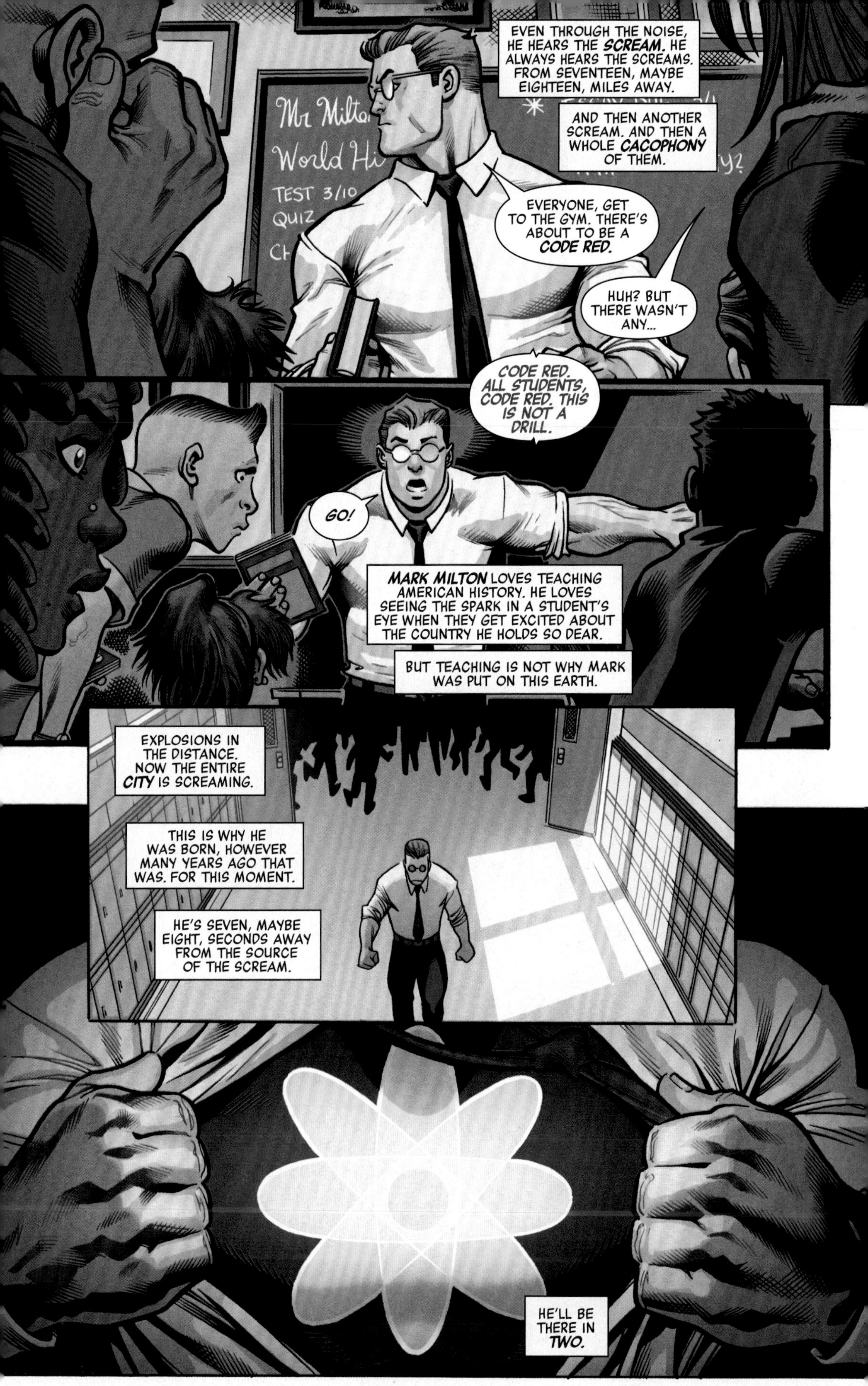

EVEN THROUGH THE NOISE, HE HEARS THE SCREAM. HE ALWAYS HEARS THE SCREAMS. FROM SEVENTEEN, MAYBE EIGHTEEN, MILES AWAY.
AND THEN ANOTHER SCREAM. AND THEN A WHOLE CACOPHONY OF THEM.
Mr Milto
World Hi
TEST 3/10
QUIZ
EVERYONE, GET TO THE GYM. THERE'S ABOUT TO BE A CODE RED.
HUH? BUT THERE WASN'T ANY...
CODE RED. ALL STUDENTS, CODE RED. THIS IS NOT A DRILL.
GO!
MARK MILTON LOVES TEACHING AMERICAN HISTORY. HE LOVES SEEING THE SPARK IN A STUDENT'S EYE WHEN THEY GET EXCITED ABOUT THE COUNTRY HE HOLDS SO DEAR.
BUT TEACHING IS NOT WHY MARK WAS PUT ON THIS EARTH.
EXPLOSIONS IN THE DISTANCE. NOW THE ENTIRE CITY IS SCREAMING.
THIS IS WHY HE WAS BORN, HOWEVER MANY YEARS AGO THAT WAS. FOR THIS MOMENT.
HE'S SEVEN, MAYBE EIGHT, SECONDS AWAY FROM THE SOURCE OF THE SCREAM.
HE'LL BE THERE IN TWO.

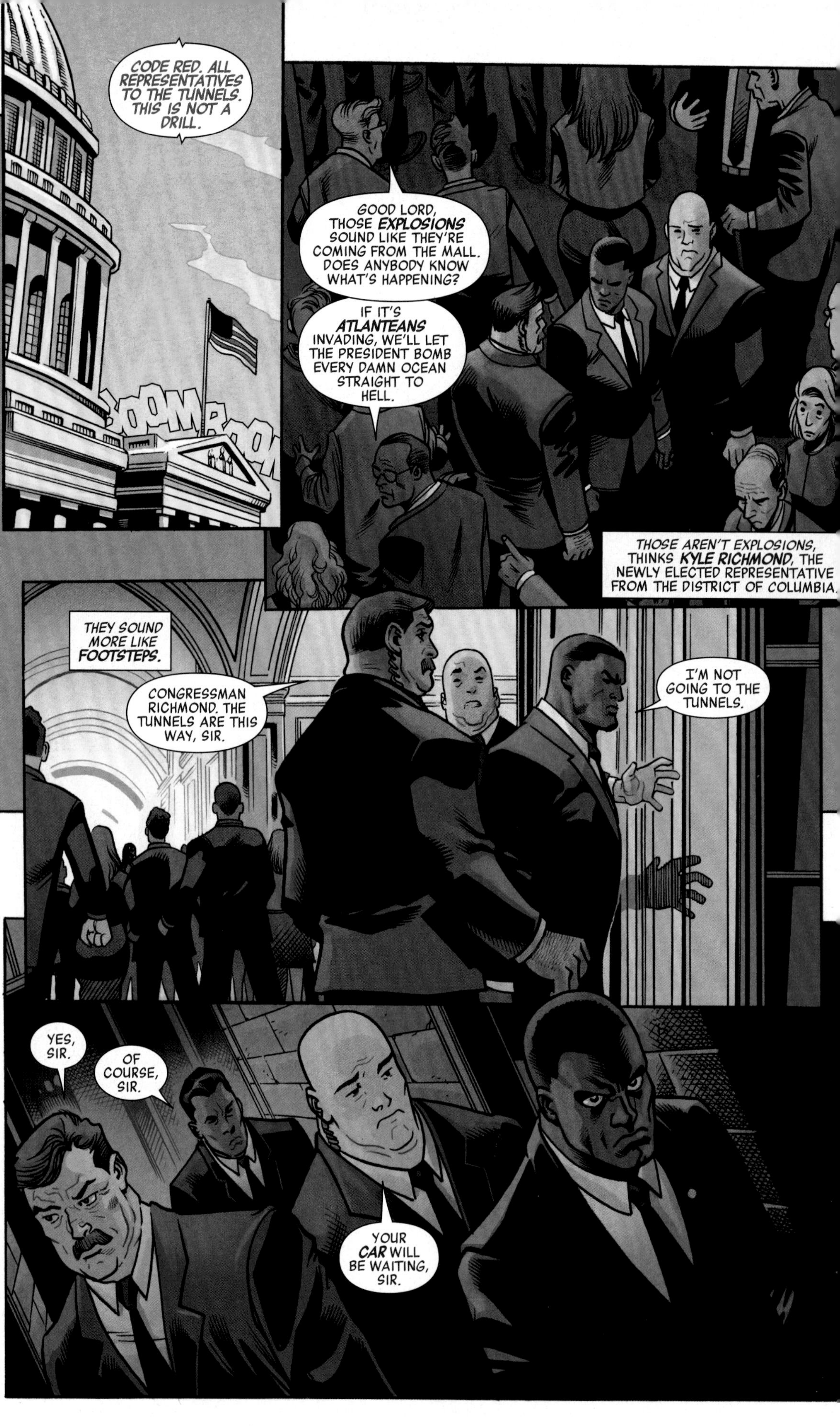
CODE RED. ALL REPRESENTATIVES TO THE TUNNELS. THIS IS NOT A DRILL.
BOOM BOOM
GOOD LORD, THOSE EXPLOSIONS SOUND LIKE THEY'RE COMING FROM THE MALL. DOES ANYBODY KNOW WHAT'S HAPPENING?
IF IT'S ATLANTEANS INVADING, WE'LL LET THE PRESIDENT BOMB EVERY DAMN OCEAN STRAIGHT TO HELL.
THOSE AREN'T EXPLOSIONS, THINKS KYLE RICHMOND, THE NEWLY ELECTED REPRESENTATIVE FROM THE DISTRICT OF COLUMBIA.
THEY SOUND MORE LIKE FOOTSTEPS.
CONGRESSMAN RICHMOND. THE TUNNELS ARE THIS WAY, SIR.
I'M NOT GOING TO THE TUNNELS.
YES, SIR.
OF COURSE, SIR.
YOUR CAR WILL BE WAITING, SIR.

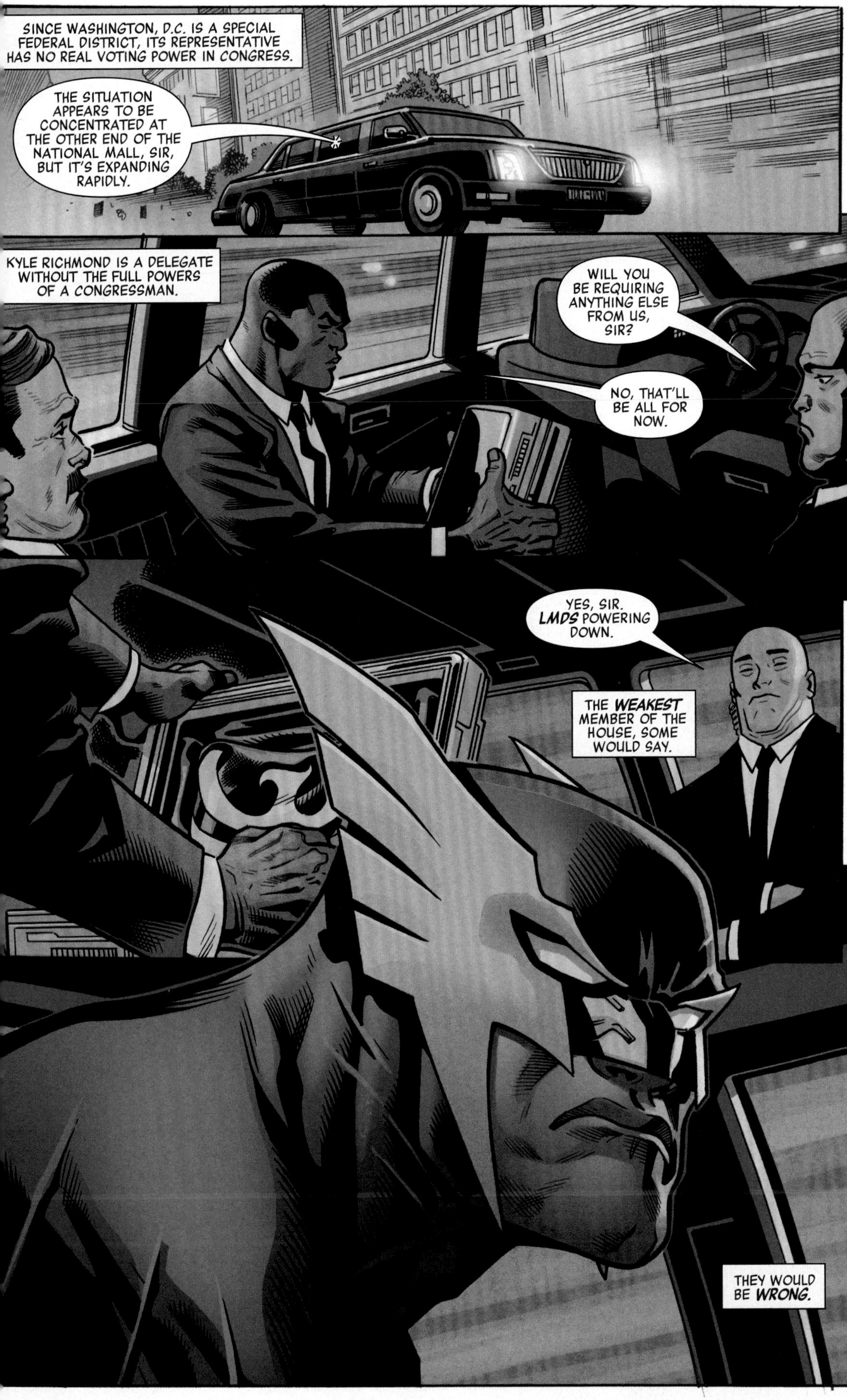
SINCE WASHINGTON, D.C. IS A SPECIAL FEDERAL DISTRICT, ITS REPRESENTATIVE HAS NO REAL VOTING POWER IN CONGRESS.
THE SITUATION APPEARS TO BE CONCENTRATED AT THE OTHER END OF THE NATIONAL MALL, SIR, BUT IT'S EXPANDING RAPIDLY.
KYLE RICHMOND IS A DELEGATE WITHOUT THE FULL POWERS OF A CONGRESSMAN.
WILL YOU BE REQUIRING ANYTHING ELSE FROM US, SIR?
NO, THAT'LL BE ALL FOR NOW.
YES, SIR. LMDS POWERING DOWN.
THE WEAKEST MEMBER OF THE HOUSE, SOME WOULD SAY.
THEY WOULD BE WRONG.

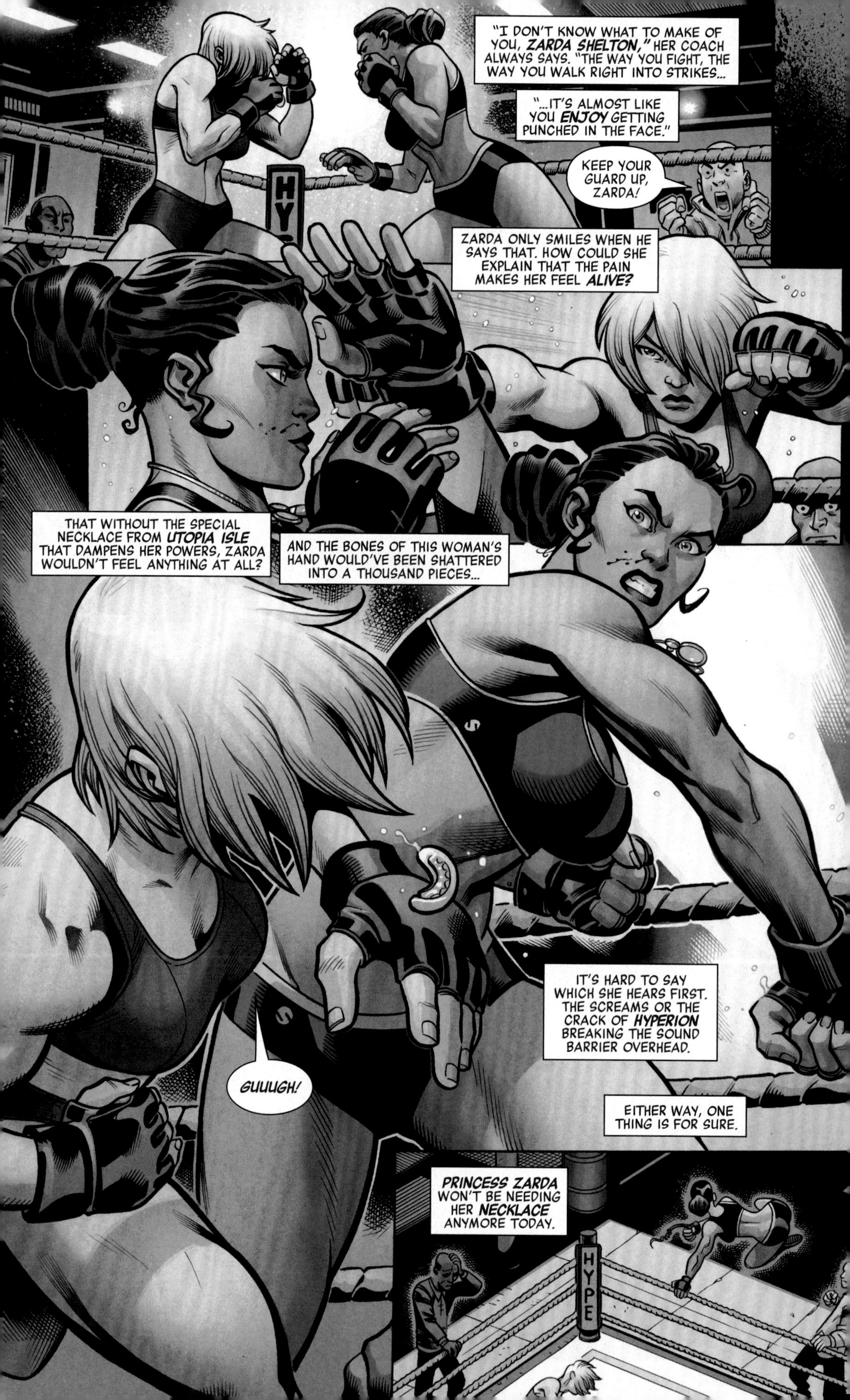
"I DON'T KNOW WHAT TO MAKE OF YOU, ZARDA SHELTON," HER COACH ALWAYS SAYS. "THE WAY YOU FIGHT, THE WAY YOU WALK RIGHT INTO STRIKES...
"...IT'S ALMOST LIKE YOU ENJOY GETTING PUNCHED IN THE FACE."
KEEP YOUR GUARD UP, ZARDA!
ZARDA ONLY SMILES WHEN HE SAYS THAT. HOW COULD SHE EXPLAIN THAT THE PAIN MAKES HER FEEL ALIVE?
THAT WITHOUT THE SPECIAL NECKLACE FROM UTOPIA ISLE THAT DAMPENS HER POWERS, ZARDA WOULDN'T FEEL ANYTHING AT ALL?
AND THE BONES OF THIS WOMAN'S HAND WOULD'VE BEEN SHATTERED INTO A THOUSAND PIECES...
GUUUGH!
IT'S HARD TO SAY WHICH SHE HEARS FIRST. THE SCREAMS OR THE CRACK OF HYPERION BREAKING THE SOUND BARRIER OVERHEAD.
EITHER WAY, ONE THING IS FOR SURE.
PRINCESS ZARDA WON'T BE NEEDING HER NECKLACE ANYMORE TODAY.
HYPE

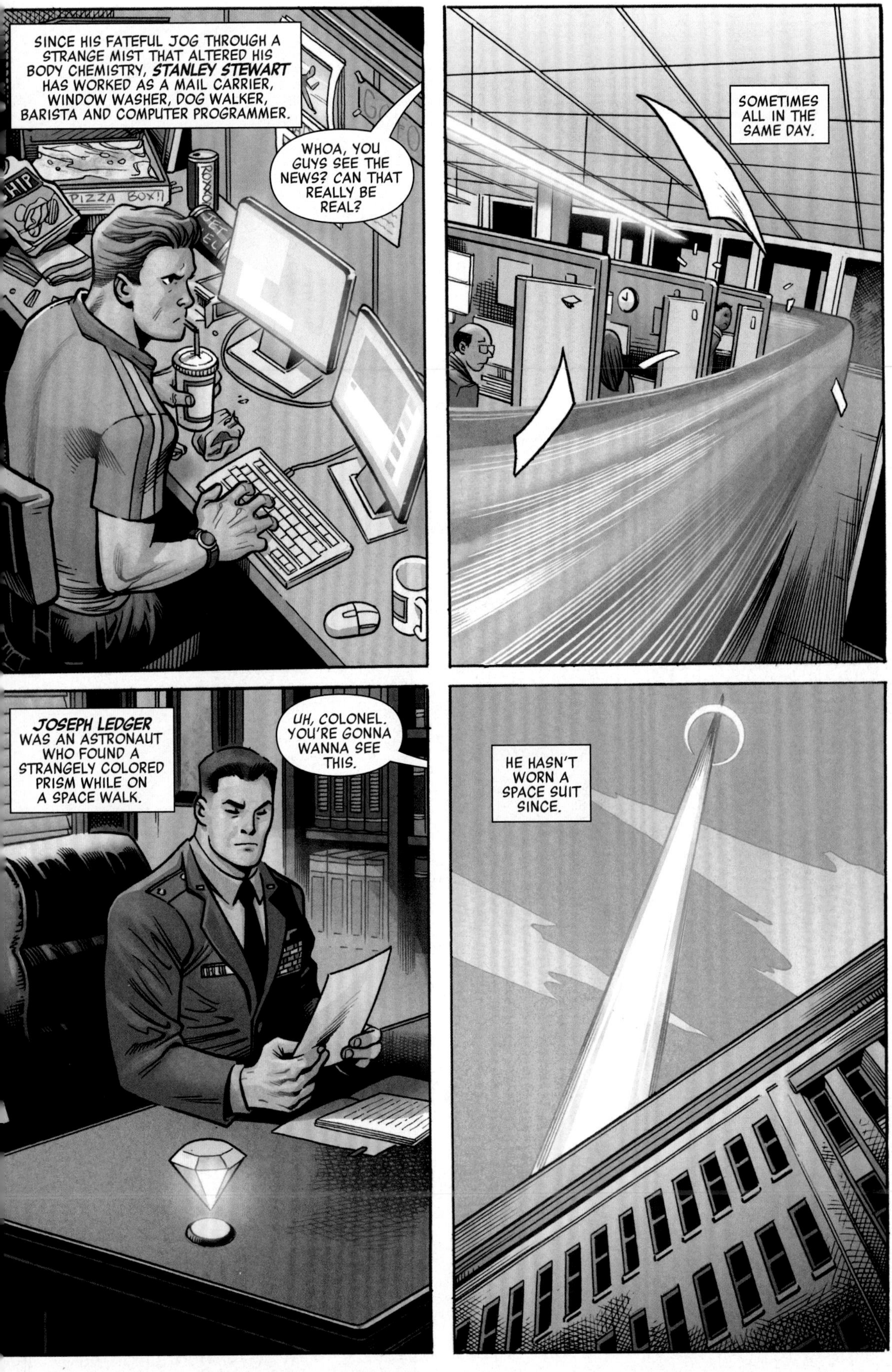
SINCE HIS FATEFUL JOG THROUGH A STRANGE MIST THAT ALTERED HIS BODY CHEMISTRY, STANLEY STEWART HAS WORKED AS A MAIL CARRIER, WINDOW WASHER, DOG WALKER, BARISTA AND COMPUTER PROGRAMMER.
WHOA, YOU GUYS SEE THE NEWS? CAN THAT REALLY BE REAL?
PIZZA BOX!!
SOMETIMES ALL IN THE SAME DAY.
JOSEPH LEDGER WAS AN ASTRONAUT WHO FOUND A STRANGELY COLORED PRISM WHILE ON A SPACE WALK.
UH, COLONEL. YOU'RE GONNA WANNA SEE THIS.
HE HASN'T WORN A SPACE SUIT SINCE.

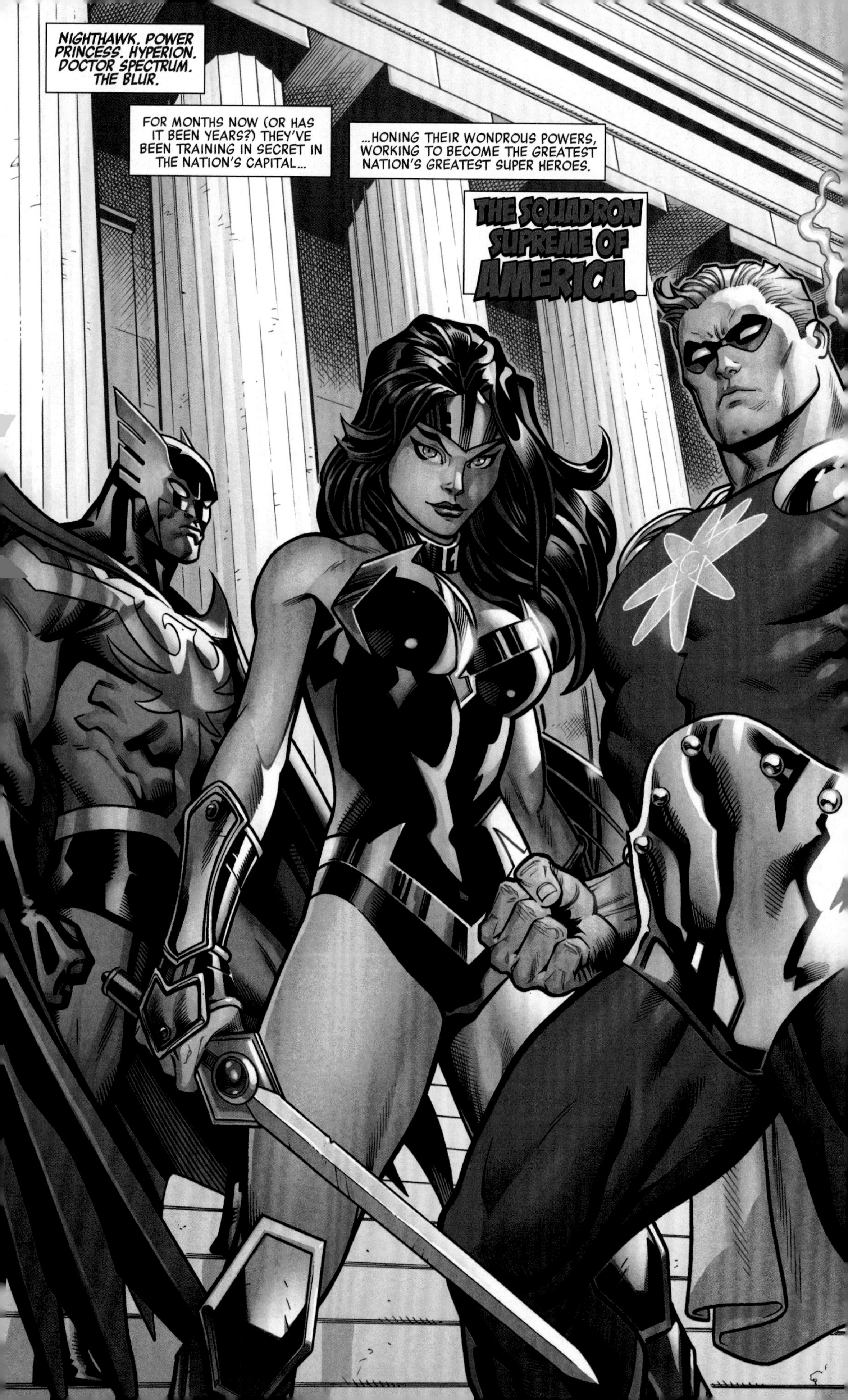
NIGHTHAWK. POWER PRINCESS. HYPERION. DOCTOR SPECTRUM. THE BLUR.
FOR MONTHS NOW (OR HAS IT BEEN YEARS?) THEY'VE BEEN TRAINING IN SECRET IN THE NATION'S CAPITAL...
...HONING THEIR WONDROUS POWERS, WORKING TO BECOME THE GREATEST NATION'S GREATEST SUPER HEROES.
THE SQUADRON SUPREME OF AMERICA.

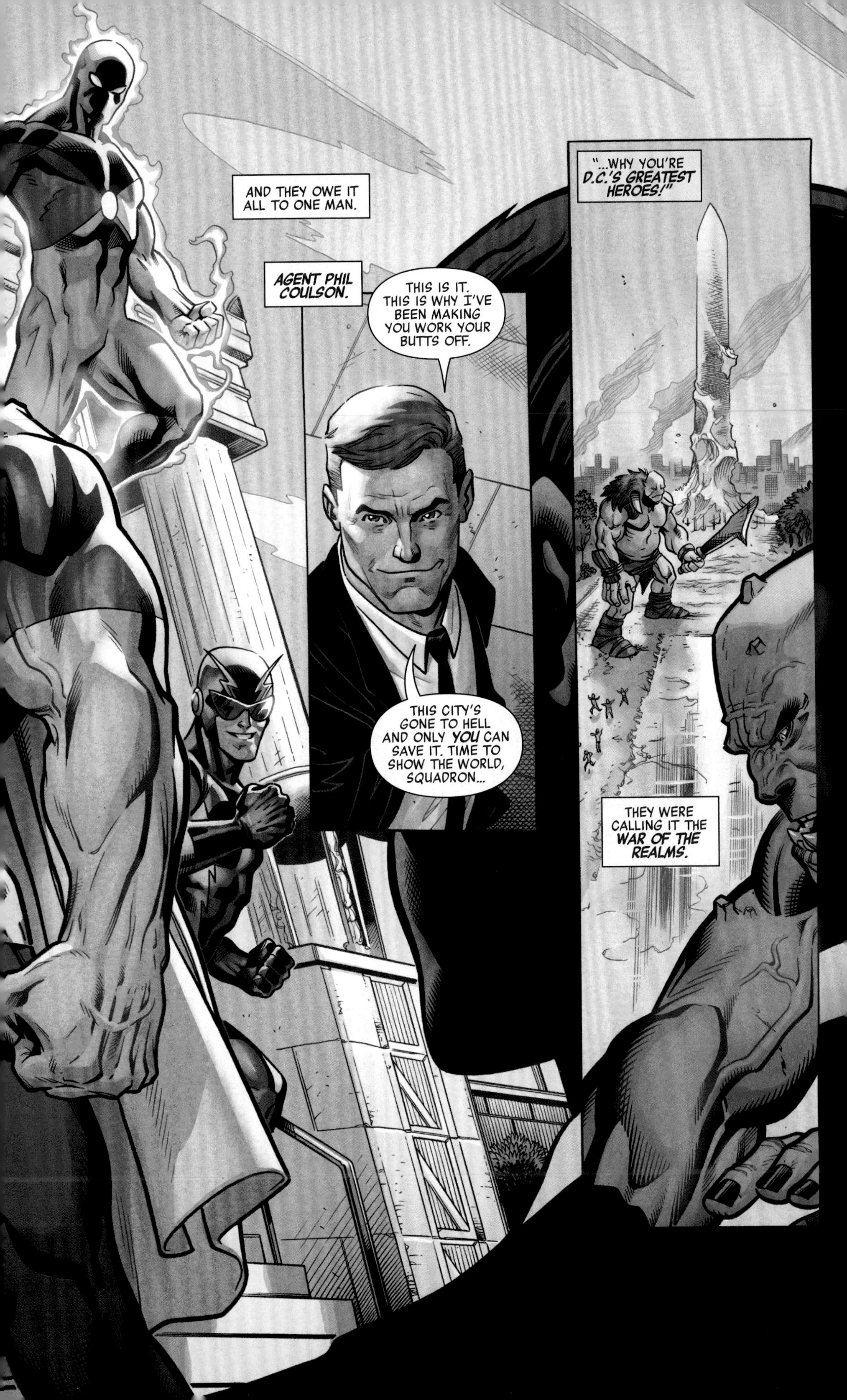
AND THEY OWE IT ALL TO ONE MAN.
AGENT PHIL COULSON.
THIS IS IT. THIS IS WHY I'VE BEEN MAKING YOU WORK YOUR BUTTS OFF.
THIS CITY'S GONE TO HELL AND ONLY YOU CAN SAVE IT. TIME TO SHOW THE WORLD, SQUADRON...
"...WHY YOU'RE D.C.'S GREATEST HEROES!"
THEY WERE CALLING IT THE WAR OF THE REALMS.

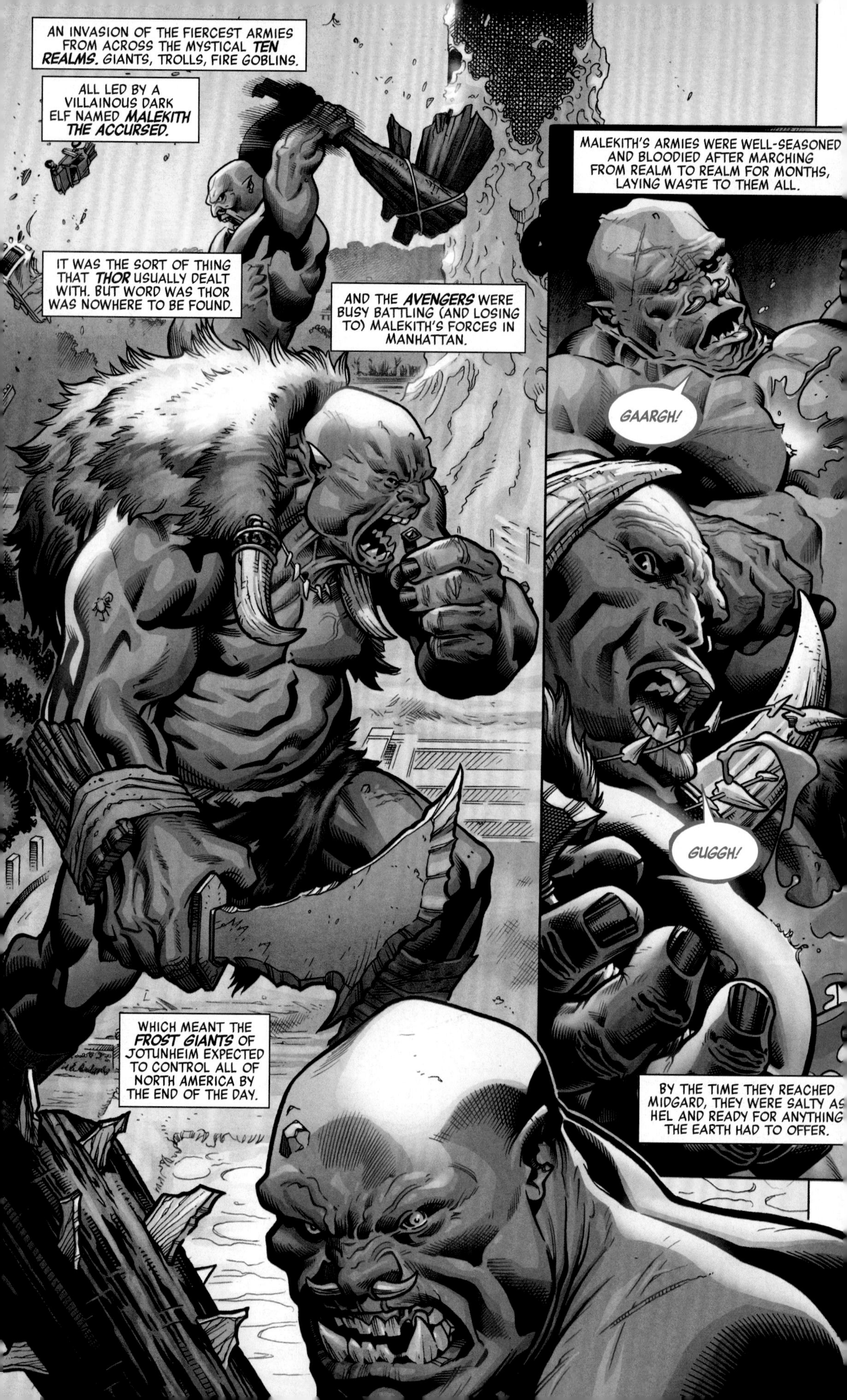
AN INVASION OF THE FIERCEST ARMIES FROM ACROSS THE MYSTICAL TEN REALMS. GIANTS, TROLLS, FIRE GOBLINS.
ALL LED BY A VILLAINOUS DARK ELF NAMED MALEKITH THE ACCURSED.
IT WAS THE SORT OF THING THAT THOR USUALLY DEALT WITH. BUT WORD WAS THOR WAS NOWHERE TO BE FOUND.
AND THE AVENGERS WERE BUSY BATTLING (AND LOSING TO) MALEKITH'S FORCES IN MANHATTAN.
WHICH MEANT THE FROST GIANTS OF JOTUNHEIM EXPECTED TO CONTROL ALL OF NORTH AMERICA BY THE END OF THE DAY.
MALEKITH'S ARMIES WERE WELL-SEASONED AND BLOODIED AFTER MARCHING FROM REALM TO REALM FOR MONTHS, LAYING WASTE TO THEM ALL.
GAARGH!
GUGGH!
BY THE TIME THEY REACHED MIDGARD, THEY WERE SALTY AS HEL AND READY FOR ANYTHING THE EARTH HAD TO OFFER.

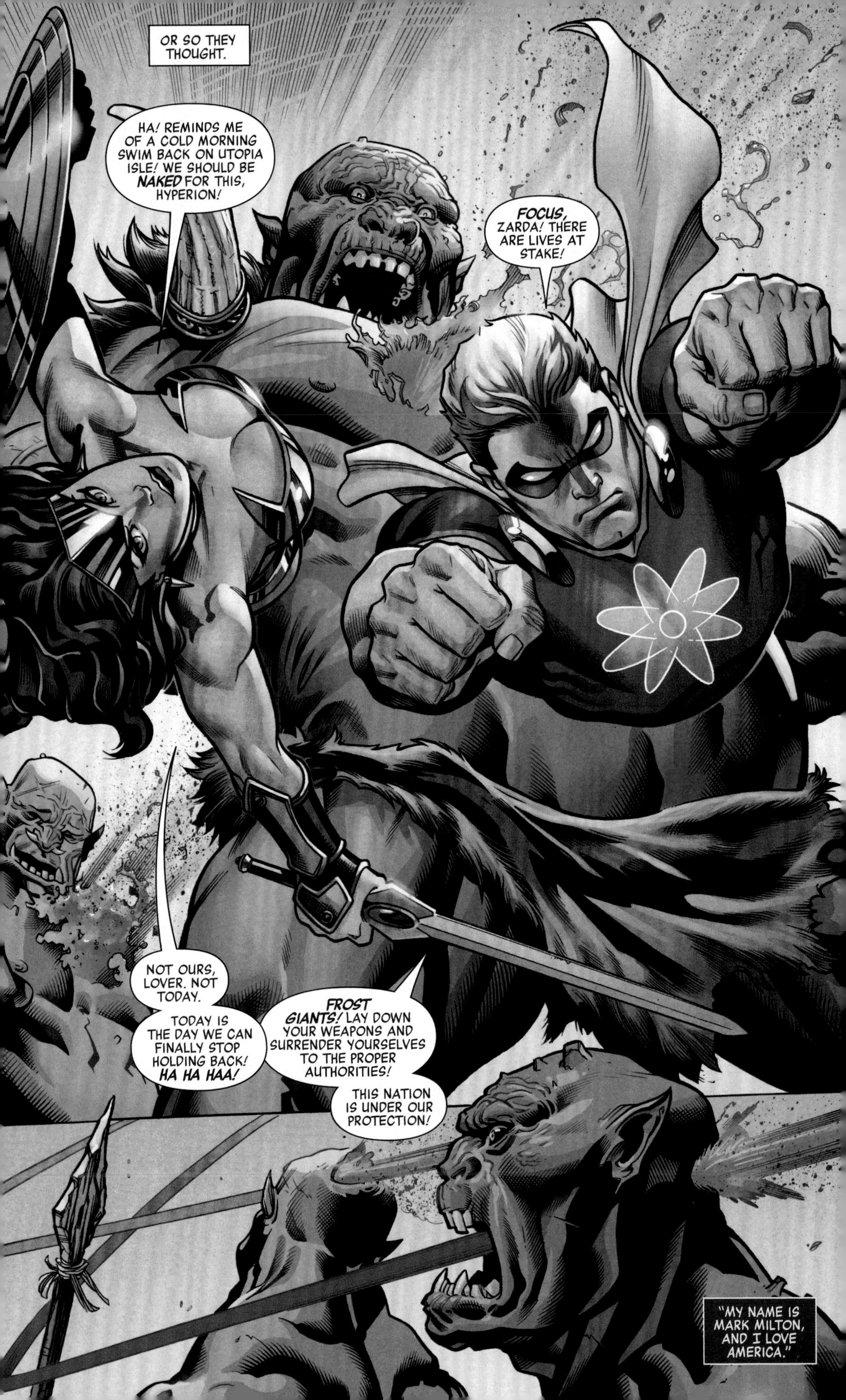
OR SO THEY THOUGHT.
HA! REMINDS ME OF A COLD MORNING SWIM BACK ON UTOPIA ISLE! WE SHOULD BE NAKED FOR THIS, HYPERION!
FOCUS, ZARDA! THERE ARE LIVES AT STAKE!
NOT OURS, LOVER. NOT TODAY.
TODAY IS THE DAY WE CAN FINALLY STOP HOLDING BACK! HA HA HAA!
FROST GIANTS! LAY DOWN YOUR WEAPONS AND SURRENDER YOURSELVES TO THE PROPER AUTHORITIES!
THIS NATION IS UNDER OUR PROTECTION!
"MY NAME IS MARK MILTON, AND I LOVE AMERICA."

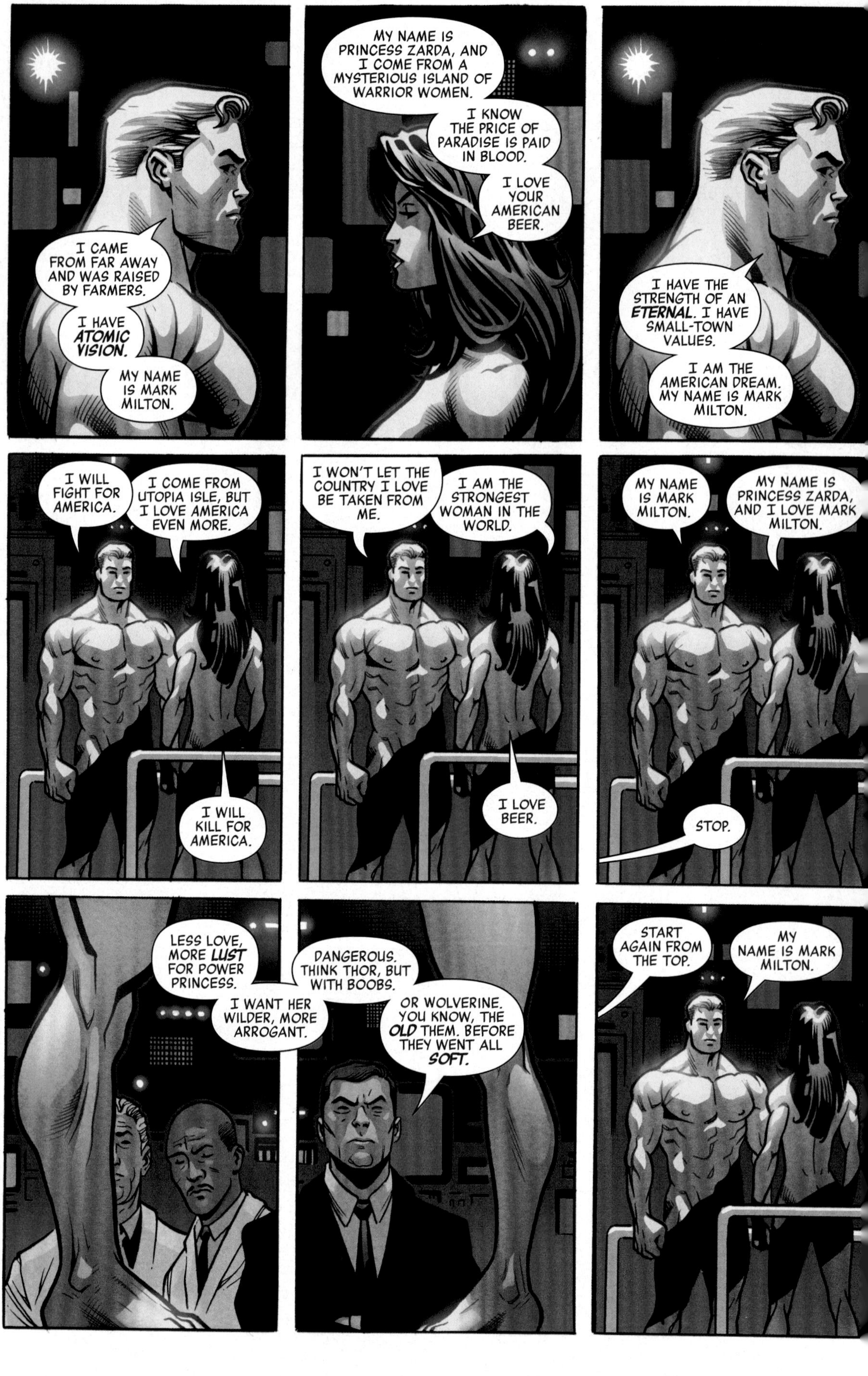

I CAME FROM FAR AWAY AND WAS RAISED BY FARMERS.
I HAVE ATOMIC VISION.
MY NAME IS MARK MILTON.
MY NAME IS PRINCESS ZARDA, AND I COME FROM A MYSTERIOUS ISLAND OF WARRIOR WOMEN.
I KNOW THE PRICE OF PARADISE IS PAID IN BLOOD.
I LOVE YOUR AMERICAN BEER.
I HAVE THE STRENGTH OF AN ETERNAL. I HAVE SMALL-TOWN VALUES.
I AM THE AMERICAN DREAM. MY NAME IS MARK MILTON.
I WILL FIGHT FOR AMERICA.
I COME FROM UTOPIA ISLE, BUT I LOVE AMERICA EVEN MORE.
I WILL KILL FOR AMERICA.
I WON'T LET THE COUNTRY I LOVE BE TAKEN FROM ME.
I AM THE STRONGEST WOMAN IN THE WORLD.
I LOVE BEER.
MY NAME IS MARK MILTON.
MY NAME IS PRINCESS ZARDA, AND I LOVE MARK MILTON.
STOP.
LESS LOVE, MORE LUST FOR POWER PRINCESS.
I WANT HER WILDER, MORE ARROGANT.
DANGEROUS. THINK THOR, BUT WITH BOOBS.
OR WOLVERINE. YOU KNOW, THE OLD THEM. BEFORE THEY WENT ALL SOFT.
START AGAIN FROM THE TOP.
MY NAME IS MARK MILTON.

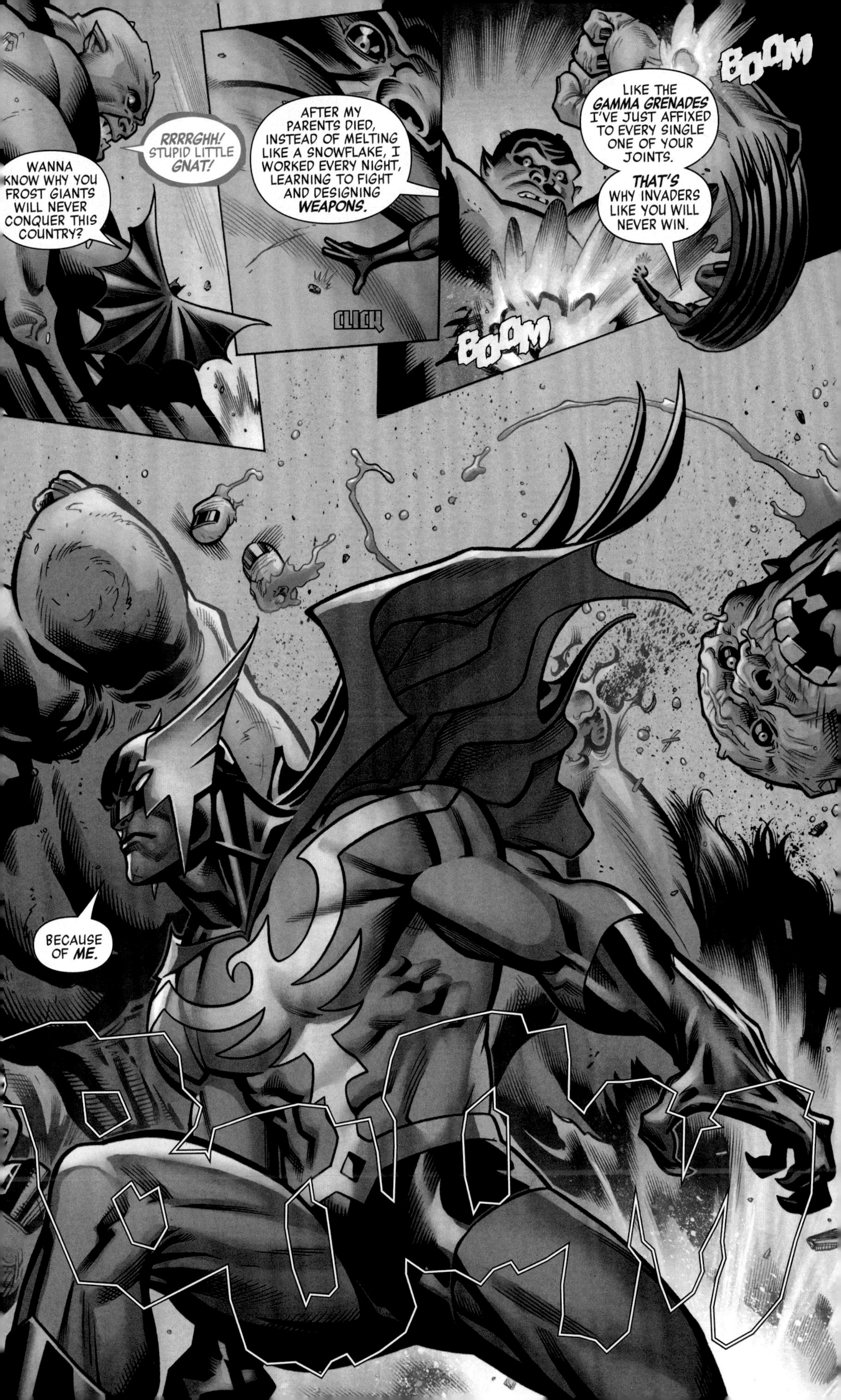
WANNA KNOW WHY YOU FROST GIANTS WILL NEVER CONQUER THIS COUNTRY?
RRRRGHH! STUPID LITTLE GNAT!
AFTER MY PARENTS DIED, INSTEAD OF MELTING LIKE A SNOWFLAKE, I WORKED EVERY NIGHT, LEARNING TO FIGHT AND DESIGNING WEAPONS.
CLICK
LIKE THE GAMMA GRENADES I'VE JUST AFFIXED TO EVERY SINGLE ONE OF YOUR JOINTS.
THAT'S WHY INVADERS LIKE YOU WILL NEVER WIN.
BOOM
BOOM
BECAUSE OF ME.

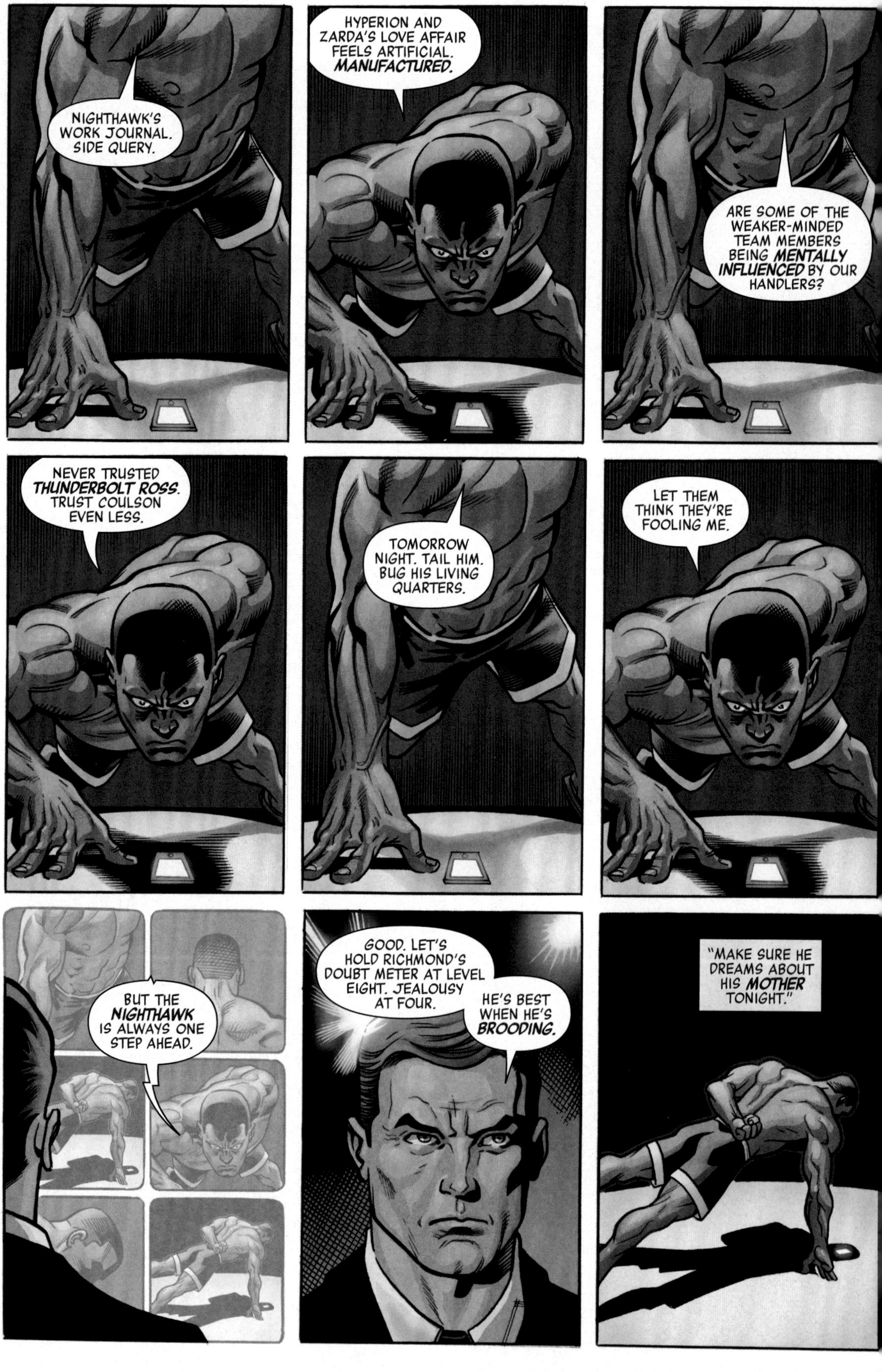
NIGHTHAWK'S WORK JOURNAL. SIDE QUERY.
HYPERION AND ZARDA'S LOVE AFFAIR FEELS ARTIFICIAL. MANUFACTURED.
ARE SOME OF THE WEAKER-MINDED TEAM MEMBERS BEING MENTALLY INFLUENCED BY OUR HANDLERS?
NEVER TRUSTED THUNDERBOLT ROSS. TRUST COULSON EVEN LESS.
TOMORROW NIGHT. TAIL HIM. BUG HIS LIVING QUARTERS.
LET THEM THINK THEY'RE FOOLING ME.
BUT THE NIGHTHAWK IS ALWAYS ONE STEP AHEAD.
GOOD. LET'S HOLD RICHMOND'S DOUBT METER AT LEVEL EIGHT. JEALOUSY AT FOUR.
HE'S BEST WHEN HE'S BROODING.
"MAKE SURE HE DREAMS ABOUT HIS MOTHER TONIGHT."

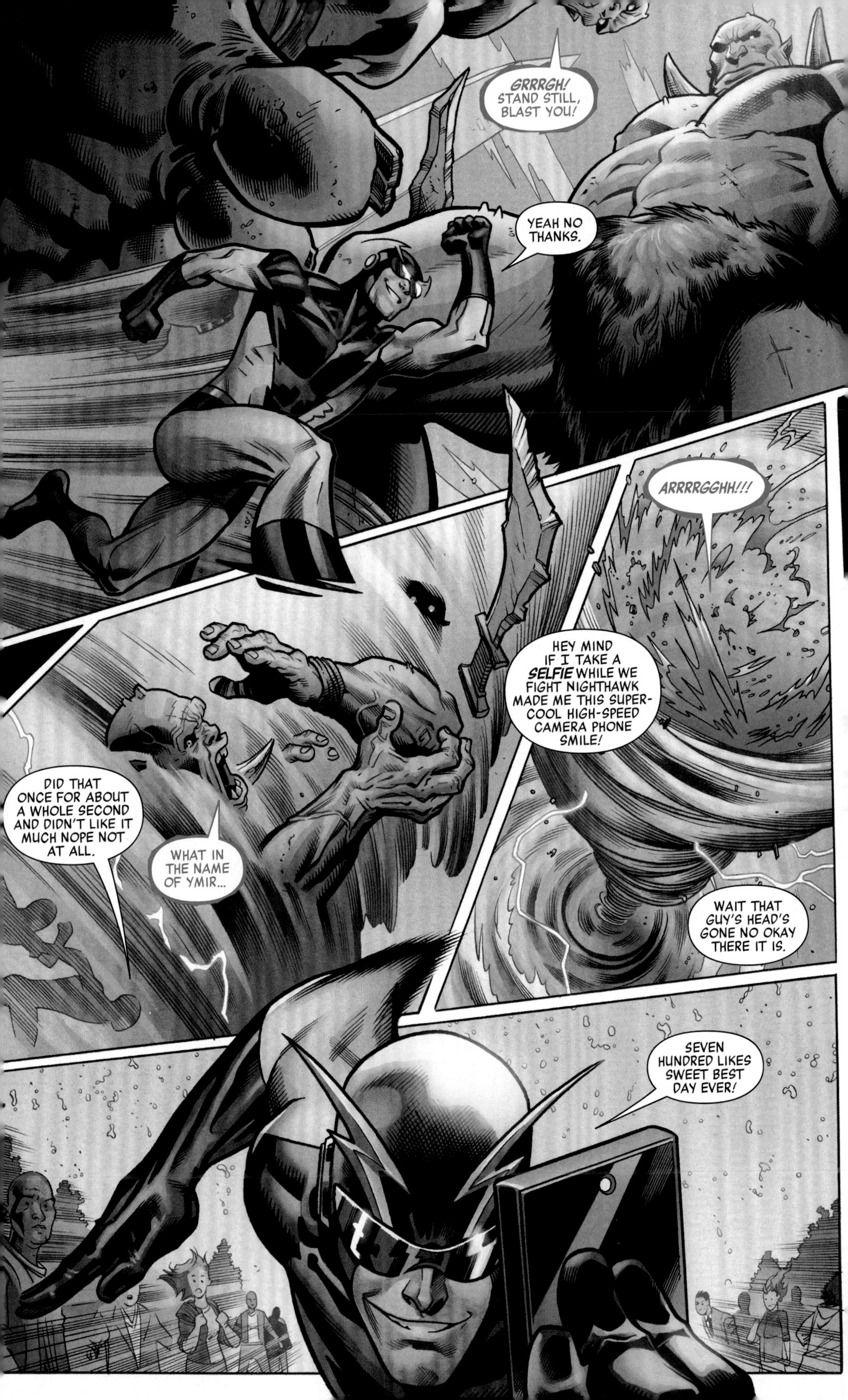
GRRRGH! STAND STILL, BLAST YOU!
YEAH NO THANKS.
ARRRRGGHH!!!
HEY MIND IF I TAKE A SELFIE WHILE WE FIGHT NIGHTHAWK MADE ME THIS SUPER-COOL HIGH-SPEED CAMERA PHONE SMILE!
DID THAT ONCE FOR ABOUT A WHOLE SECOND AND DIDN'T LIKE IT MUCH NOPE NOT AT ALL.
WHAT IN THE NAME OF YMIR...
WAIT THAT GUY'S HEAD'S GONE NO OKAY THERE IT IS.
SEVEN HUNDRED LIKES SWEET BEST DAY EVER!

BLUR'S ON HOUR 27.

WE HAD TO LOOP IN MORE SERVERS JUST TO KEEP UP WITH THE SPEED OF HIS BRAIN.

RIGHT NOW HE'S ON A MIX OF JIHADIST EXECUTION VIDEOS AND SECRET CELEBRITY SEX TAPES FROM THE OLD S.H.I.E.L.D. ARCHIVES.

WHO KNEW VISION WAS SUCH A FREAK IN THE SHEETS? HASHTAG, I DID.

I DON'T LIKE IT, COULSON.

I'M ALL FOR HOOKING CAR BATTERIES TO TERRORISTS' PRIVATES IF THAT'S WHAT IT TAKES TO KEEP THE COUNTRY SAFE.

BUT TORTURING OUR OWN CITIZENS? THAT CROSSES THE LINE.

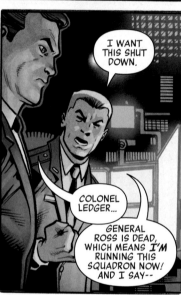

I WANT THIS SHUT DOWN.

COLONEL LEDGER...

GENERAL ROSS IS DEAD, WHICH MEANS I'M RUNNING THIS SQUADRON NOW! AND I SAY--

DOESN'T IT REMIND YOU OF WHAT YOUR MOTHER'S SECOND COUSIN ONCE REMOVED ALWAYS SAID?

IT...REMINDS ME OF WHAT MY MOTHER'S SECOND COUSIN ONCE REMOVED ALWAYS SAID.

WHAT... WHAT WAS THAT AGAIN?

CARRY ON, AGENT COULSON.

EXACTLY.

CARRY ON, AGENT COULSON.

HA! FASTER!

THERE'S NO STOPPING US NOW!

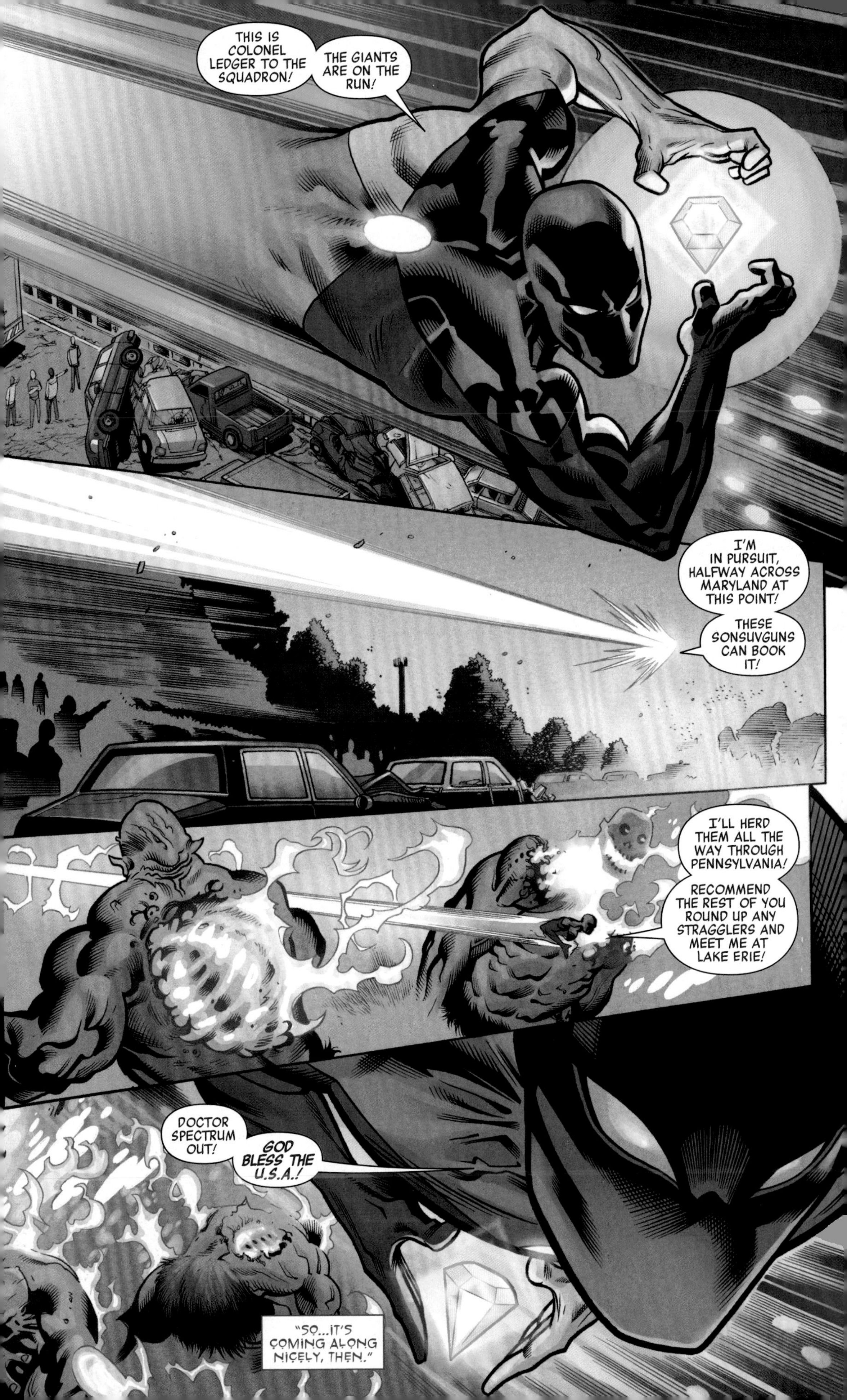
THIS IS COLONEL LEDGER TO THE SQUADRON!
THE GIANTS ARE ON THE RUN!
I'M IN PURSUIT, HALFWAY ACROSS MARYLAND AT THIS POINT!
THESE SONSUVGUNS CAN BOOK IT!
I'LL HERD THEM ALL THE WAY THROUGH PENNSYLVANIA!
RECOMMEND THE REST OF YOU ROUND UP ANY STRAGGLERS AND MEET ME AT LAKE ERIE!
DOCTOR SPECTRUM OUT!
GOD BLESS THE U.S.A.!
"SO...IT'S COMING ALONG NICELY, THEN."

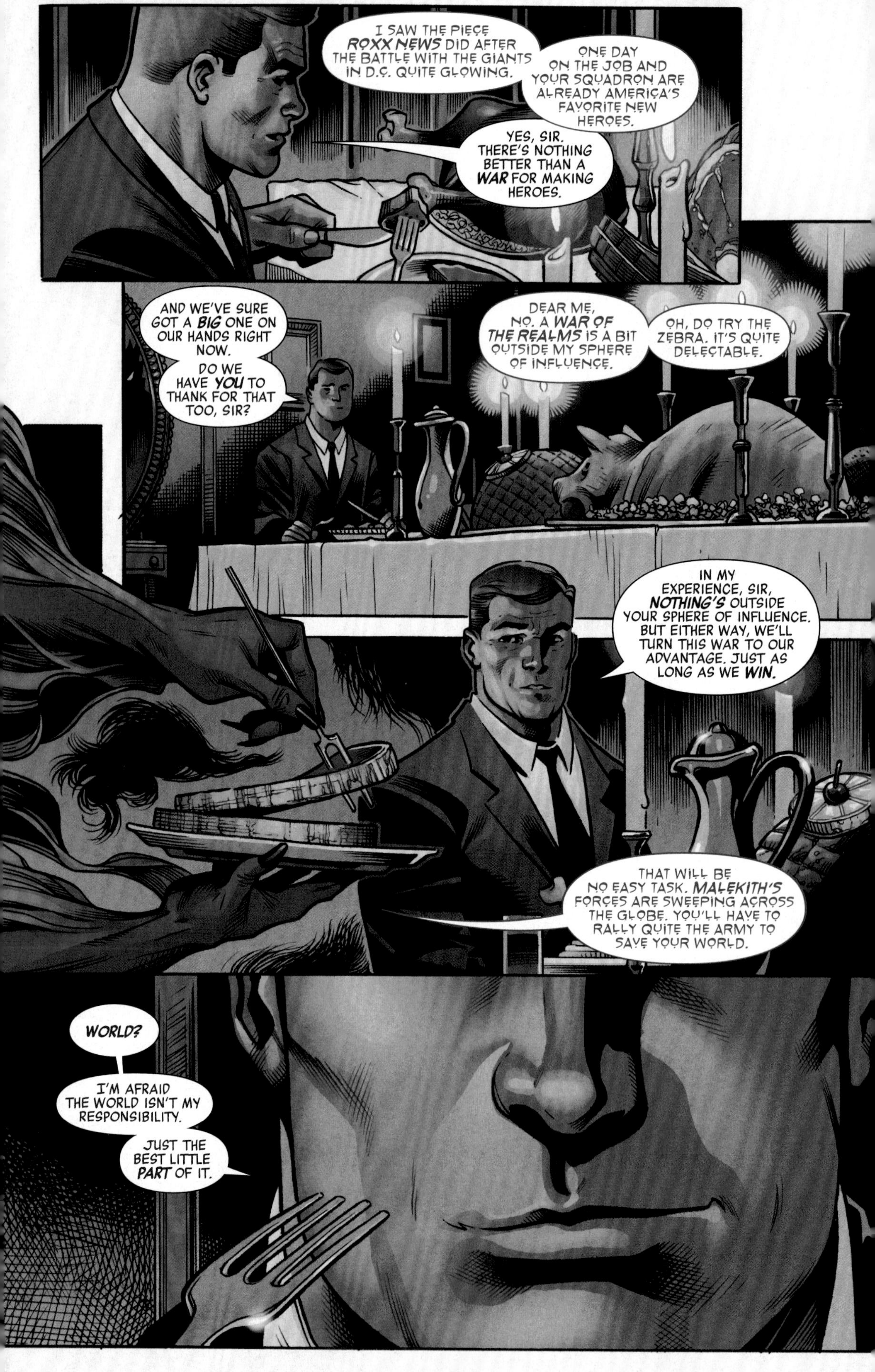

I SAW THE PIECE ROXX NEWS DID AFTER THE BATTLE WITH THE GIANTS IN D.C. QUITE GLOWING.
ONE DAY ON THE JOB AND YOUR SQUADRON ARE ALREADY AMERICA'S FAVORITE NEW HEROES.
YES, SIR. THERE'S NOTHING BETTER THAN A WAR FOR MAKING HEROES.
AND WE'VE SURE GOT A BIG ONE ON OUR HANDS RIGHT NOW.
DO WE HAVE YOU TO THANK FOR THAT TOO, SIR?
DEAR ME, NO. A WAR OF THE REALMS IS A BIT OUTSIDE MY SPHERE OF INFLUENCE.
OH, DO TRY THE ZEBRA. IT'S QUITE DELECTABLE.
IN MY EXPERIENCE, SIR, NOTHING'S OUTSIDE YOUR SPHERE OF INFLUENCE. BUT EITHER WAY, WE'LL TURN THIS WAR TO OUR ADVANTAGE. JUST AS LONG AS WE WIN.
THAT WILL BE NO EASY TASK. MALEKITH'S FORCES ARE SWEEPING ACROSS THE GLOBE. YOU'LL HAVE TO RALLY QUITE THE ARMY TO SAVE YOUR WORLD.
WORLD?
I'M AFRAID THE WORLD ISN'T MY RESPONSIBILITY.
JUST THE BEST LITTLE PART OF IT.

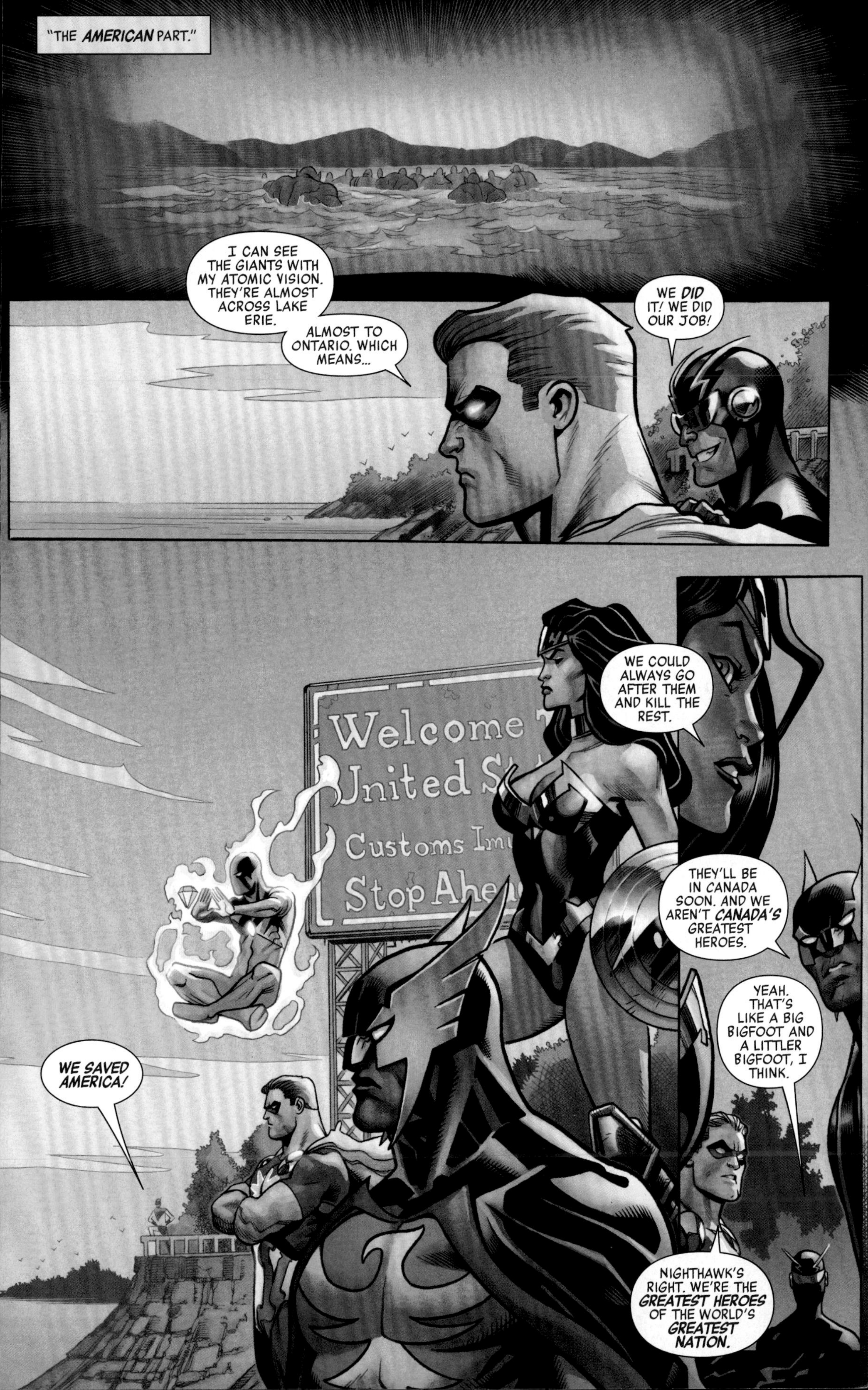

"THE AMERICAN PART."
I CAN SEE THE GIANTS WITH MY ATOMIC VISION. THEY'RE ALMOST ACROSS LAKE ERIE.
ALMOST TO ONTARIO. WHICH MEANS...
WE DID IT! WE DID OUR JOB!
Welcome T
United St
Customs Imm
Stop Ahe
WE COULD ALWAYS GO AFTER THEM AND KILL THE REST.
THEY'LL BE IN CANADA SOON. AND WE AREN'T CANADA'S GREATEST HEROES.
YEAH. THAT'S LIKE A BIG BIGFOOT AND A LITTLER BIGFOOT, I THINK.
WE SAVED AMERICA!
NIGHTHAWK'S RIGHT. WE'RE THE GREATEST HEROES OF THE WORLD'S GREATEST NATION.

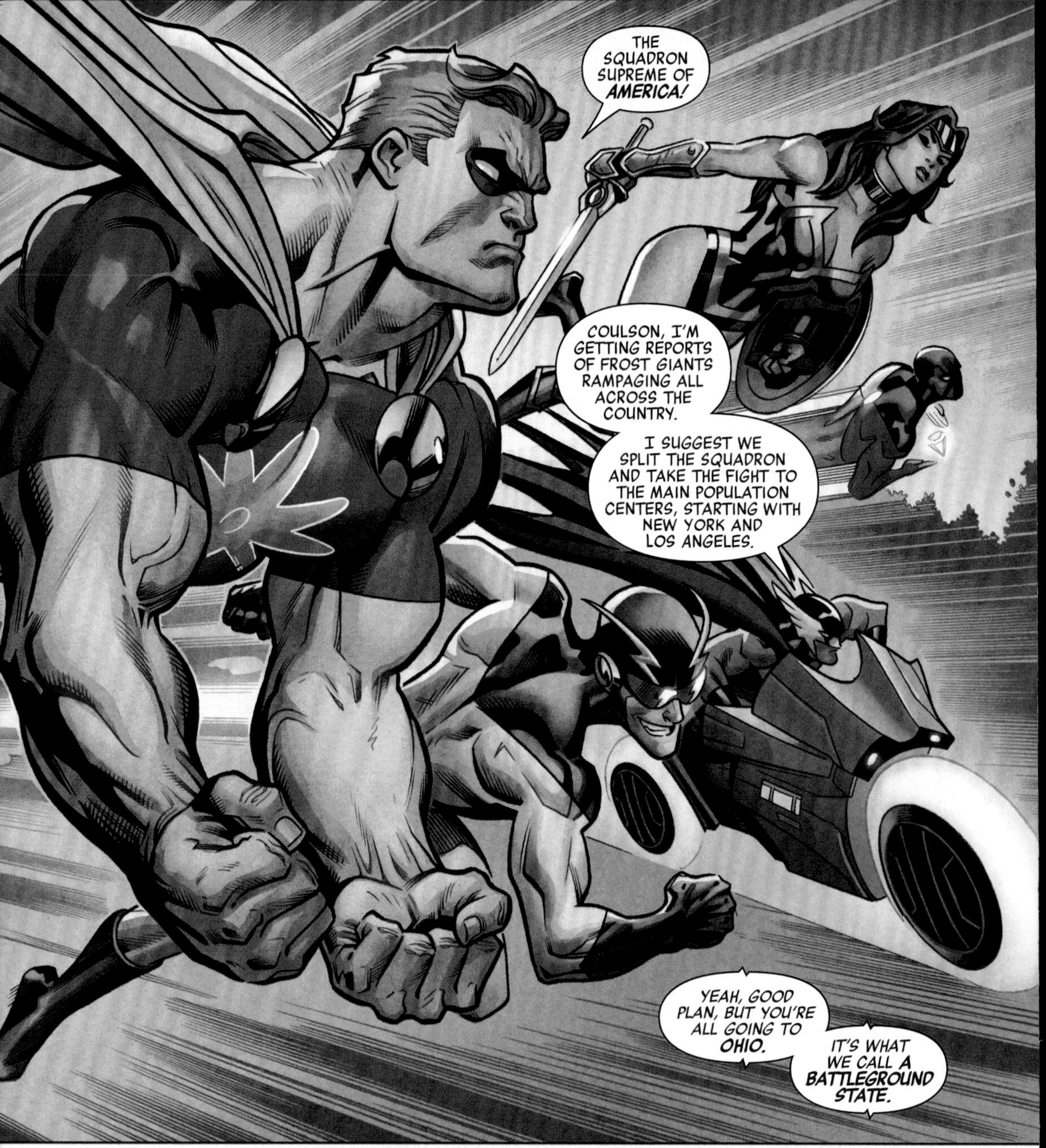
THE SQUADRON SUPREME OF AMERICA!
COULSON, I'M GETTING REPORTS OF FROST GIANTS RAMPAGING ALL ACROSS THE COUNTRY.
I SUGGEST WE SPLIT THE SQUADRON AND TAKE THE FIGHT TO THE MAIN POPULATION CENTERS, STARTING WITH NEW YORK AND LOS ANGELES.
YEAH, GOOD PLAN, BUT YOU'RE ALL GOING TO OHIO.
IT'S WHAT WE CALL A BATTLEGROUND STATE.

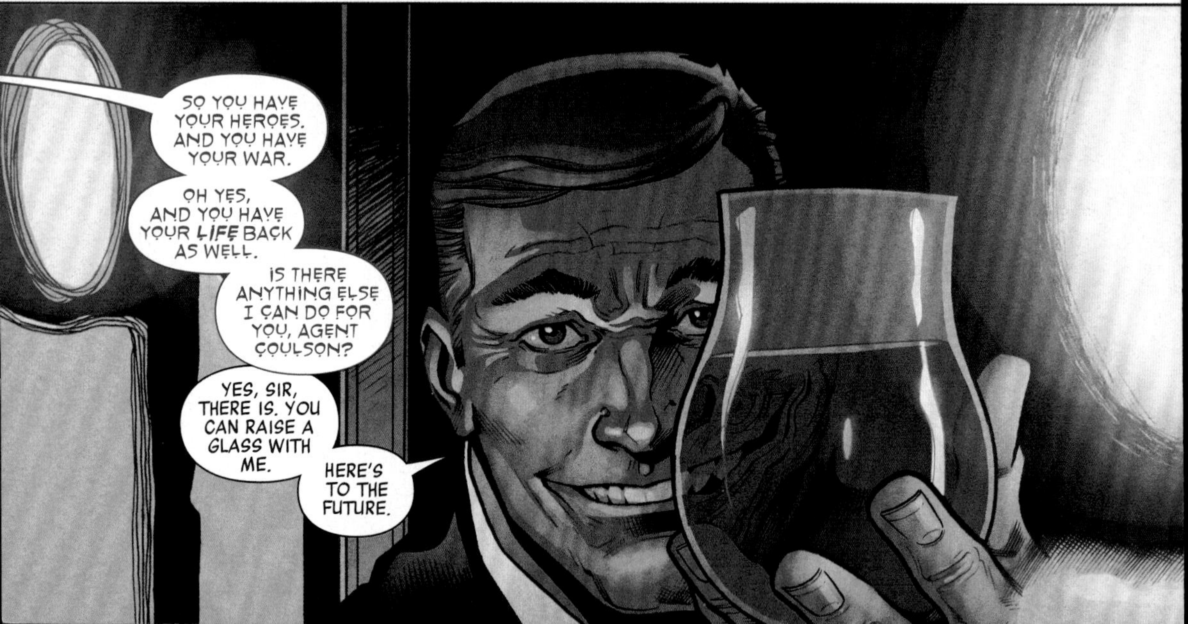
SO YOU HAVE YOUR HEROES. AND YOU HAVE YOUR WAR.
OH YES, AND YOU HAVE YOUR LIFE BACK AS WELL.
IS THERE ANYTHING ELSE I CAN DO FOR YOU, AGENT COULSON?
YES, SIR, THERE IS. YOU CAN RAISE A GLASS WITH ME.
HERE'S TO THE FUTURE.

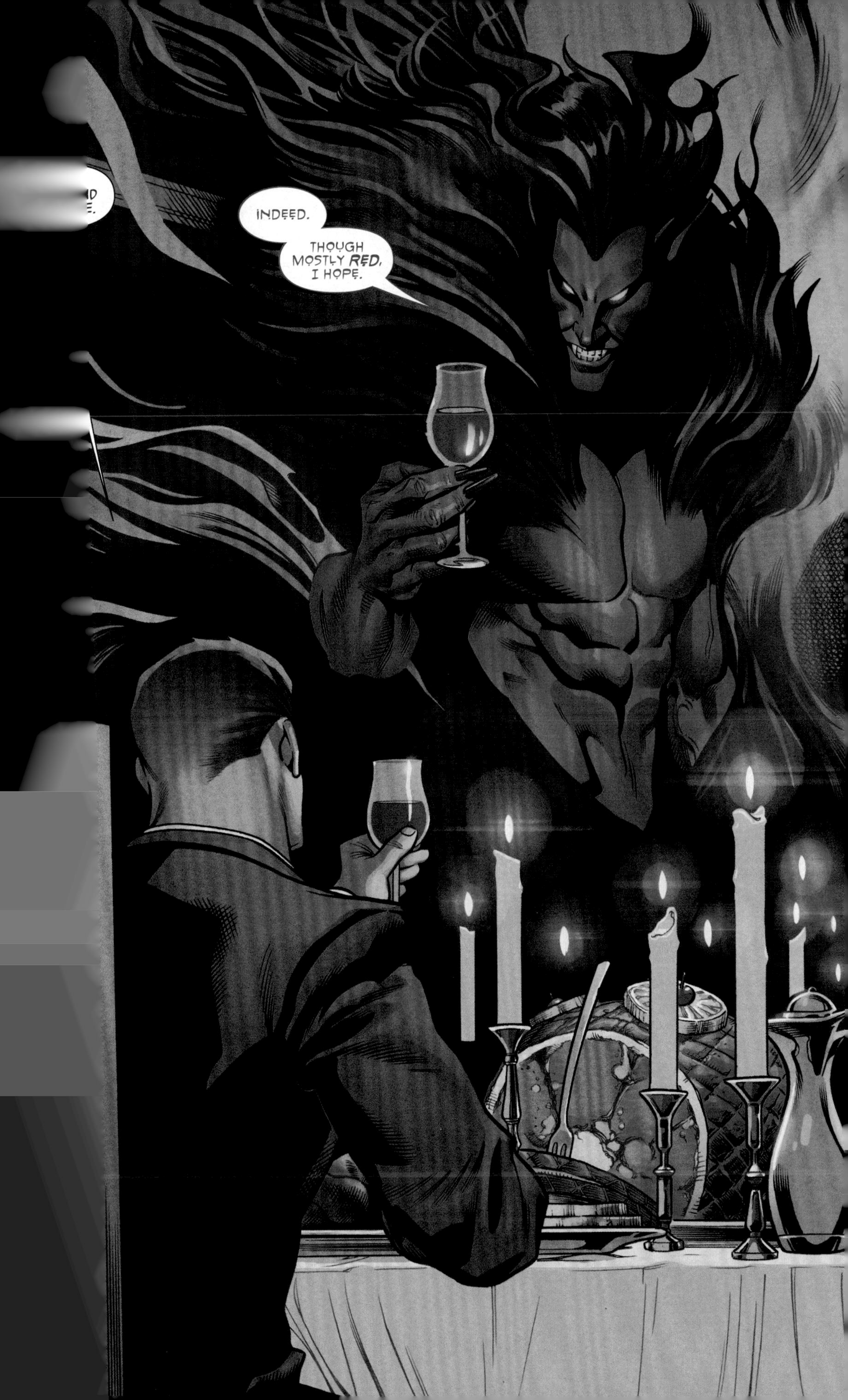
INDEED.
THOUGH MOSTLY RED, I HOPE.

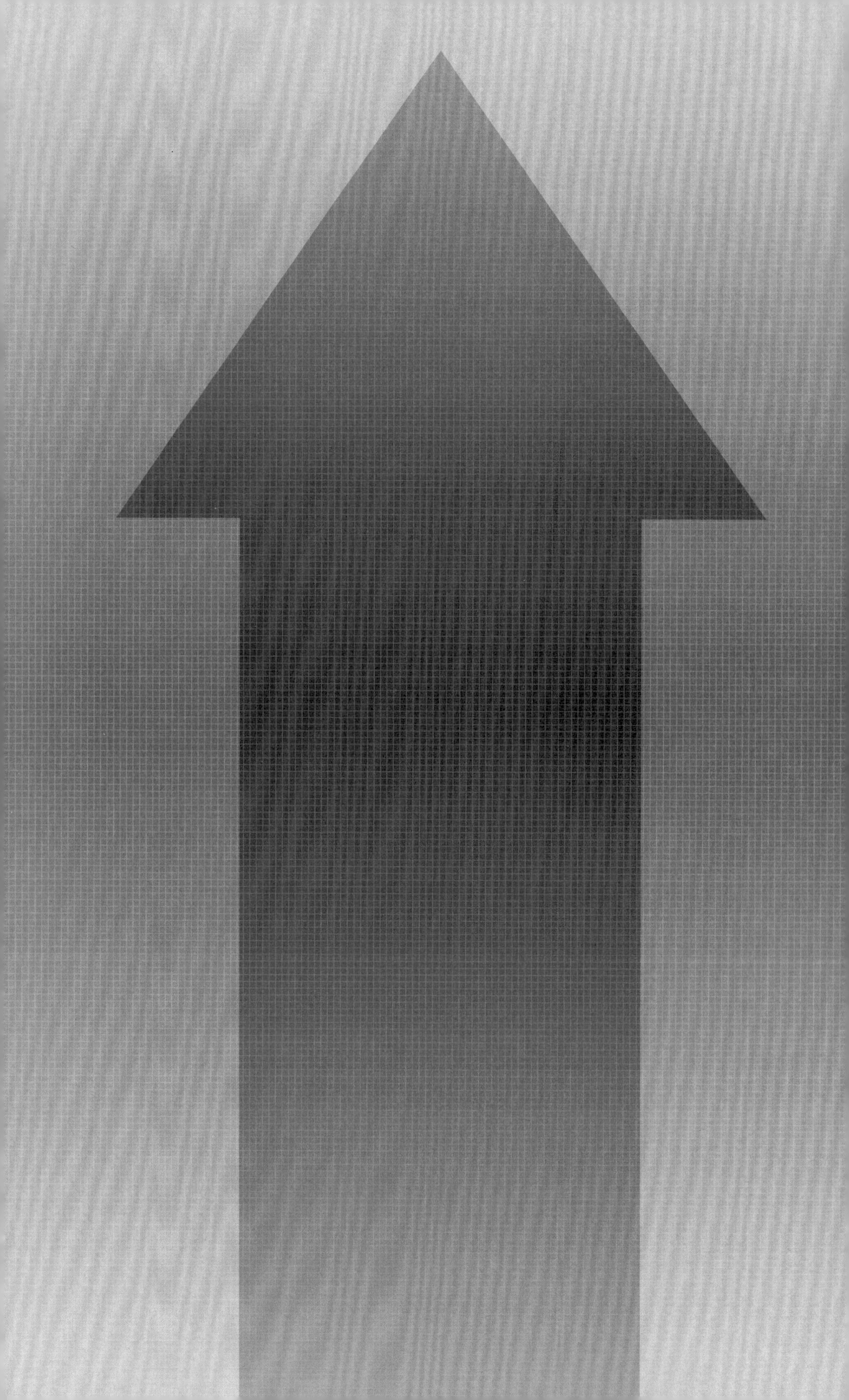

19 THE MAN IN THE MOUNTAIN

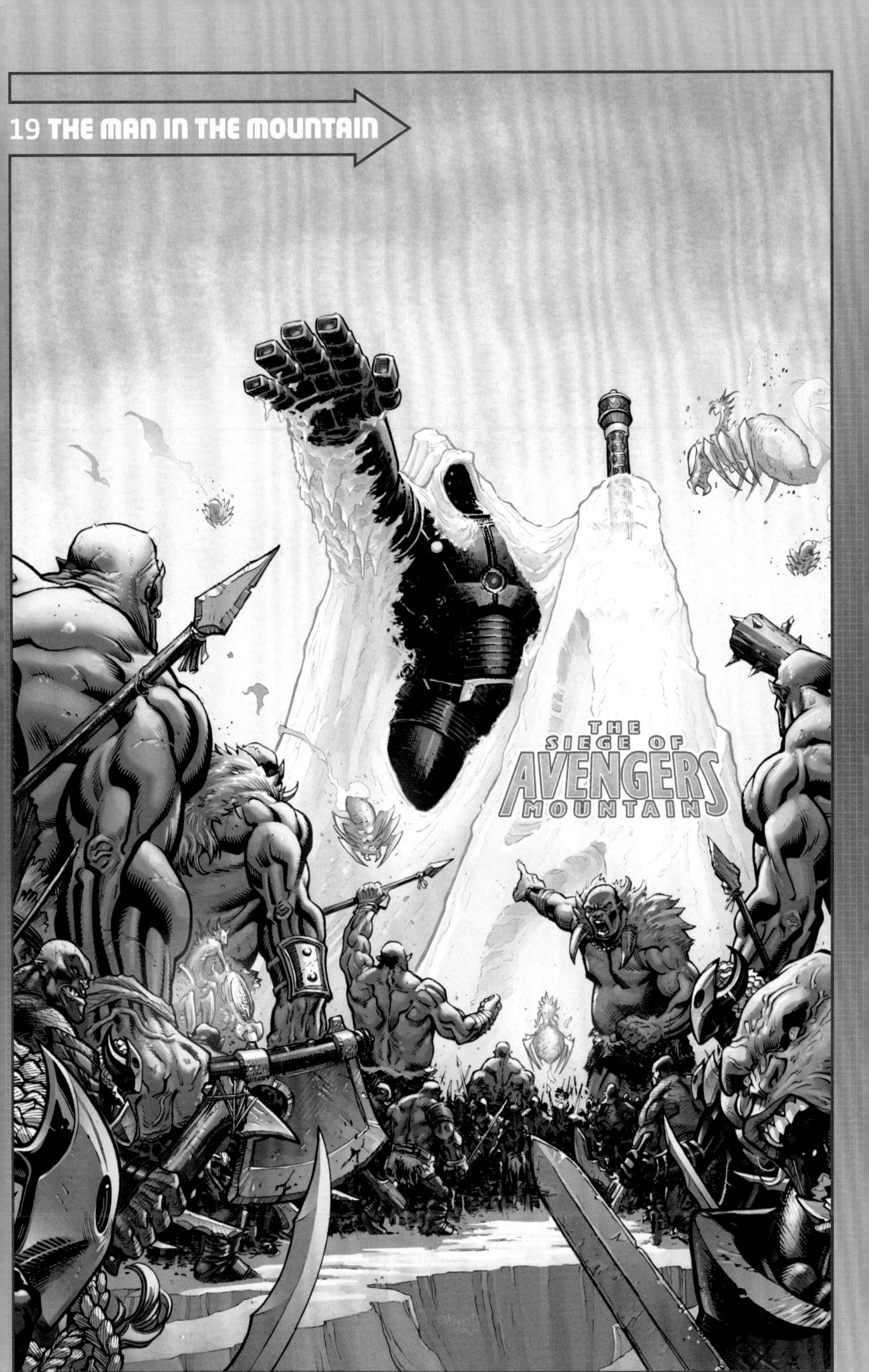
THE SIEGE OF AVENGERS MOUNTAIN

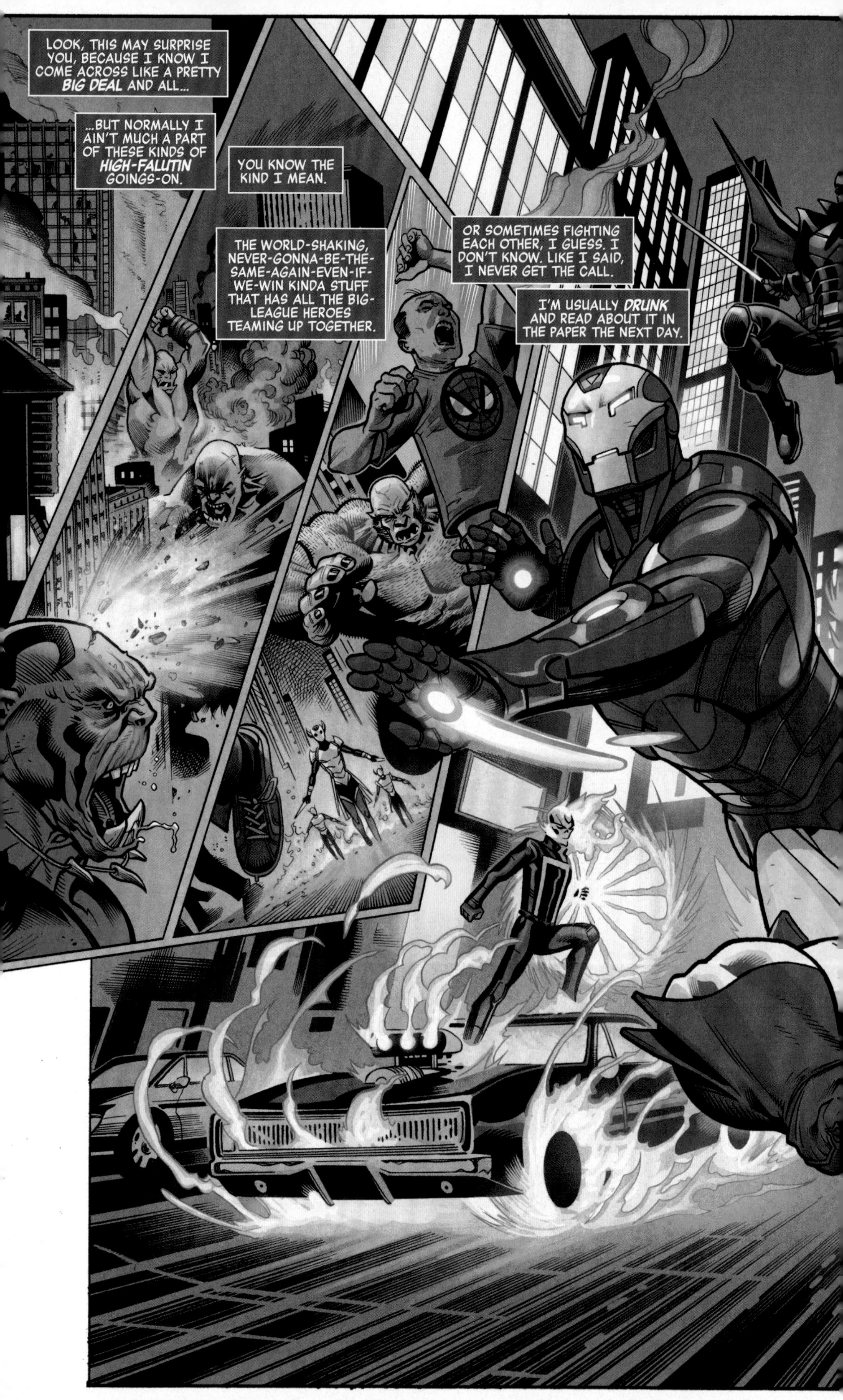

LOOK, THIS MAY SURPRISE YOU, BECAUSE I KNOW I COME ACROSS LIKE A PRETTY BIG DEAL AND ALL...
...BUT NORMALLY I AIN'T MUCH A PART OF THESE KINDS OF HIGH-FALUTIN GOINGS-ON.
YOU KNOW THE KIND I MEAN.
THE WORLD-SHAKING, NEVER-GONNA-BE-THE-SAME-AGAIN-EVEN-IF-WE-WIN KINDA STUFF THAT HAS ALL THE BIG-LEAGUE HEROES TEAMING UP TOGETHER.
OR SOMETIMES FIGHTING EACH OTHER, I GUESS. I DON'T KNOW. LIKE I SAID, I NEVER GET THE CALL.
I'M USUALLY DRUNK AND READ ABOUT IT IN THE PAPER THE NEXT DAY.

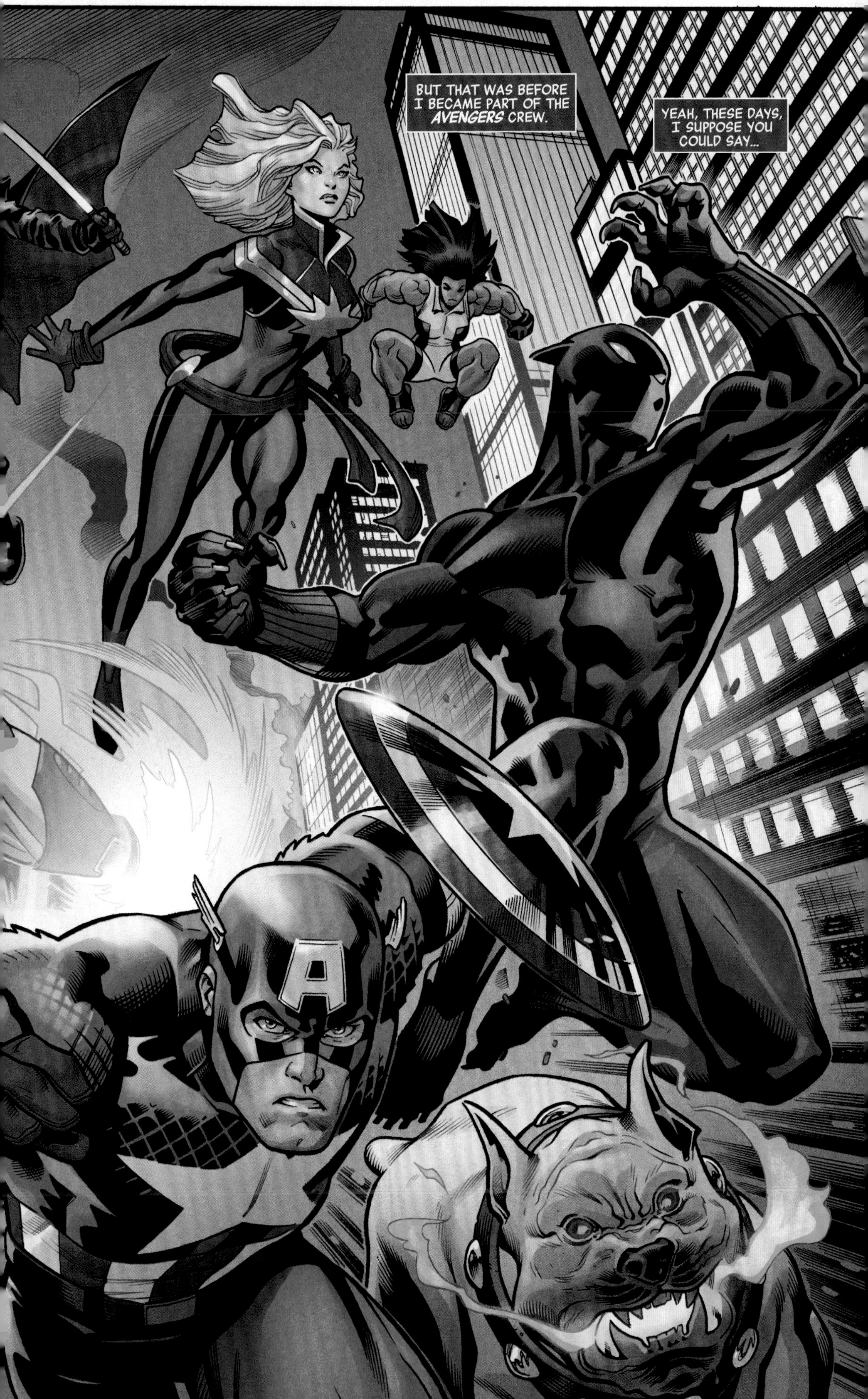
BUT THAT WAS BEFORE I BECAME PART OF THE *AVENGERS* CREW.
YEAH, THESE DAYS, I SUPPOSE YOU COULD SAY...

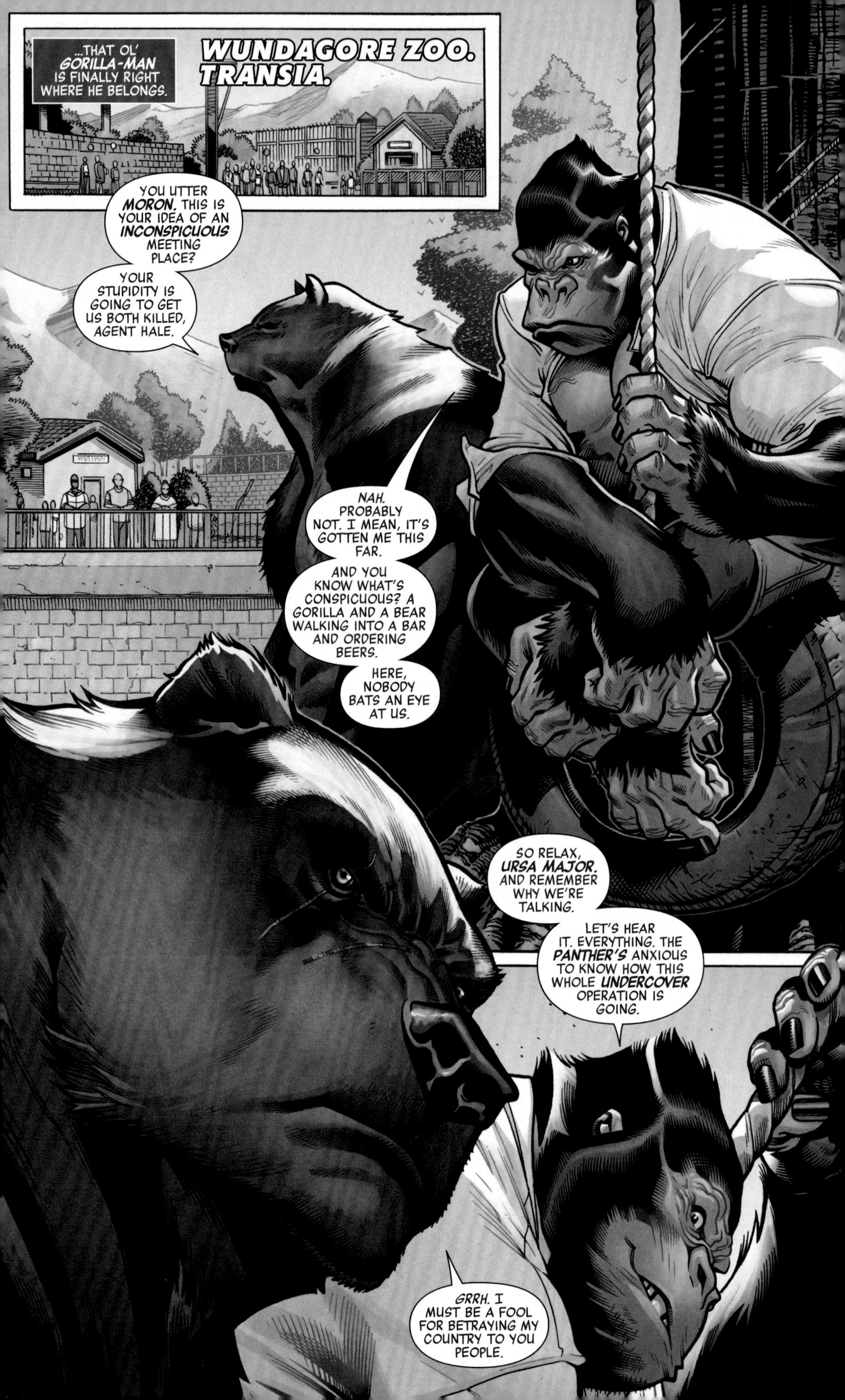

...THAT OL' *GORILLA-MAN* IS FINALLY RIGHT WHERE HE BELONGS.
WUNDAGORE ZOO. TRANSIA.
YOU UTTER ***MORON.*** THIS IS YOUR IDEA OF AN ***INCONSPICUOUS*** MEETING PLACE?
YOUR STUPIDITY IS GOING TO GET US BOTH KILLED, AGENT HALE.
NAH. PROBABLY NOT. I MEAN, IT'S GOTTEN ME THIS FAR.
AND YOU KNOW WHAT'S CONSPICUOUS? A GORILLA AND A BEAR WALKING INTO A BAR AND ORDERING BEERS.
HERE, NOBODY BATS AN EYE AT US.
SO RELAX, ***URSA MAJOR.*** AND REMEMBER WHY WE'RE TALKING.
LET'S HEAR IT. EVERYTHING. THE ***PANTHER'S*** ANXIOUS TO KNOW HOW THIS WHOLE ***UNDERCOVER*** OPERATION IS GOING.
GRRH. I MUST BE A FOOL FOR BETRAYING MY COUNTRY TO YOU PEOPLE.

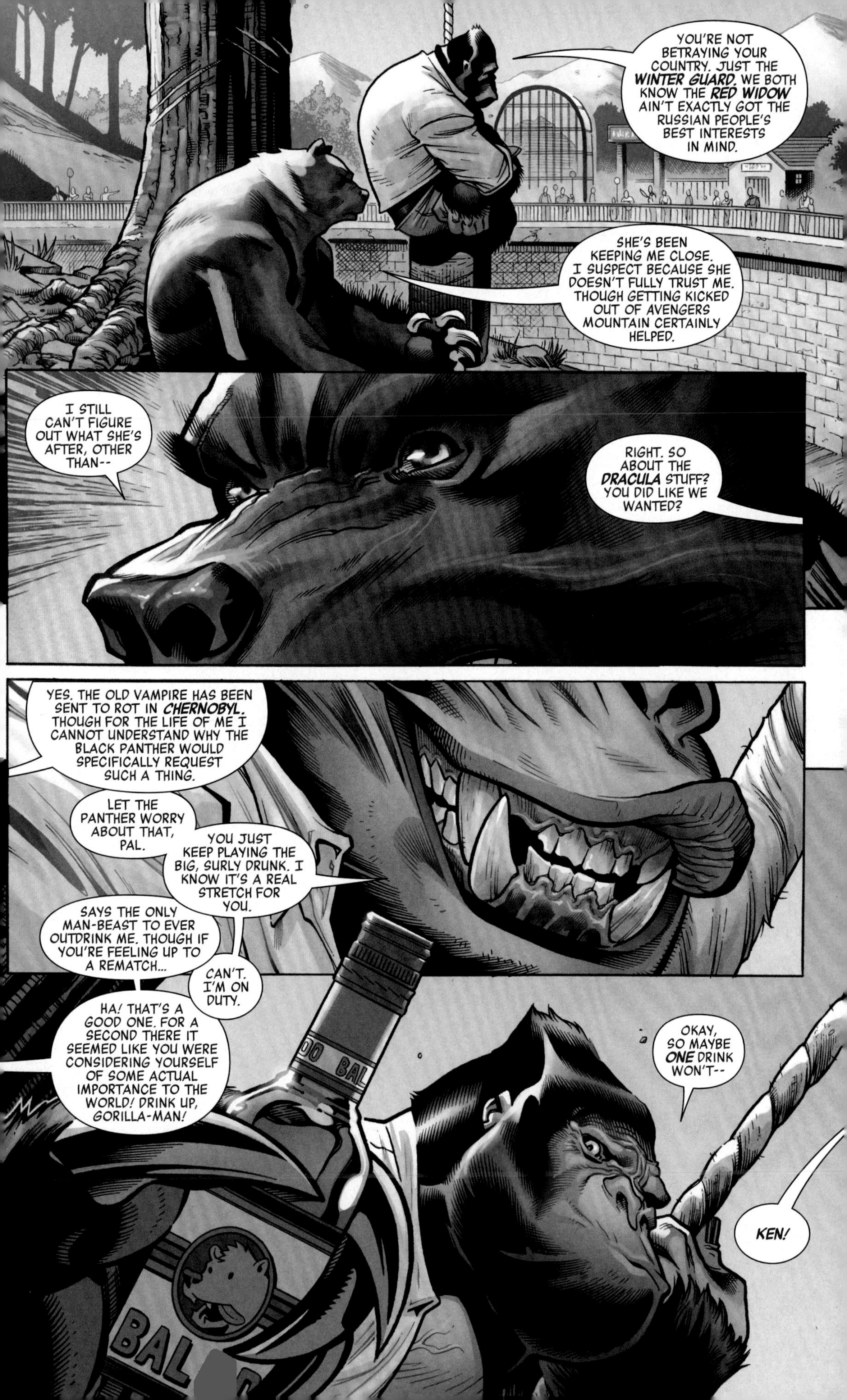
YOU'RE NOT BETRAYING YOUR COUNTRY. JUST THE WINTER GUARD. WE BOTH KNOW THE RED WIDOW AIN'T EXACTLY GOT THE RUSSIAN PEOPLE'S BEST INTERESTS IN MIND.
SHE'S BEEN KEEPING ME CLOSE. I SUSPECT BECAUSE SHE DOESN'T FULLY TRUST ME. THOUGH GETTING KICKED OUT OF AVENGERS MOUNTAIN CERTAINLY HELPED.
I STILL CAN'T FIGURE OUT WHAT SHE'S AFTER, OTHER THAN--
RIGHT. SO ABOUT THE DRACULA STUFF? YOU DID LIKE WE WANTED?
YES. THE OLD VAMPIRE HAS BEEN SENT TO ROT IN CHERNOBYL. THOUGH FOR THE LIFE OF ME I CANNOT UNDERSTAND WHY THE BLACK PANTHER WOULD SPECIFICALLY REQUEST SUCH A THING.
LET THE PANTHER WORRY ABOUT THAT, PAL.
YOU JUST KEEP PLAYING THE BIG, SURLY DRUNK. I KNOW IT'S A REAL STRETCH FOR YOU.
SAYS THE ONLY MAN-BEAST TO EVER OUTDRINK ME. THOUGH IF YOU'RE FEELING UP TO A REMATCH...
CAN'T. I'M ON DUTY.
HA! THAT'S A GOOD ONE. FOR A SECOND THERE IT SEEMED LIKE YOU WERE CONSIDERING YOURSELF OF SOME ACTUAL IMPORTANCE TO THE WORLD! DRINK UP, GORILLA-MAN!
OKAY, SO MAYBE ONE DRINK WON'T--
KEN!

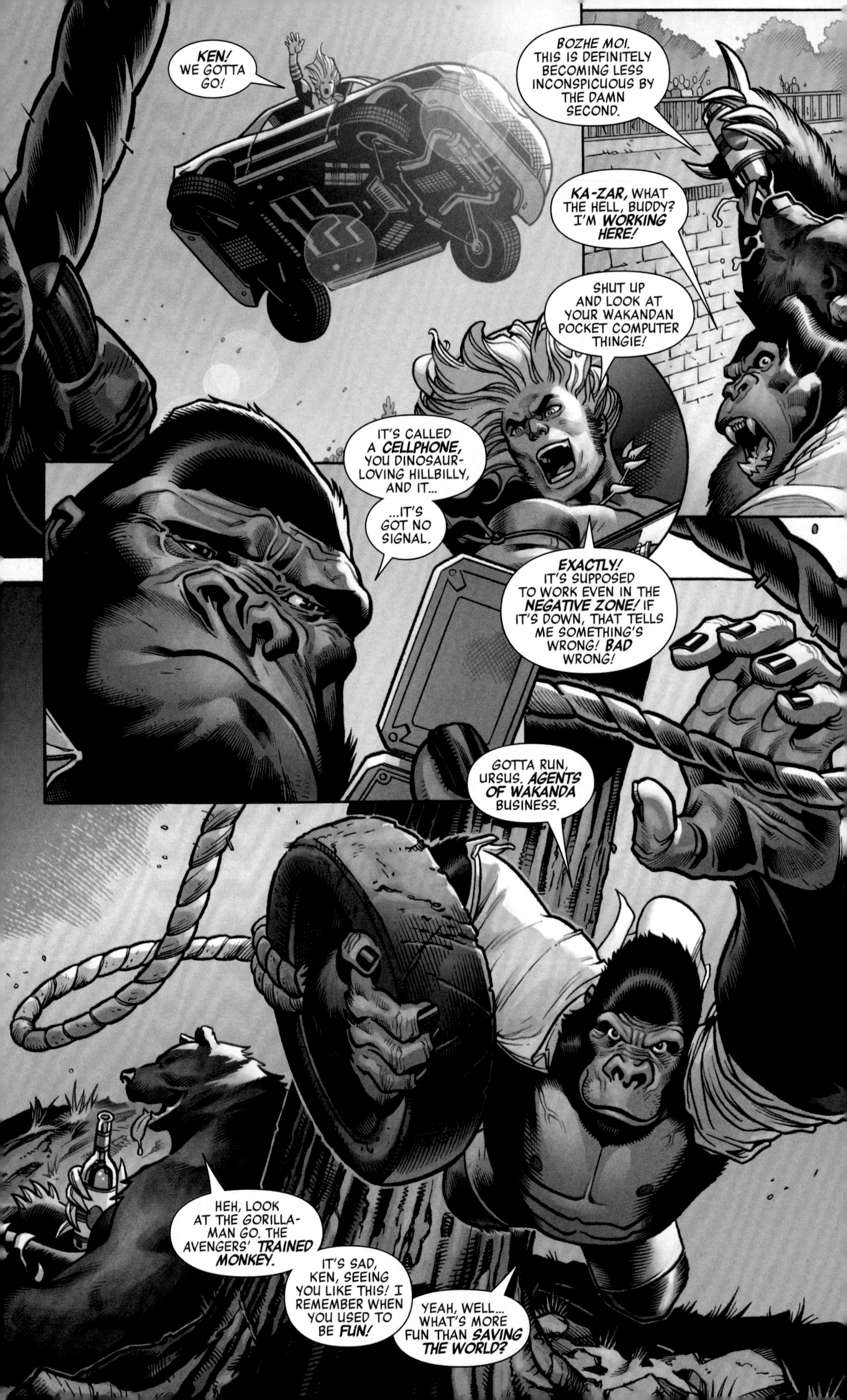
KEN! WE GOTTA GO!
BOZHE MOI. THIS IS DEFINITELY BECOMING LESS INCONSPICUOUS BY THE DAMN SECOND.
KA-ZAR, WHAT THE HELL, BUDDY? I'M WORKING HERE!
SHUT UP AND LOOK AT YOUR WAKANDAN POCKET COMPUTER THINGIE!
IT'S CALLED A CELLPHONE, YOU DINOSAUR-LOVING HILLBILLY, AND IT...
...IT'S GOT NO SIGNAL.
EXACTLY! IT'S SUPPOSED TO WORK EVEN IN THE NEGATIVE ZONE! IF IT'S DOWN, THAT TELLS ME SOMETHING'S WRONG! BAD WRONG!
GOTTA RUN, URSUS. AGENTS OF WAKANDA BUSINESS.
HEH, LOOK AT THE GORILLA-MAN GO. THE AVENGERS' TRAINED MONKEY.
IT'S SAD, KEN, SEEING YOU LIKE THIS! I REMEMBER WHEN YOU USED TO BE FUN!
YEAH, WELL... WHAT'S MORE FUN THAN SAVING THE WORLD?

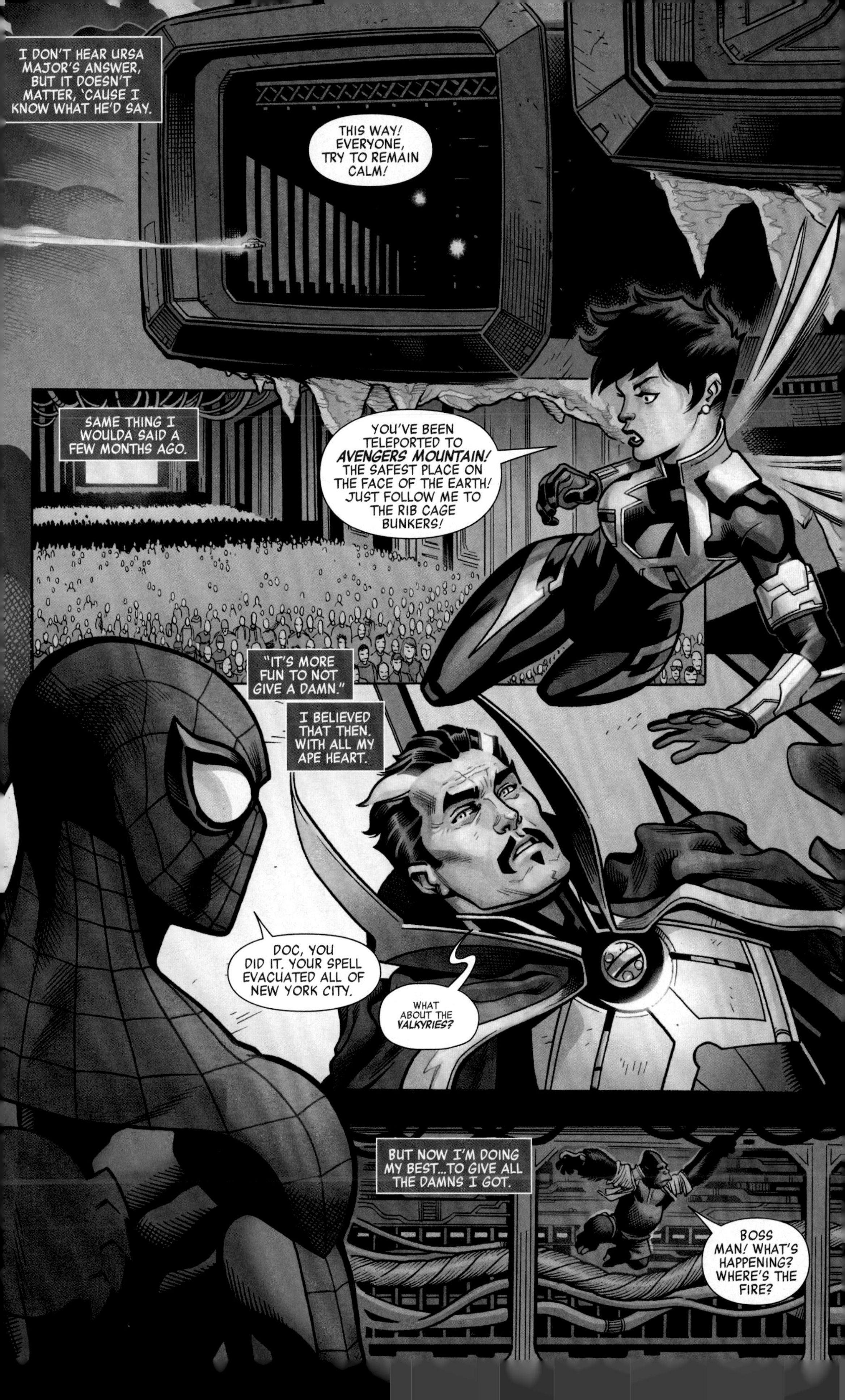
I DON'T HEAR URSA MAJOR'S ANSWER, BUT IT DOESN'T MATTER, 'CAUSE I KNOW WHAT HE'D SAY.
THIS WAY! EVERYONE, TRY TO REMAIN CALM!
SAME THING I WOULDA SAID A FEW MONTHS AGO.
YOU'VE BEEN TELEPORTED TO AVENGERS MOUNTAIN! THE SAFEST PLACE ON THE FACE OF THE EARTH! JUST FOLLOW ME TO THE RIB CAGE BUNKERS!
"IT'S MORE FUN TO NOT GIVE A DAMN."
I BELIEVED THAT THEN. WITH ALL MY APE HEART.
DOC, YOU DID IT. YOUR SPELL EVACUATED ALL OF NEW YORK CITY.
WHAT ABOUT THE VALKYRIES?
BUT NOW I'M DOING MY BEST...TO GIVE ALL THE DAMNS I GOT.
BOSS MAN! WHAT'S HAPPENING? WHERE'S THE FIRE?

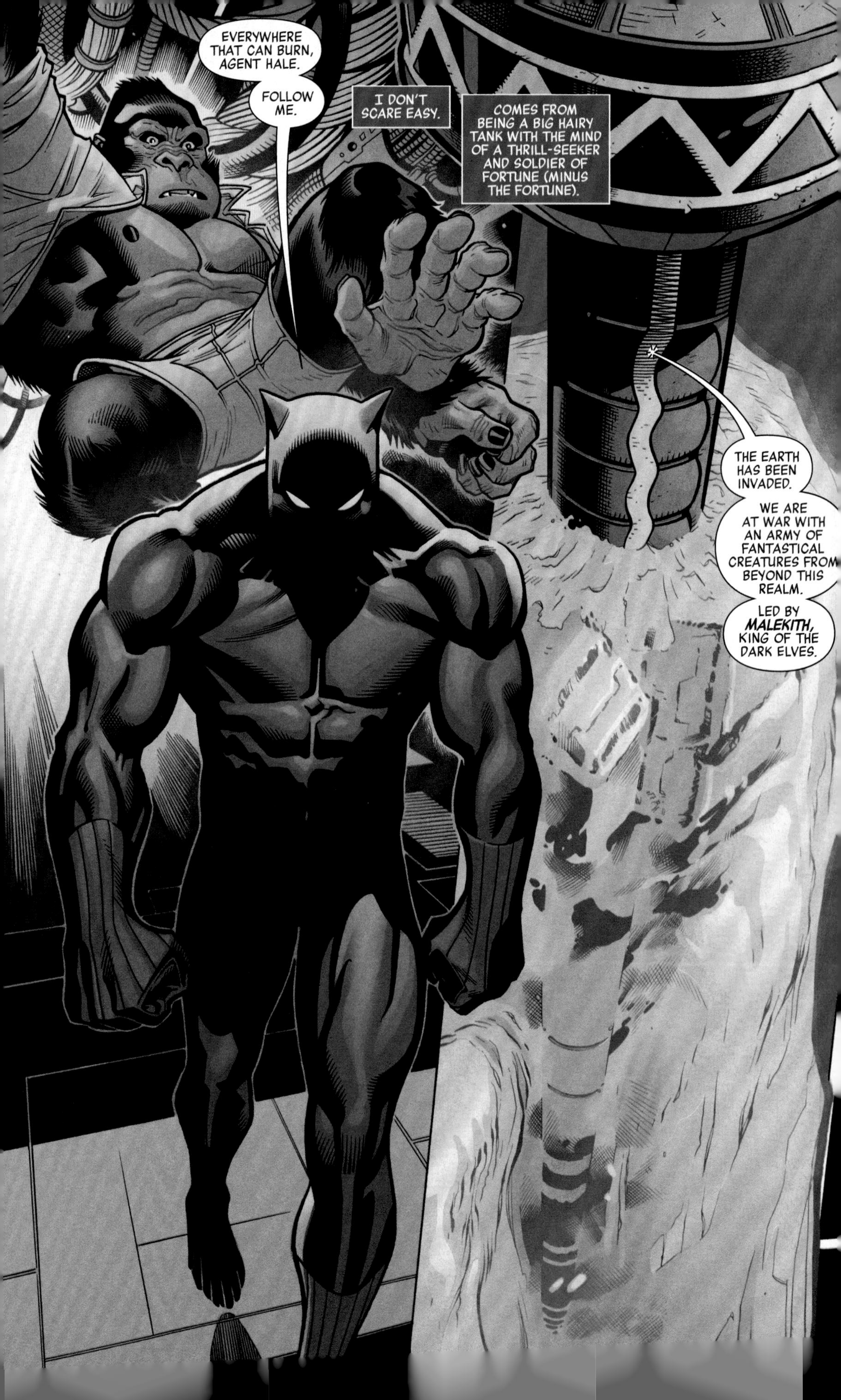
EVERYWHERE THAT CAN BURN, AGENT HALE.
FOLLOW ME.
I DON'T SCARE EASY.
COMES FROM BEING A BIG HAIRY TANK WITH THE MIND OF A THRILL-SEEKER AND SOLDIER OF FORTUNE (MINUS THE FORTUNE).
THE EARTH HAS BEEN INVADED.
WE ARE AT WAR WITH AN ARMY OF FANTASTICAL CREATURES FROM BEYOND THIS REALM.
LED BY *MALEKITH,* KING OF THE DARK ELVES.

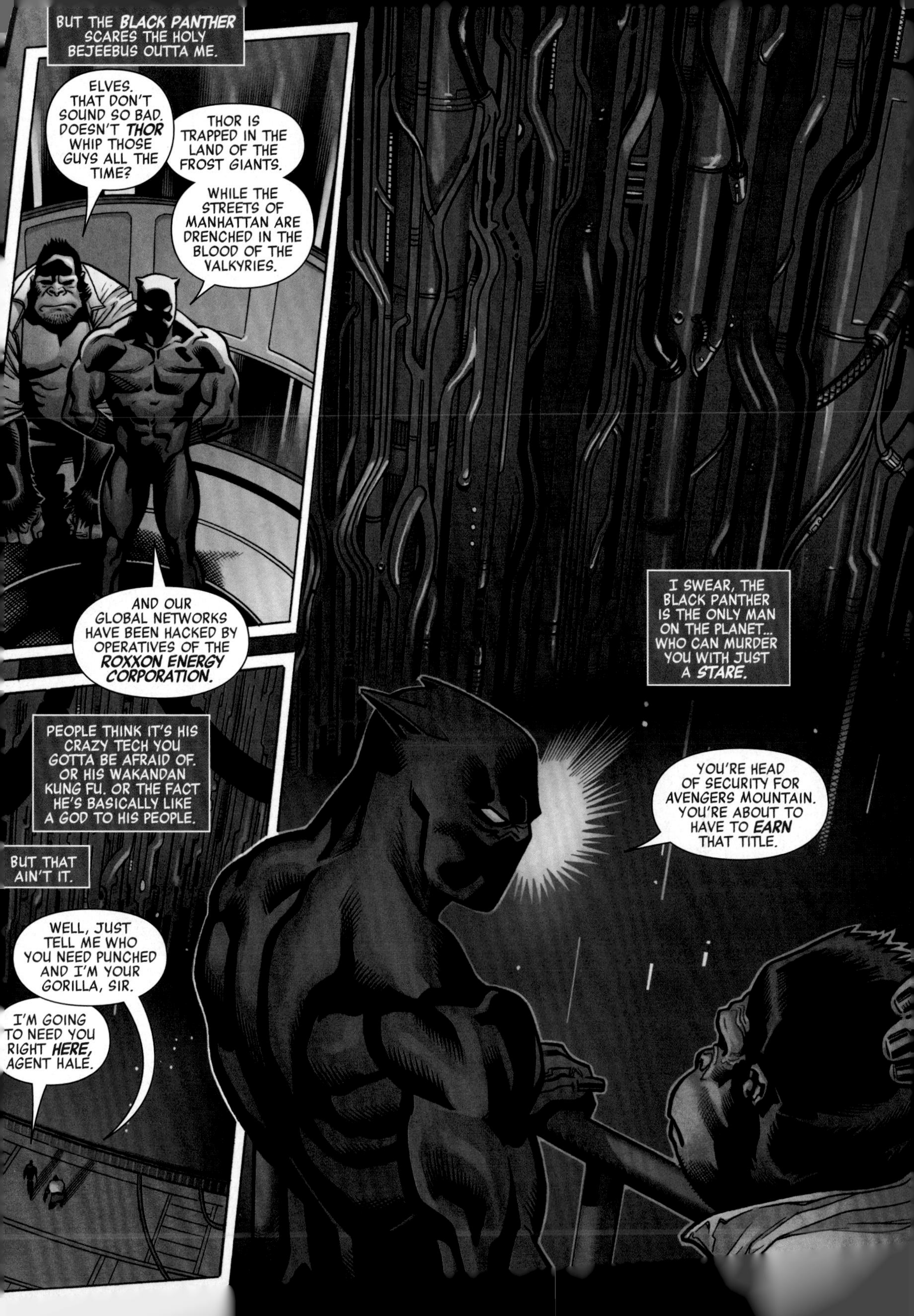

BUT THE BLACK PANTHER SCARES THE HOLY BEJEEBUS OUTTA ME.
ELVES. THAT DON'T SOUND SO BAD. DOESN'T THOR WHIP THOSE GUYS ALL THE TIME?
THOR IS TRAPPED IN THE LAND OF THE FROST GIANTS.
WHILE THE STREETS OF MANHATTAN ARE DRENCHED IN THE BLOOD OF THE VALKYRIES.
AND OUR GLOBAL NETWORKS HAVE BEEN HACKED BY OPERATIVES OF THE ROXXON ENERGY CORPORATION.
PEOPLE THINK IT'S HIS CRAZY TECH YOU GOTTA BE AFRAID OF. OR HIS WAKANDAN KUNG FU. OR THE FACT HE'S BASICALLY LIKE A GOD TO HIS PEOPLE.
BUT THAT AIN'T IT.
WELL, JUST TELL ME WHO YOU NEED PUNCHED AND I'M YOUR GORILLA, SIR.
I'M GOING TO NEED YOU RIGHT HERE, AGENT HALE.
I SWEAR, THE BLACK PANTHER IS THE ONLY MAN ON THE PLANET... WHO CAN MURDER YOU WITH JUST A STARE.
YOU'RE HEAD OF SECURITY FOR AVENGERS MOUNTAIN. YOU'RE ABOUT TO HAVE TO EARN THAT TITLE.

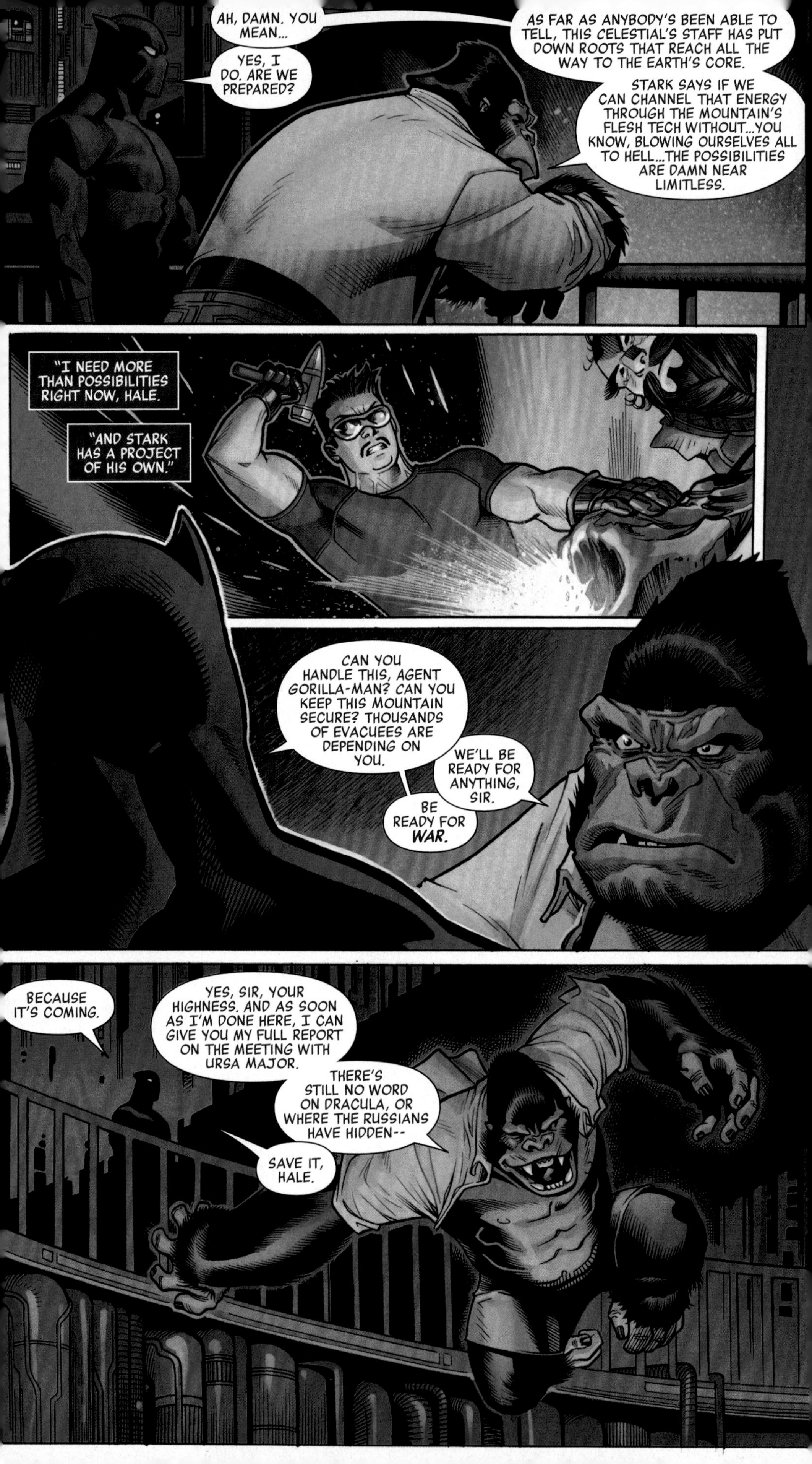
AH, DAMN. YOU MEAN...
AS FAR AS ANYBODY'S BEEN ABLE TO TELL, THIS CELESTIAL'S STAFF HAS PUT DOWN ROOTS THAT REACH ALL THE WAY TO THE EARTH'S CORE.
STARK SAYS IF WE CAN CHANNEL THAT ENERGY THROUGH THE MOUNTAIN'S FLESH TECH WITHOUT...YOU KNOW, BLOWING OURSELVES ALL TO HELL...THE POSSIBILITIES ARE DAMN NEAR LIMITLESS.
YES, I DO. ARE WE PREPARED?
"I NEED MORE THAN POSSIBILITIES RIGHT NOW, HALE.
"AND STARK HAS A PROJECT OF HIS OWN."
CAN YOU HANDLE THIS, AGENT GORILLA-MAN? CAN YOU KEEP THIS MOUNTAIN SECURE? THOUSANDS OF EVACUEES ARE DEPENDING ON YOU.
WE'LL BE READY FOR ANYTHING, SIR.
BE READY FOR **WAR.**
BECAUSE IT'S COMING.
YES, SIR, YOUR HIGHNESS. AND AS SOON AS I'M DONE HERE, I CAN GIVE YOU MY FULL REPORT ON THE MEETING WITH URSA MAJOR.
THERE'S STILL NO WORD ON DRACULA, OR WHERE THE RUSSIANS HAVE HIDDEN--
SAVE IT, HALE.

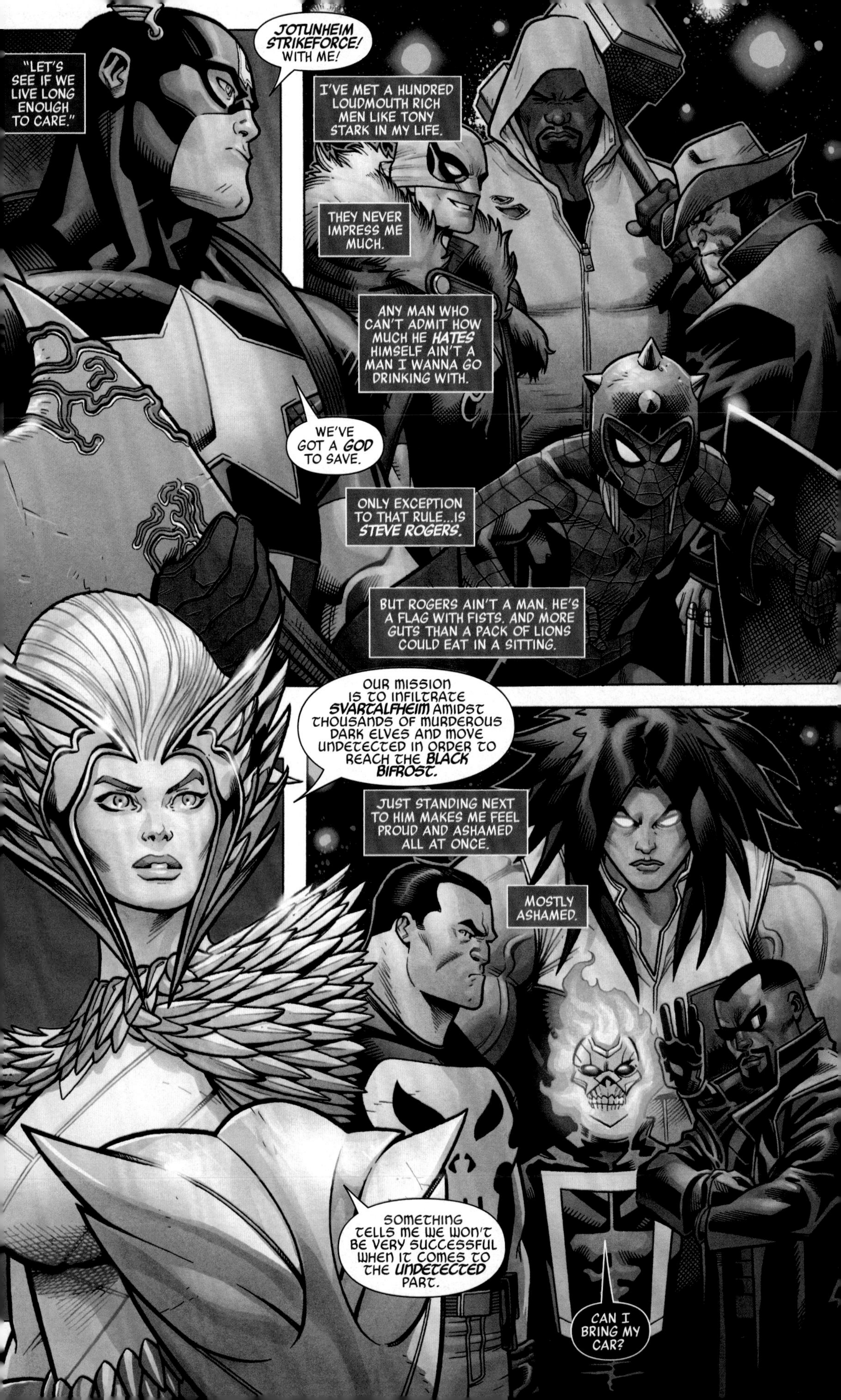
"LET'S SEE IF WE LIVE LONG ENOUGH TO CARE."
JOTUNHEIM STRIKEFORCE! WITH ME!
I'VE MET A HUNDRED LOUDMOUTH RICH MEN LIKE TONY STARK IN MY LIFE.
THEY NEVER IMPRESS ME MUCH.
ANY MAN WHO CAN'T ADMIT HOW MUCH HE HATES HIMSELF AIN'T A MAN I WANNA GO DRINKING WITH.
WE'VE GOT A GOD TO SAVE.
ONLY EXCEPTION TO THAT RULE...IS STEVE ROGERS.
BUT ROGERS AIN'T A MAN. HE'S A FLAG WITH FISTS. AND MORE GUTS THAN A PACK OF LIONS COULD EAT IN A SITTING.
OUR MISSION IS TO INFILTRATE SVARTALFHEIM AMIDST THOUSANDS OF MURDEROUS DARK ELVES AND MOVE UNDETECTED IN ORDER TO REACH THE BLACK BIFROST.
JUST STANDING NEXT TO HIM MAKES ME FEEL PROUD AND ASHAMED ALL AT ONCE.
MOSTLY ASHAMED.
SOMETHING TELLS ME WE WON'T BE VERY SUCCESSFUL WHEN IT COMES TO THE UNDETECTED PART.
CAN I BRING MY CAR?

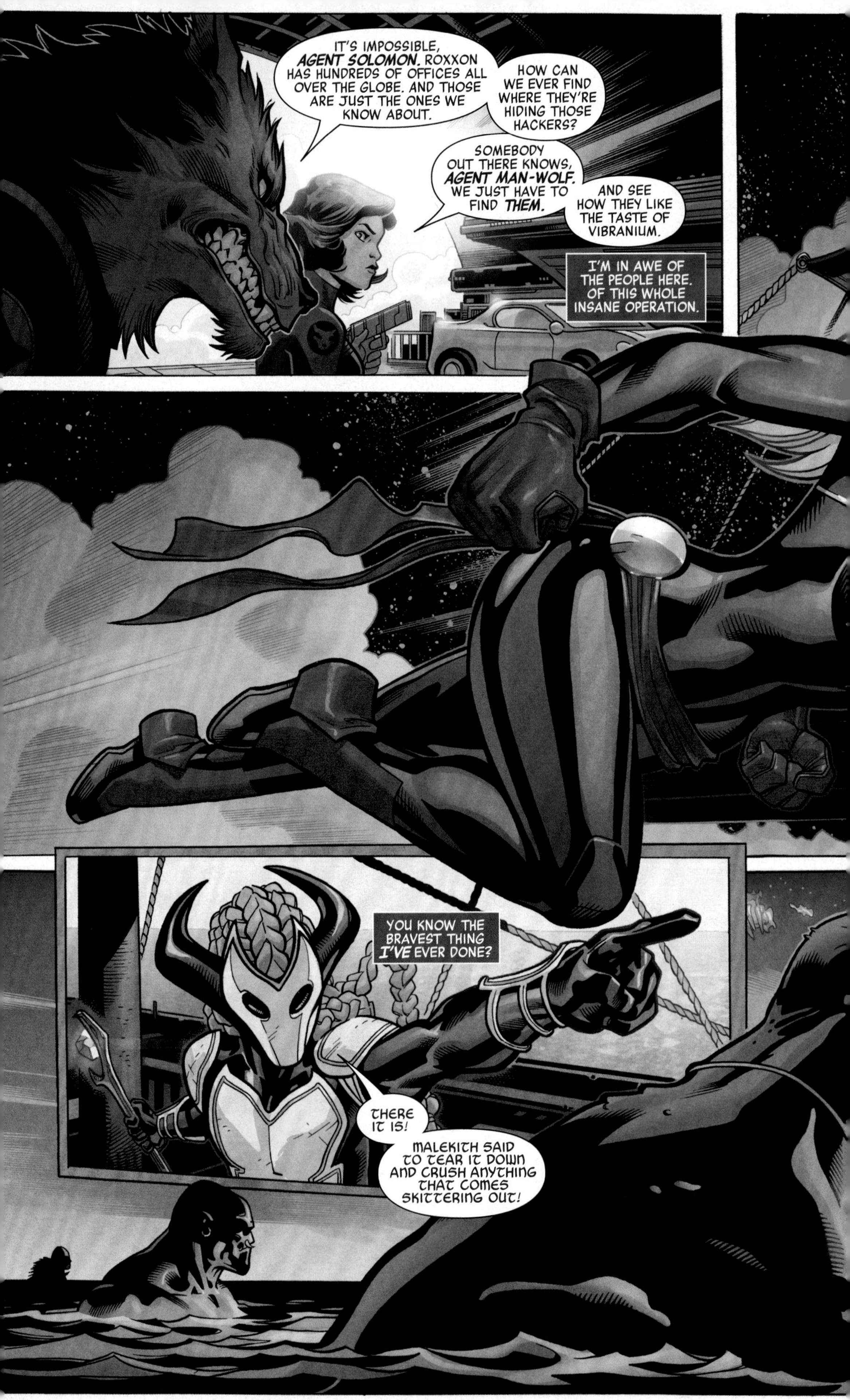
IT'S IMPOSSIBLE, AGENT SOLOMON. ROXXON HAS HUNDREDS OF OFFICES ALL OVER THE GLOBE. AND THOSE ARE JUST THE ONES WE KNOW ABOUT.
HOW CAN WE EVER FIND WHERE THEY'RE HIDING THOSE HACKERS?
SOMEBODY OUT THERE KNOWS, AGENT MAN-WOLF. WE JUST HAVE TO FIND THEM.
AND SEE HOW THEY LIKE THE TASTE OF VIBRANIUM.
I'M IN AWE OF THE PEOPLE HERE. OF THIS WHOLE INSANE OPERATION.
YOU KNOW THE BRAVEST THING I'VE EVER DONE?
THERE IT IS!
MALEKITH SAID TO TEAR IT DOWN AND CRUSH ANYTHING THAT COMES SKITTERING OUT!

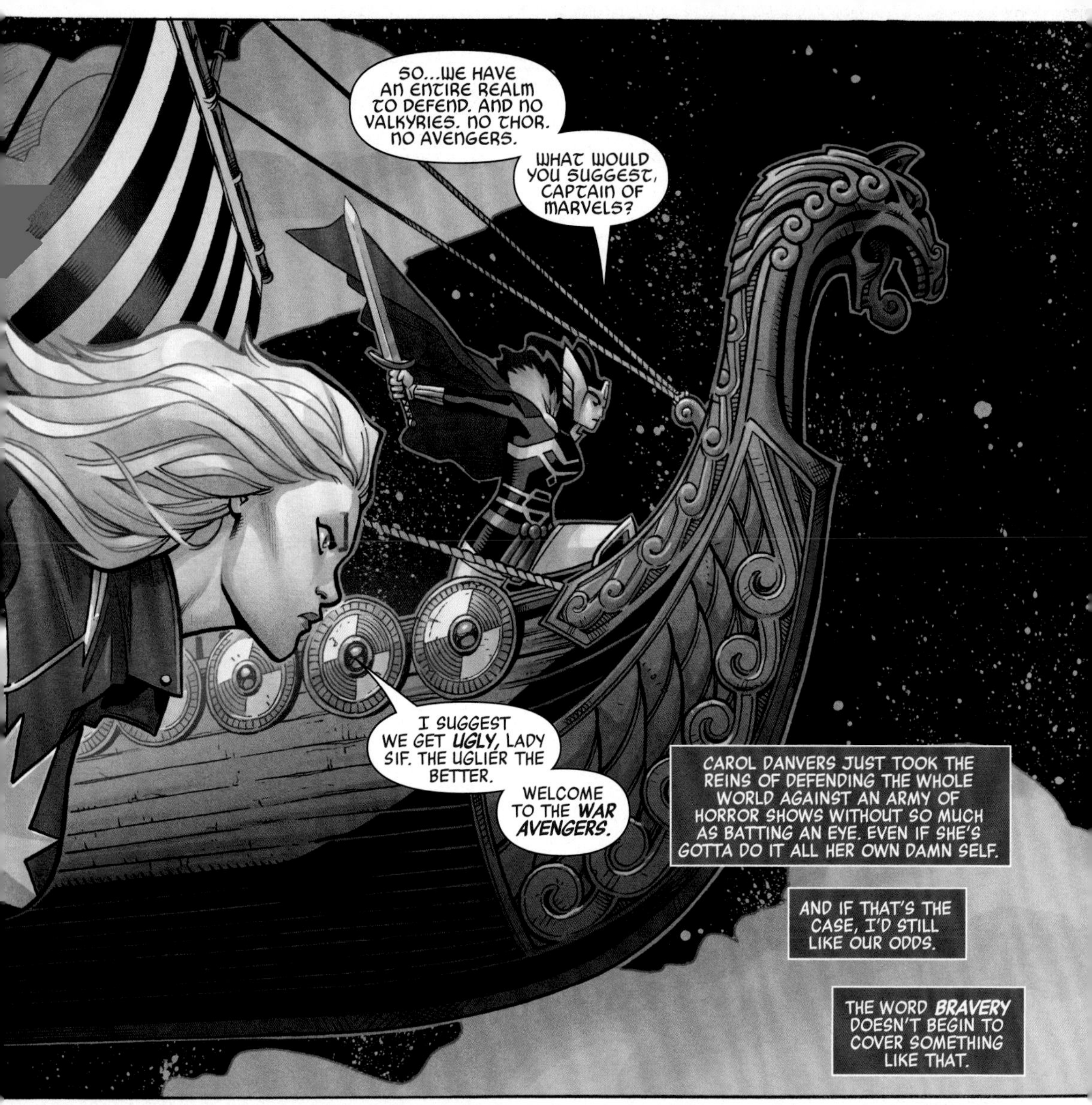
SO...WE HAVE AN ENTIRE REALM TO DEFEND. AND NO VALKYRIES. NO THOR. NO AVENGERS.
WHAT WOULD YOU SUGGEST, CAPTAIN OF MARVELS?
I SUGGEST WE GET UGLY, LADY SIF. THE UGLIER THE BETTER.
WELCOME TO THE WAR AVENGERS.
CAROL DANVERS JUST TOOK THE REINS OF DEFENDING THE WHOLE WORLD AGAINST AN ARMY OF HORROR SHOWS WITHOUT SO MUCH AS BATTING AN EYE. EVEN IF SHE'S GOTTA DO IT ALL HER OWN DAMN SELF.
AND IF THAT'S THE CASE, I'D STILL LIKE OUR ODDS.
THE WORD BRAVERY DOESN'T BEGIN TO COVER SOMETHING LIKE THAT.

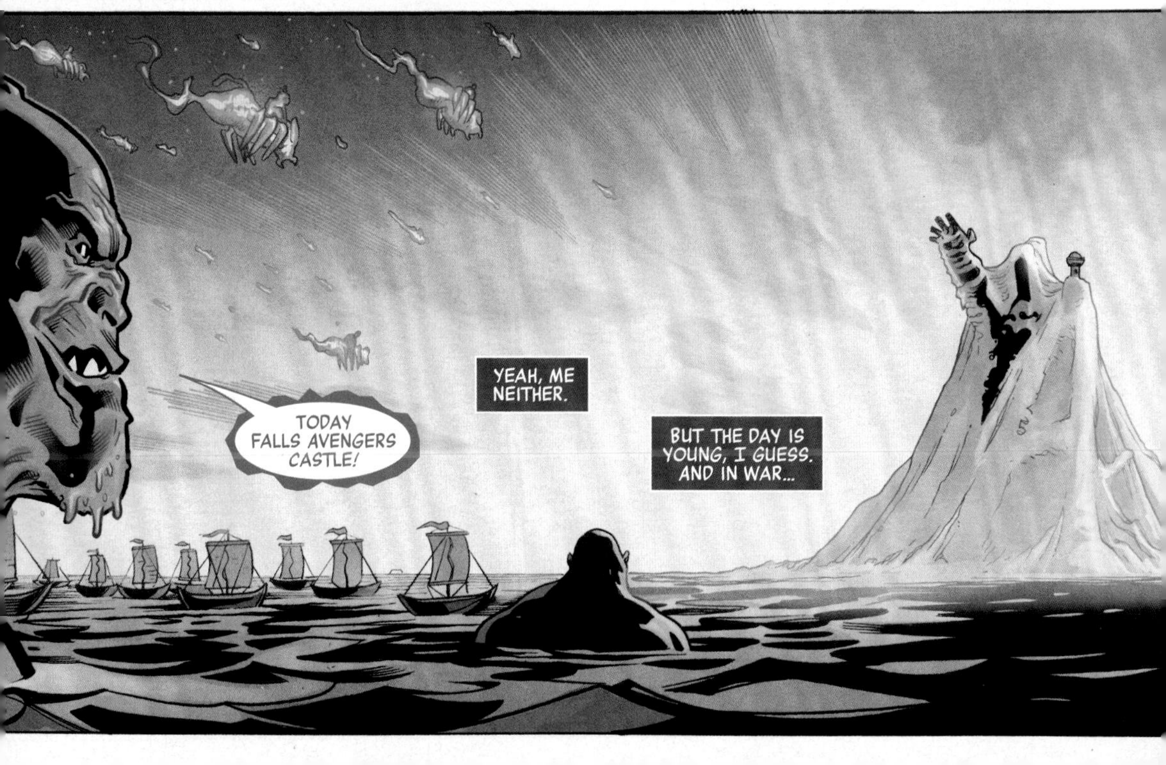
YEAH, ME NEITHER.
TODAY FALLS AVENGERS CASTLE!
BUT THE DAY IS YOUNG, I GUESS. AND IN WAR...

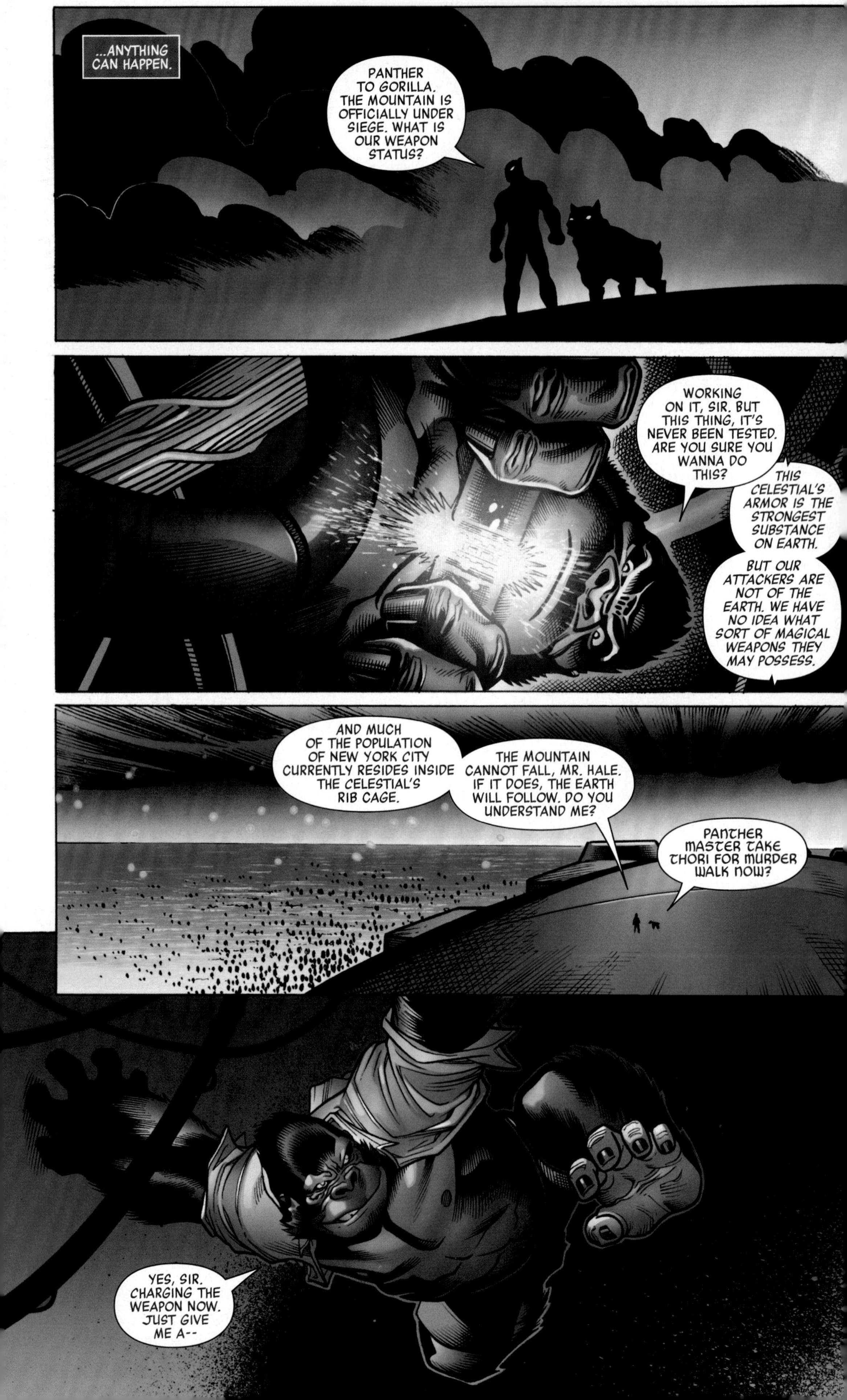
...ANYTHING CAN HAPPEN.
PANTHER TO GORILLA. THE MOUNTAIN IS OFFICIALLY UNDER SIEGE. WHAT IS OUR WEAPON STATUS?
WORKING ON IT, SIR. BUT THIS THING, IT'S NEVER BEEN TESTED. ARE YOU SURE YOU WANNA DO THIS?
THIS CELESTIAL'S ARMOR IS THE STRONGEST SUBSTANCE ON EARTH.
BUT OUR ATTACKERS ARE NOT OF THE EARTH. WE HAVE NO IDEA WHAT SORT OF MAGICAL WEAPONS THEY MAY POSSESS.
AND MUCH OF THE POPULATION OF NEW YORK CITY CURRENTLY RESIDES INSIDE THE CELESTIAL'S RIB CAGE.
THE MOUNTAIN CANNOT FALL, MR. HALE. IF IT DOES, THE EARTH WILL FOLLOW. DO YOU UNDERSTAND ME?
PANTHER MASTER TAKE THORI FOR MURDER WALK NOW?
YES, SIR. CHARGING THE WEAPON NOW. JUST GIVE ME A--

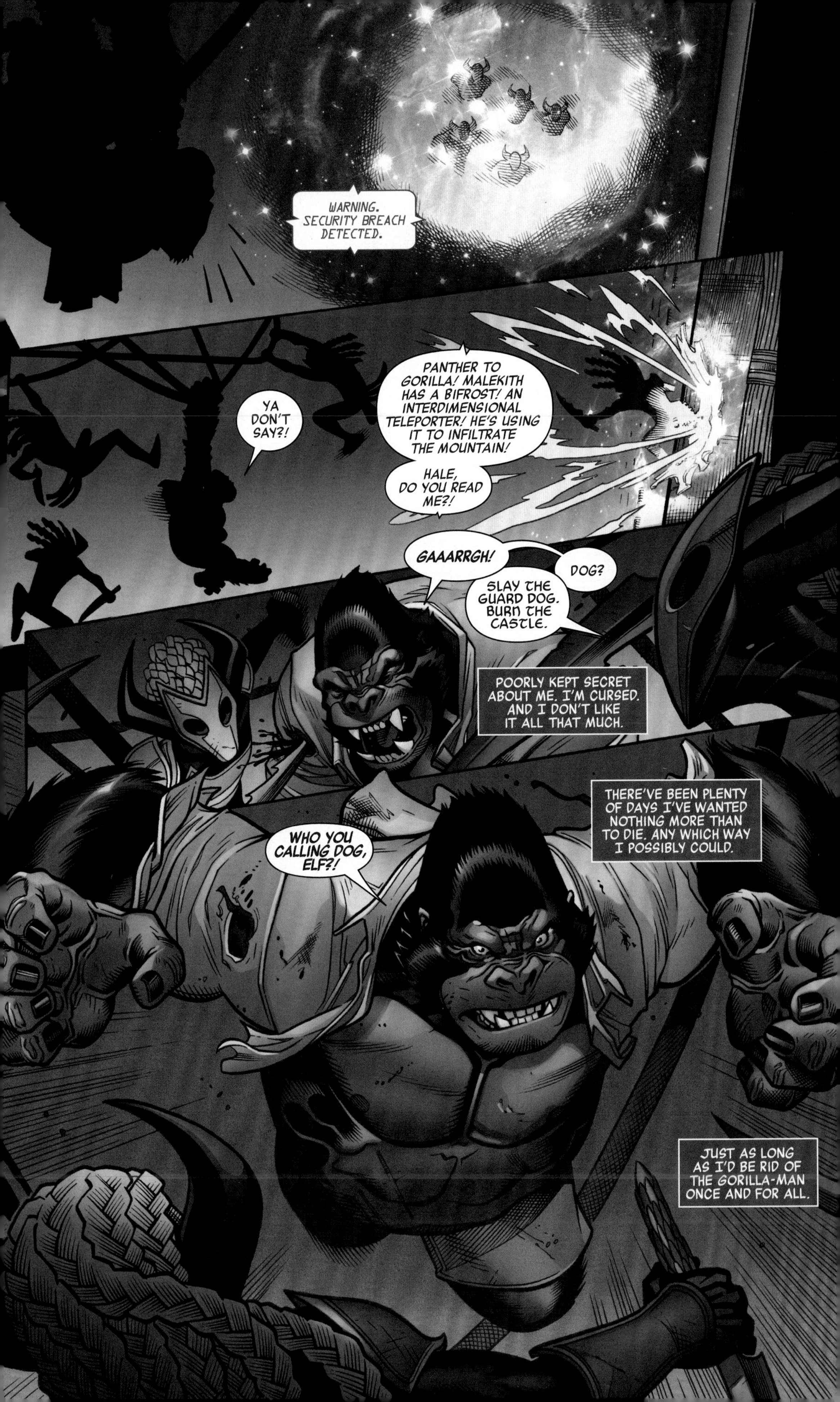
WARNING. SECURITY BREACH DETECTED.
YA DON'T SAY?!
PANTHER TO GORILLA! MALEKITH HAS A BIFROST! AN INTERDIMENSIONAL TELEPORTER! HE'S USING IT TO INFILTRATE THE MOUNTAIN!
HALE, DO YOU READ ME?!
GAAARRGH!
DOG?
SLAY THE GUARD DOG. BURN THE CASTLE.
POORLY KEPT SECRET ABOUT ME. I'M CURSED. AND I DON'T LIKE IT ALL THAT MUCH.
THERE'VE BEEN PLENTY OF DAYS I'VE WANTED NOTHING MORE THAN TO DIE. ANY WHICH WAY I POSSIBLY COULD.
WHO YOU CALLING DOG, ELF?!
JUST AS LONG AS I'D BE RID OF THE GORILLA-MAN ONCE AND FOR ALL.

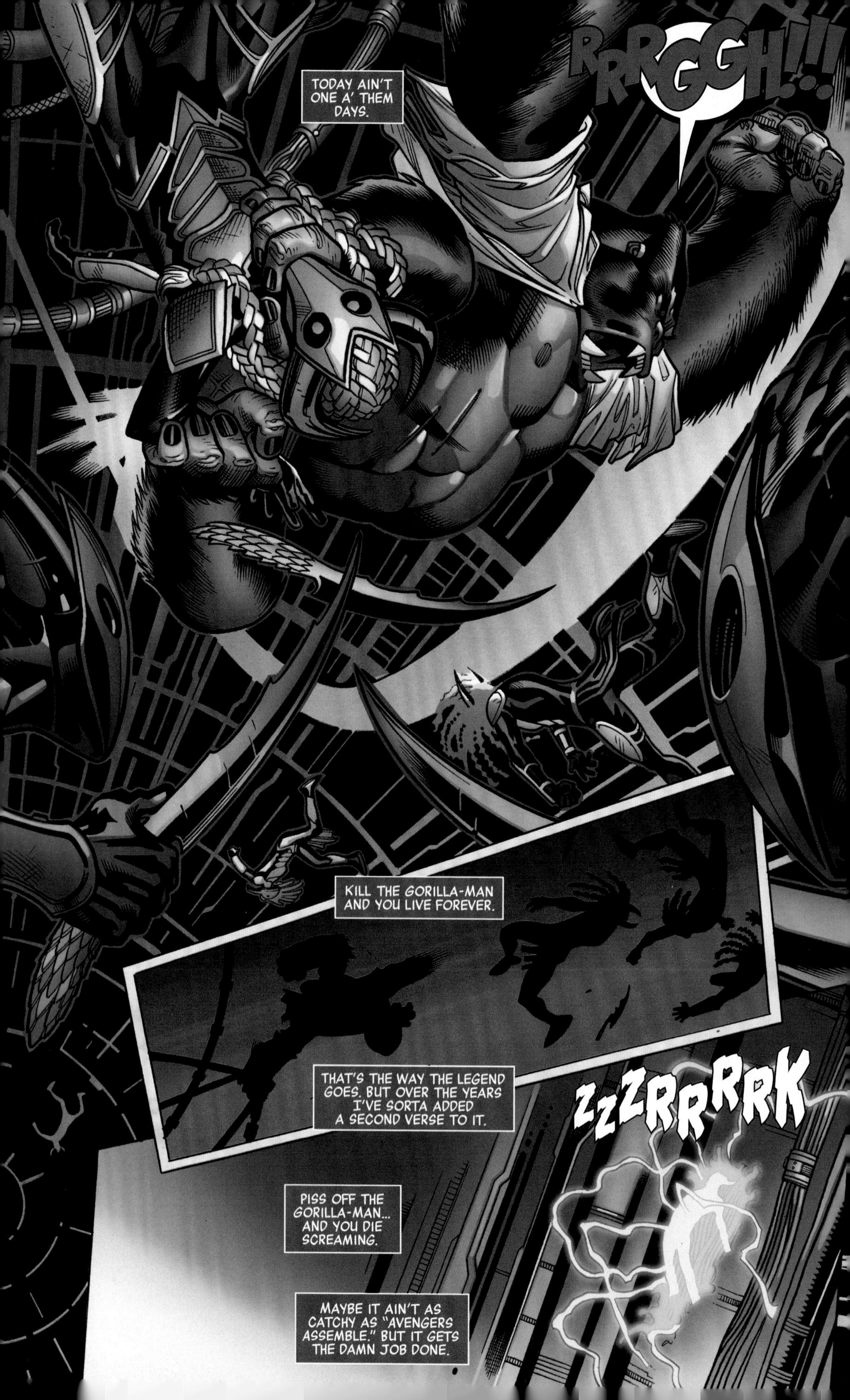
TODAY AIN'T ONE A' THEM DAYS.
RRRGGH!!!
KILL THE GORILLA-MAN AND YOU LIVE FOREVER.
THAT'S THE WAY THE LEGEND GOES. BUT OVER THE YEARS I'VE SORTA ADDED A SECOND VERSE TO IT.
ZZZRRRRRK
PISS OFF THE GORILLA-MAN... AND YOU DIE SCREAMING.
MAYBE IT AIN'T AS CATCHY AS "AVENGERS ASSEMBLE," BUT IT GETS THE DAMN JOB DONE.

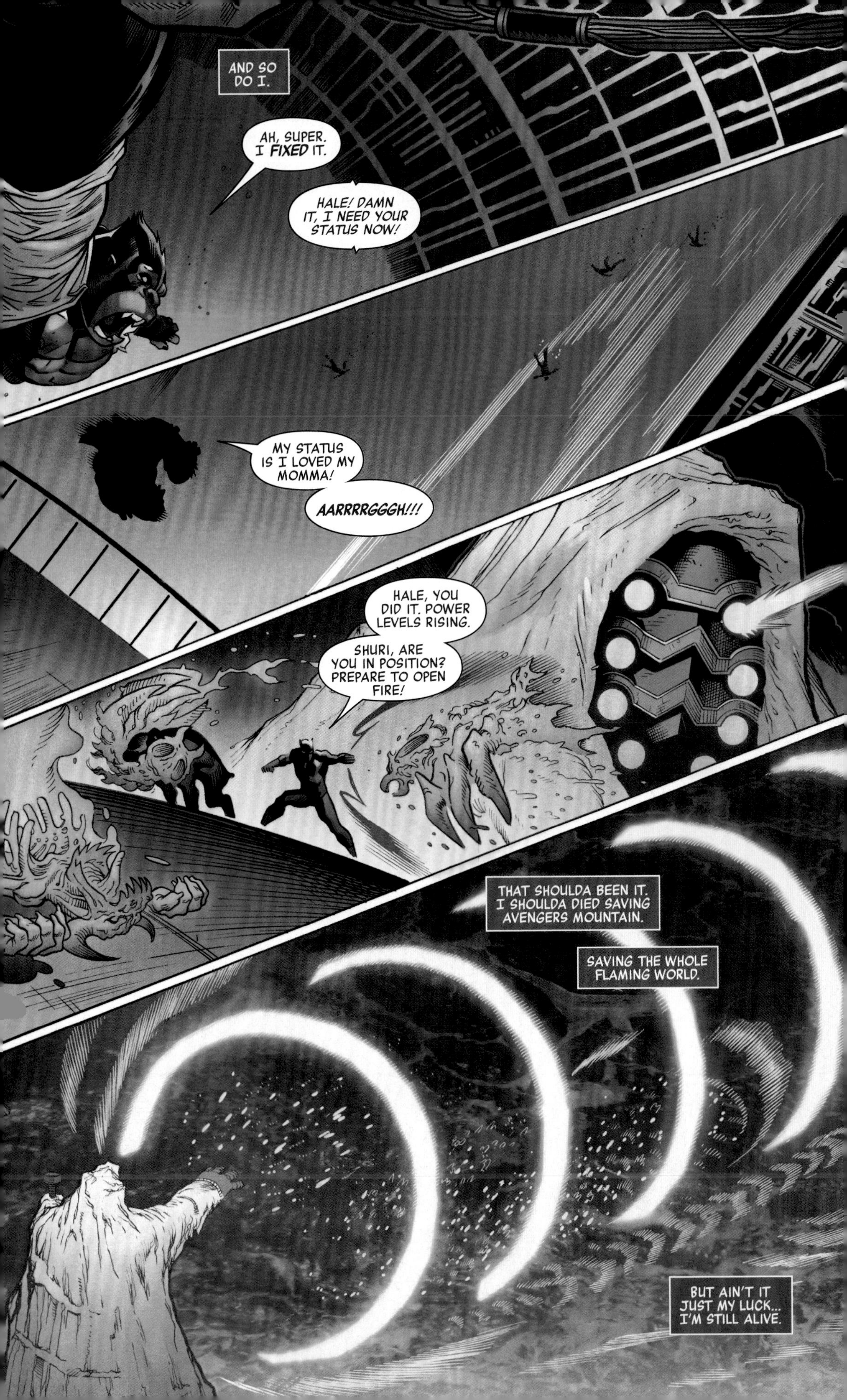
AND SO DO I.
AH, SUPER. I FIXED IT.
HALE! DAMN IT, I NEED YOUR STATUS NOW!
MY STATUS IS I LOVED MY MOMMA!
AARRRRGGGH!!!
HALE, YOU DID IT. POWER LEVELS RISING.
SHURI, ARE YOU IN POSITION? PREPARE TO OPEN FIRE!
THAT SHOULDA BEEN IT. I SHOULDA DIED SAVING AVENGERS MOUNTAIN.
SAVING THE WHOLE FLAMING WORLD.
BUT AIN'T IT JUST MY LUCK... I'M STILL ALIVE.

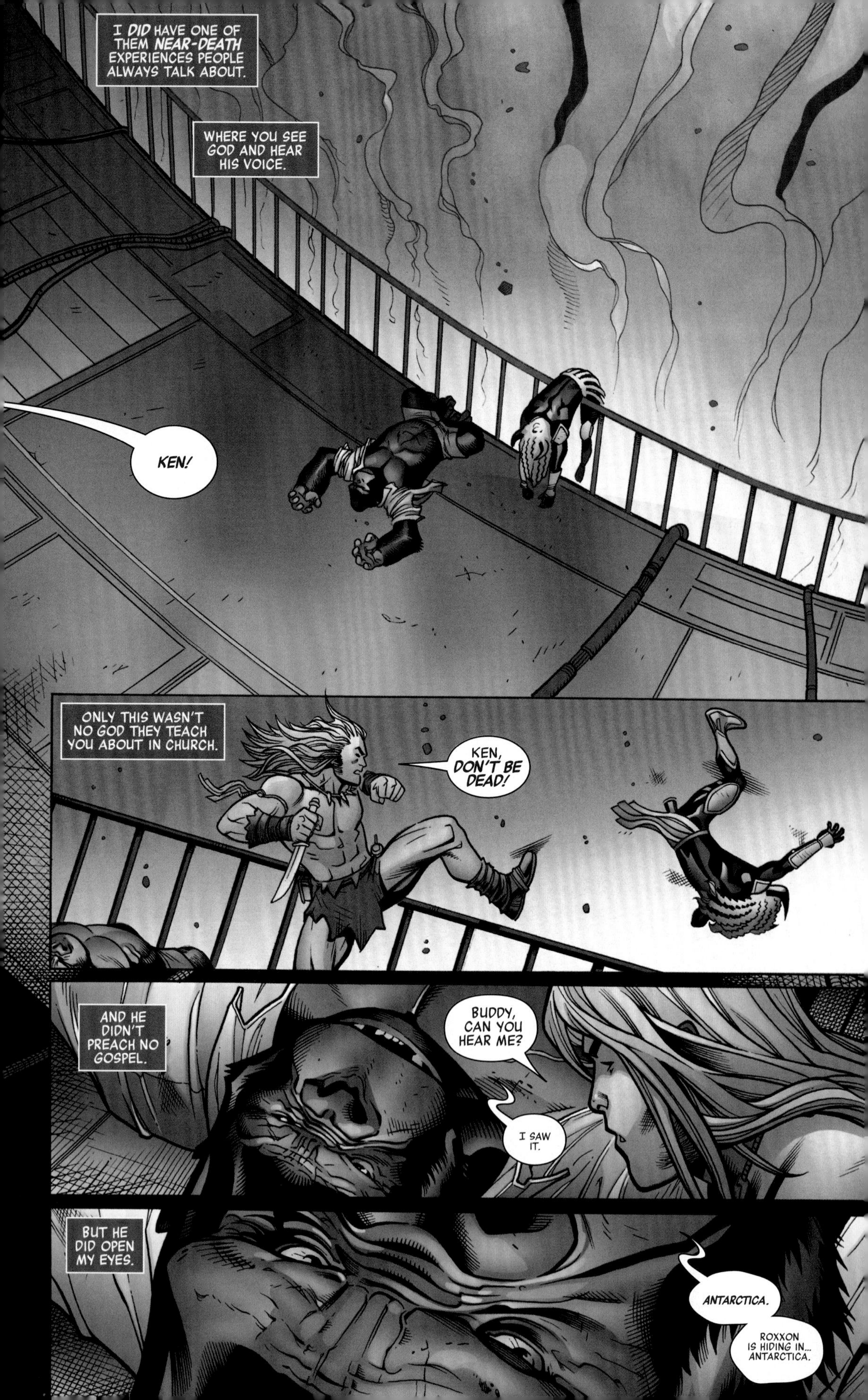
I DID HAVE ONE OF THEM NEAR-DEATH EXPERIENCES PEOPLE ALWAYS TALK ABOUT.
WHERE YOU SEE GOD AND HEAR HIS VOICE.
KEN!
ONLY THIS WASN'T NO GOD THEY TEACH YOU ABOUT IN CHURCH.
KEN, DON'T BE DEAD!
AND HE DIDN'T PREACH NO GOSPEL.
BUDDY, CAN YOU HEAR ME?
I SAW IT.
BUT HE DID OPEN MY EYES.
ANTARCTICA.
ROXXON IS HIDING IN... ANTARCTICA.

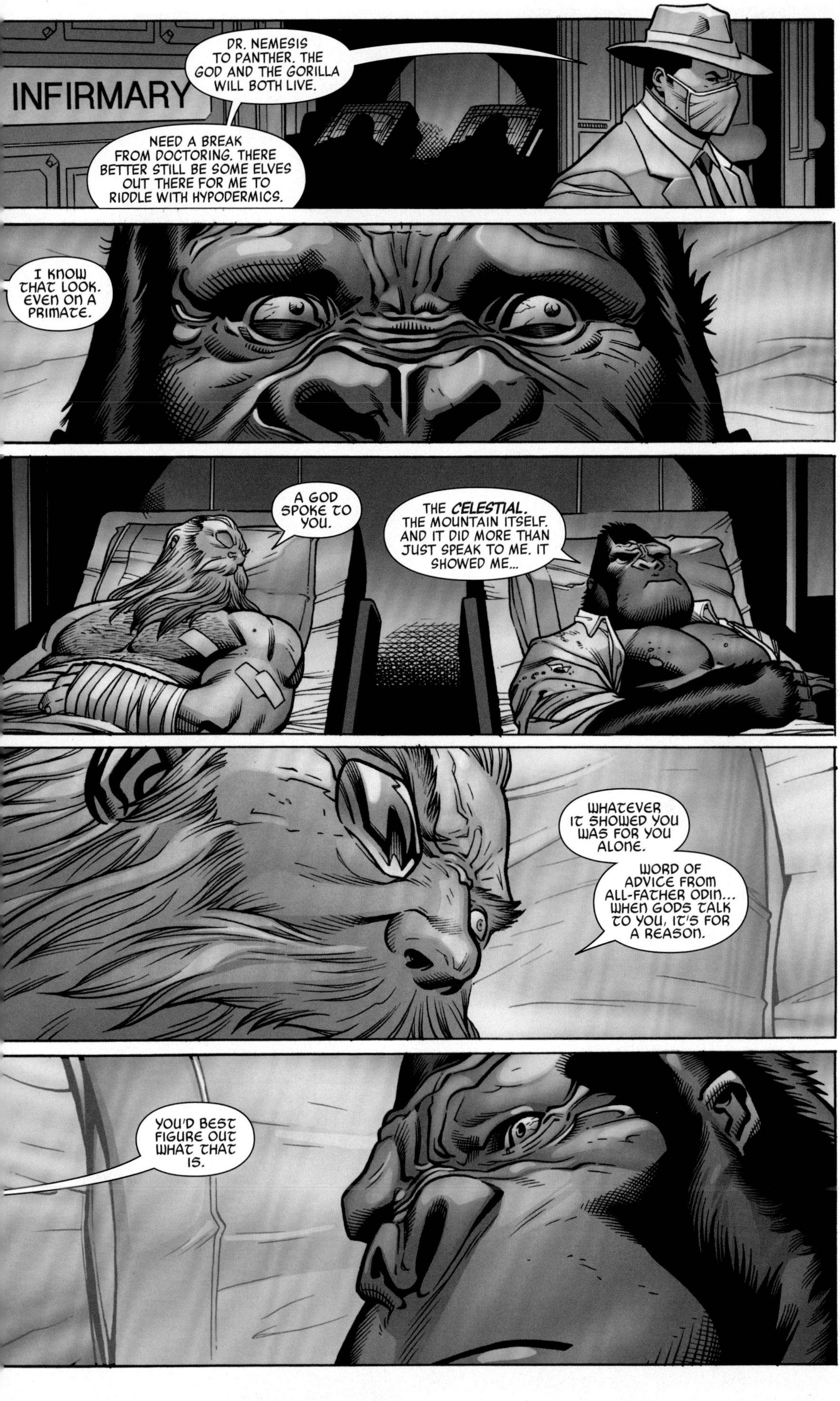
INFIRMARY
DR. NEMESIS TO PANTHER. THE GOD AND THE GORILLA WILL BOTH LIVE.
NEED A BREAK FROM DOCTORING. THERE BETTER STILL BE SOME ELVES OUT THERE FOR ME TO RIDDLE WITH HYPODERMICS.
I KNOW THAT LOOK. EVEN ON A PRIMATE.
A GOD SPOKE TO YOU.
THE CELESTIAL. THE MOUNTAIN ITSELF. AND IT DID MORE THAN JUST SPEAK TO ME. IT SHOWED ME...
WHATEVER IT SHOWED YOU WAS FOR YOU ALONE.
WORD OF ADVICE FROM ALL-FATHER ODIN... WHEN GODS TALK TO YOU, IT'S FOR A REASON.
YOU'D BEST FIGURE OUT WHAT THAT IS.

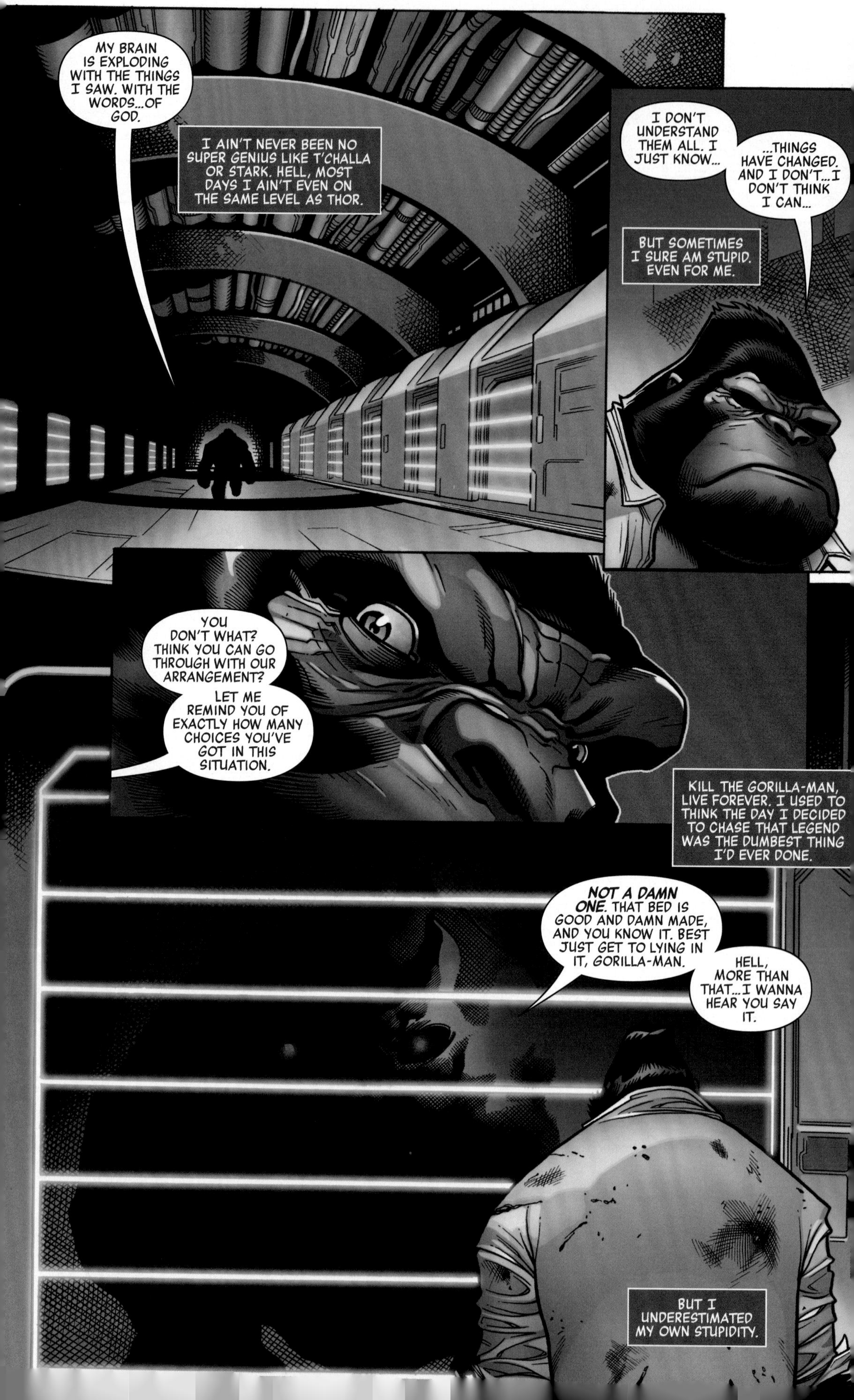
MY BRAIN IS EXPLODING WITH THE THINGS I SAW. WITH THE WORDS...OF GOD.
I AIN'T NEVER BEEN NO SUPER GENIUS LIKE T'CHALLA OR STARK. HELL, MOST DAYS I AIN'T EVEN ON THE SAME LEVEL AS THOR.
I DON'T UNDERSTAND THEM ALL. I JUST KNOW...
...THINGS HAVE CHANGED. AND I DON'T...I DON'T THINK I CAN...
BUT SOMETIMES I SURE AM STUPID. EVEN FOR ME.
YOU DON'T WHAT? THINK YOU CAN GO THROUGH WITH OUR ARRANGEMENT?
LET ME REMIND YOU OF EXACTLY HOW MANY CHOICES YOU'VE GOT IN THIS SITUATION.
KILL THE GORILLA-MAN, LIVE FOREVER. I USED TO THINK THE DAY I DECIDED TO CHASE THAT LEGEND WAS THE DUMBEST THING I'D EVER DONE.
NOT A DAMN ONE. THAT BED IS GOOD AND DAMN MADE, AND YOU KNOW IT. BEST JUST GET TO LYING IN IT, GORILLA-MAN.
HELL, MORE THAN THAT...I WANNA HEAR YOU SAY IT.
BUT I UNDERESTIMATED MY OWN STUPIDITY.

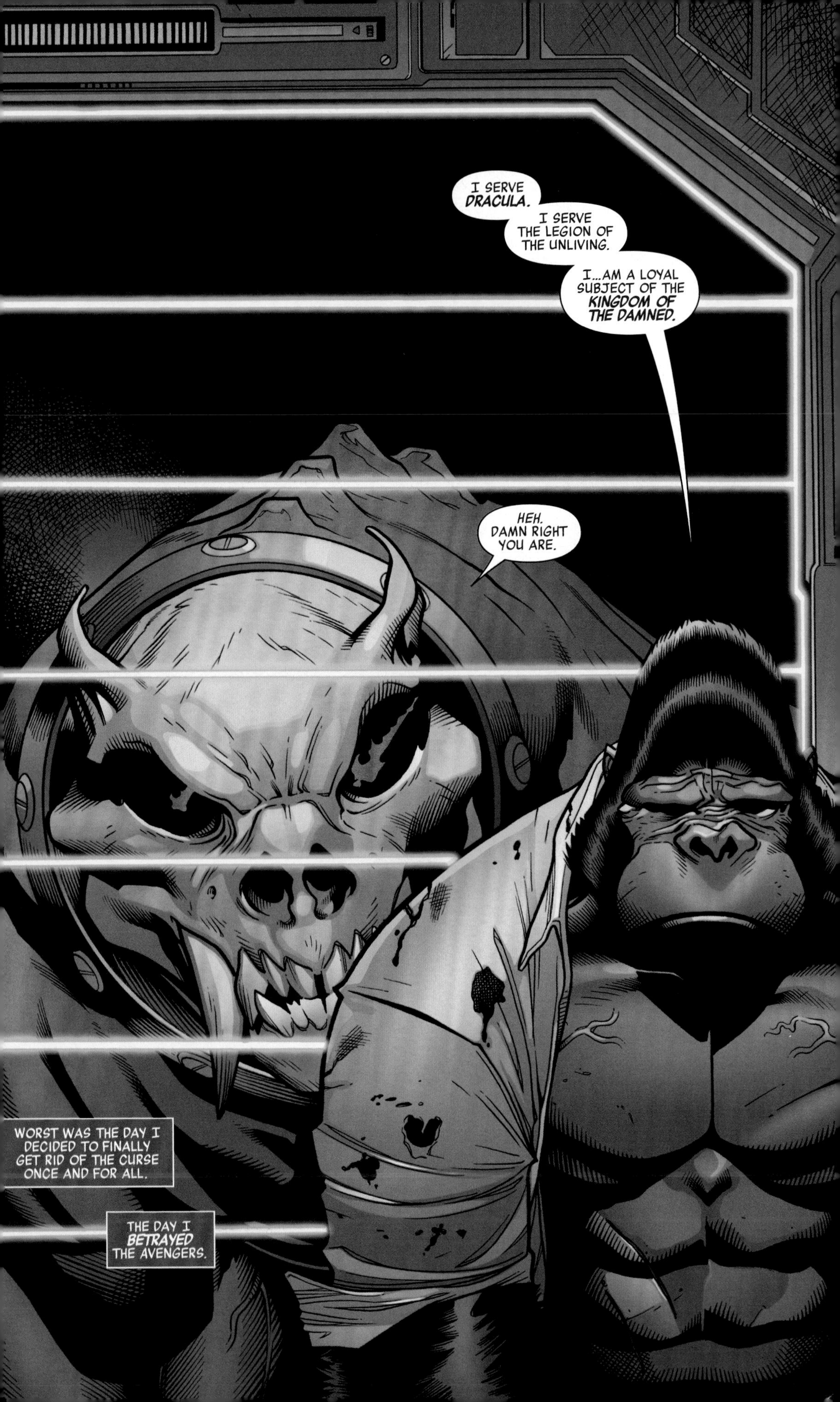
I SERVE DRACULA.
I SERVE THE LEGION OF THE UNLIVING.
I...AM A LOYAL SUBJECT OF THE KINGDOM OF THE DAMNED.
HEH. DAMN RIGHT YOU ARE.
WORST WAS THE DAY I DECIDED TO FINALLY GET RID OF THE CURSE ONCE AND FOR ALL.
THE DAY I BETRAYED THE AVENGERS.

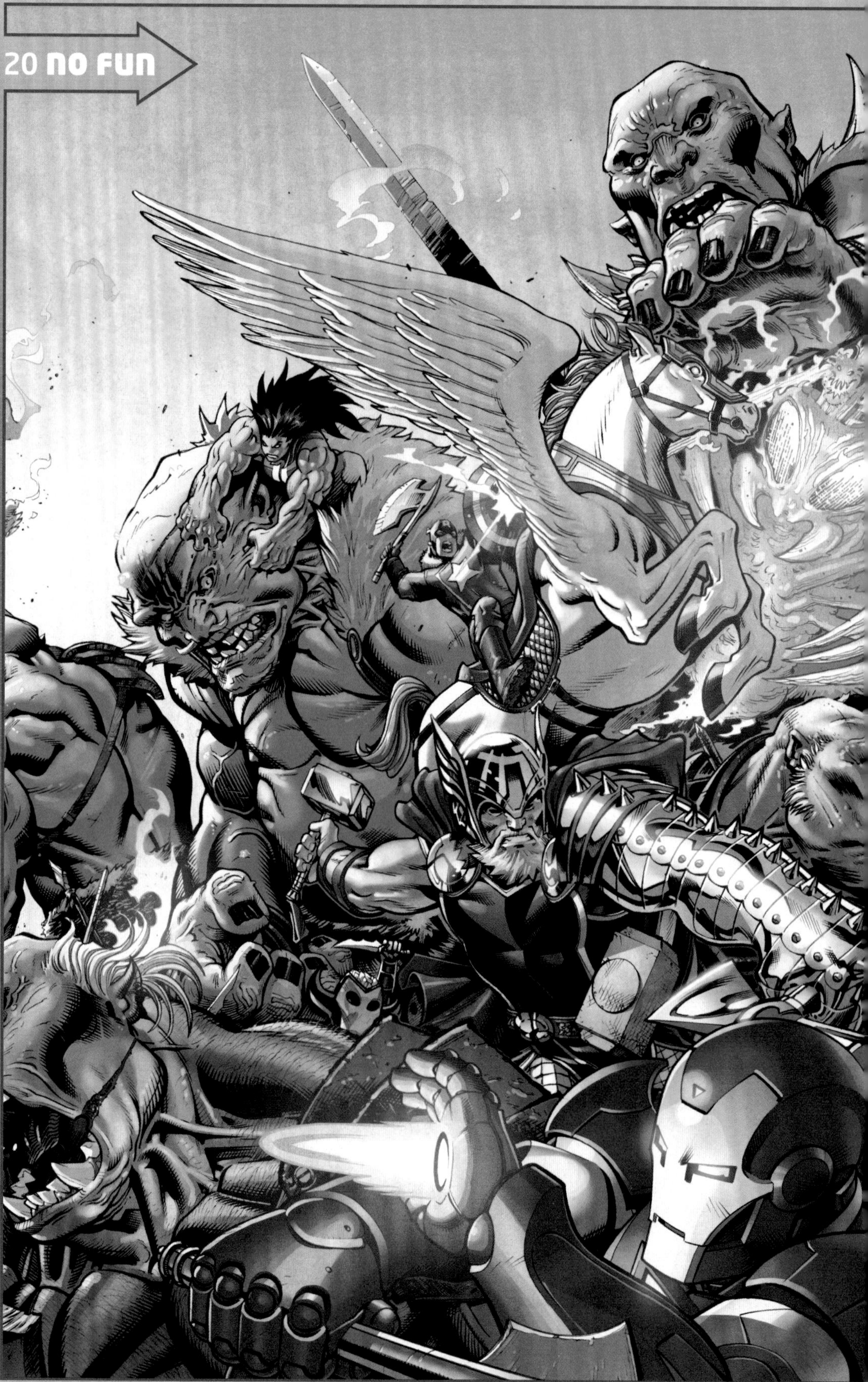

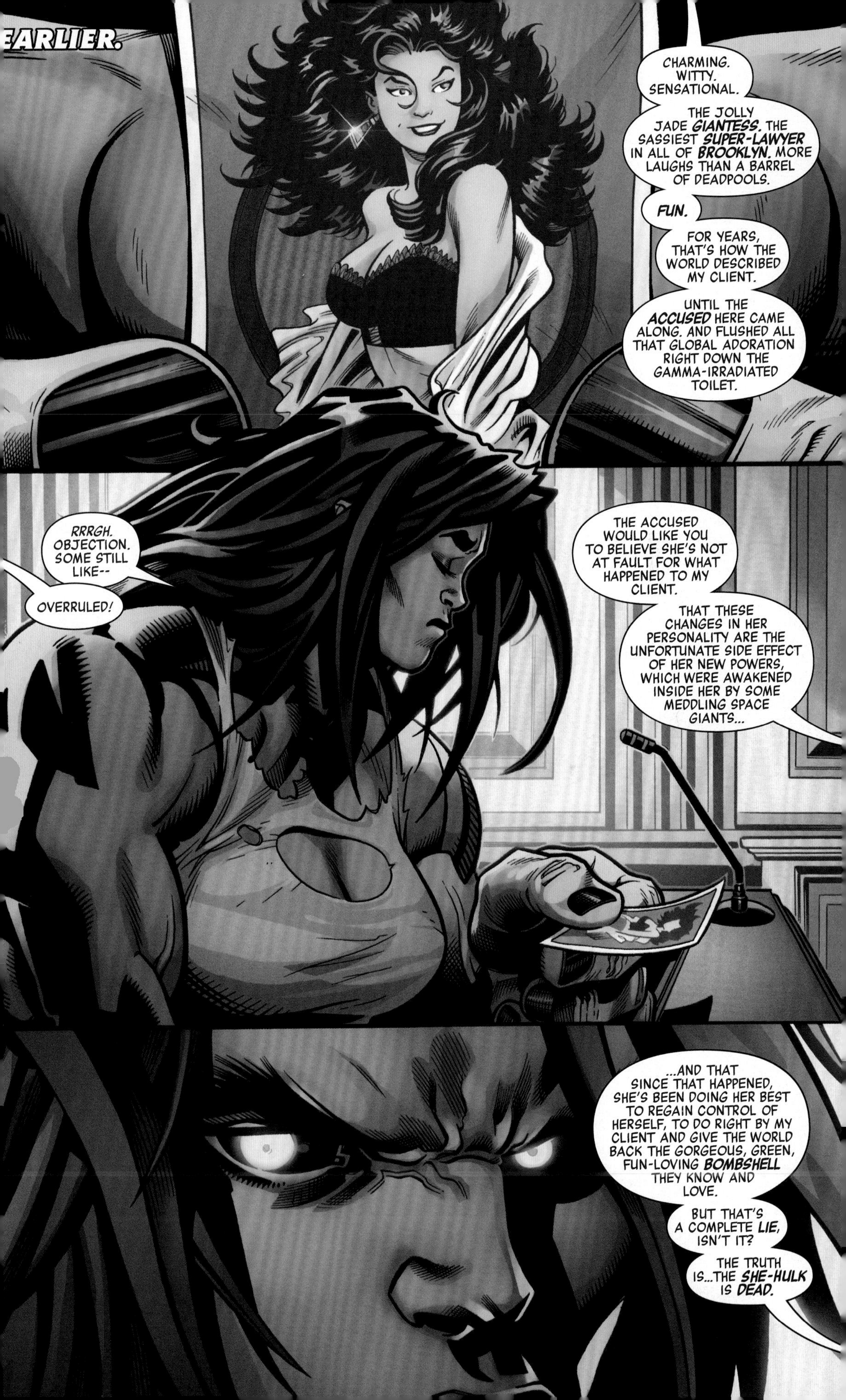
EARLIER.
CHARMING. WITTY. SENSATIONAL.
THE JOLLY JADE GIANTESS. THE SASSIEST SUPER-LAWYER IN ALL OF BROOKLYN. MORE LAUGHS THAN A BARREL OF DEADPOOLS.
FUN.
FOR YEARS, THAT'S HOW THE WORLD DESCRIBED MY CLIENT.
UNTIL THE ACCUSED HERE CAME ALONG. AND FLUSHED ALL THAT GLOBAL ADORATION RIGHT DOWN THE GAMMA-IRRADIATED TOILET.
RRRGH. OBJECTION. SOME STILL LIKE--
OVERRULED!
THE ACCUSED WOULD LIKE YOU TO BELIEVE SHE'S NOT AT FAULT FOR WHAT HAPPENED TO MY CLIENT.
THAT THESE CHANGES IN HER PERSONALITY ARE THE UNFORTUNATE SIDE EFFECT OF HER NEW POWERS, WHICH WERE AWAKENED INSIDE HER BY SOME MEDDLING SPACE GIANTS...
...AND THAT SINCE THAT HAPPENED, SHE'S BEEN DOING HER BEST TO REGAIN CONTROL OF HERSELF, TO DO RIGHT BY MY CLIENT AND GIVE THE WORLD BACK THE GORGEOUS, GREEN, FUN-LOVING BOMBSHELL THEY KNOW AND LOVE.
BUT THAT'S A COMPLETE LIE, ISN'T IT?
THE TRUTH IS...THE SHE-HULK IS DEAD.

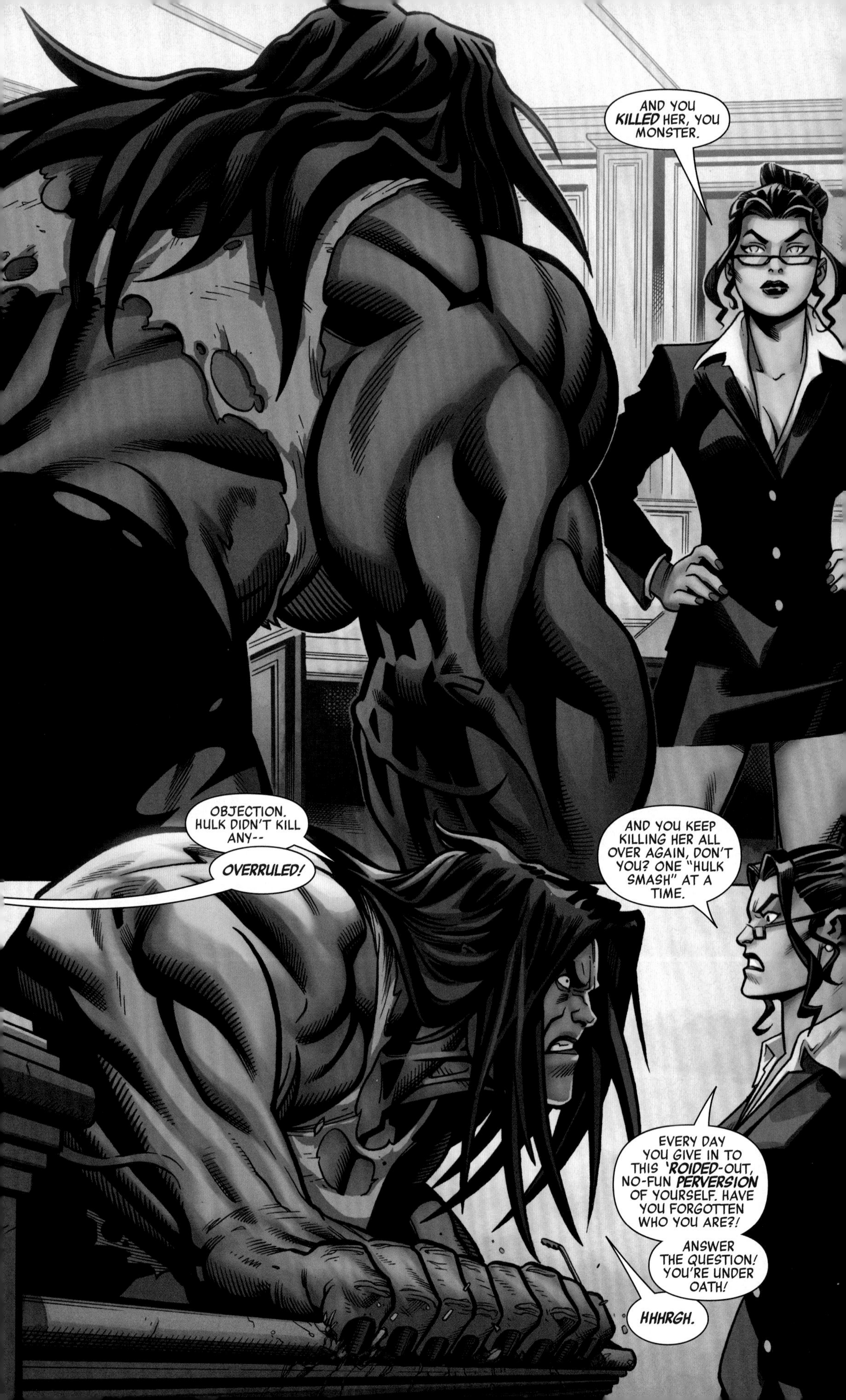
AND YOU KILLED HER, YOU MONSTER.
OBJECTION. HULK DIDN'T KILL ANY--
OVERRULED!
AND YOU KEEP KILLING HER ALL OVER AGAIN, DON'T YOU? ONE "HULK SMASH" AT A TIME.
EVERY DAY YOU GIVE IN TO THIS 'ROIDED-OUT, NO-FUN PERVERSION OF YOURSELF. HAVE YOU FORGOTTEN WHO YOU ARE?!
ANSWER THE QUESTION! YOU'RE UNDER OATH!
HHHRGH.

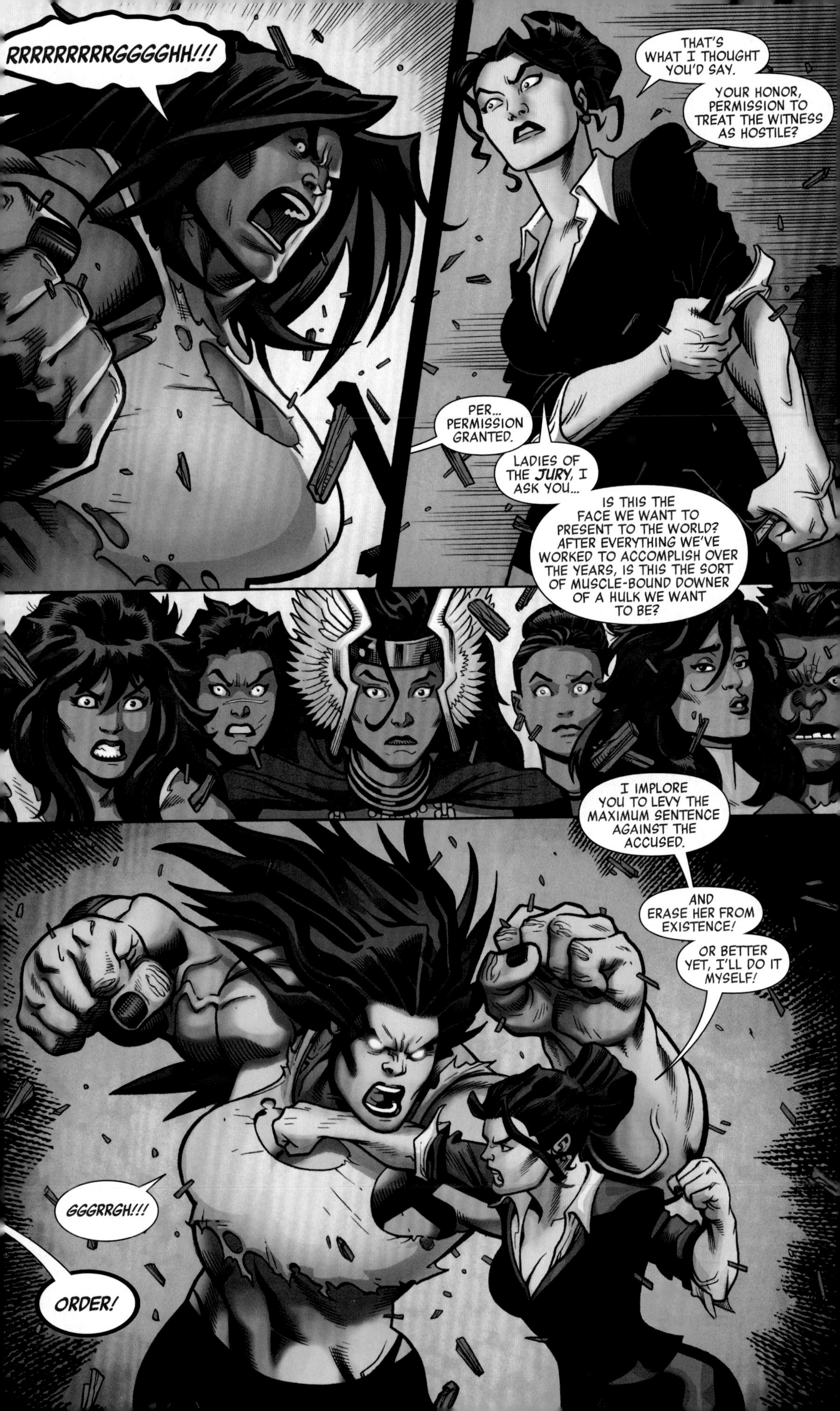
RRRRRRRRRGGGGHH!!!
THAT'S WHAT I THOUGHT YOU'D SAY.
YOUR HONOR, PERMISSION TO TREAT THE WITNESS AS HOSTILE?
PER... PERMISSION GRANTED.
LADIES OF THE JURY, I ASK YOU...
IS THIS THE FACE WE WANT TO PRESENT TO THE WORLD? AFTER EVERYTHING WE'VE WORKED TO ACCOMPLISH OVER THE YEARS, IS THIS THE SORT OF MUSCLE-BOUND DOWNER OF A HULK WE WANT TO BE?
I IMPLORE YOU TO LEVY THE MAXIMUM SENTENCE AGAINST THE ACCUSED.
AND ERASE HER FROM EXISTENCE!
OR BETTER YET, I'LL DO IT MYSELF!
GGGRRGH!!!
ORDER!

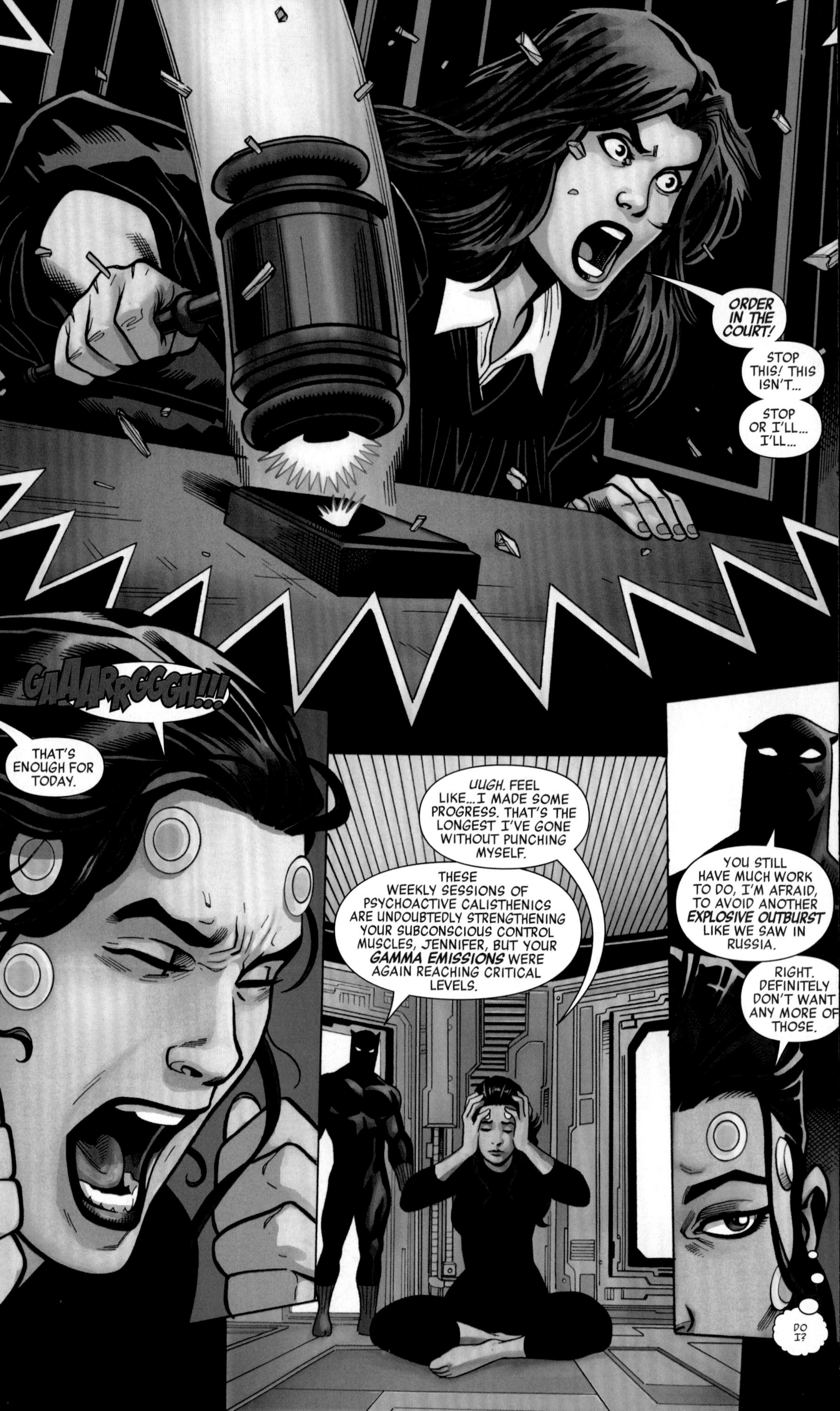
ORDER IN THE COURT!
STOP THIS! THIS ISN'T...
STOP OR I'LL... I'LL...
GAAARRGGGH!!!
THAT'S ENOUGH FOR TODAY.
UUGH. FEEL LIKE...I MADE SOME PROGRESS. THAT'S THE LONGEST I'VE GONE WITHOUT PUNCHING MYSELF.
THESE WEEKLY SESSIONS OF PSYCHOACTIVE CALISTHENICS ARE UNDOUBTEDLY STRENGTHENING YOUR SUBCONSCIOUS CONTROL MUSCLES, JENNIFER, BUT YOUR GAMMA EMISSIONS WERE AGAIN REACHING CRITICAL LEVELS.
YOU STILL HAVE MUCH WORK TO DO, I'M AFRAID, TO AVOID ANOTHER EXPLOSIVE OUTBURST LIKE WE SAW IN RUSSIA.
RIGHT. DEFINITELY DON'T WANT ANY MORE OF THOSE.
DO I?

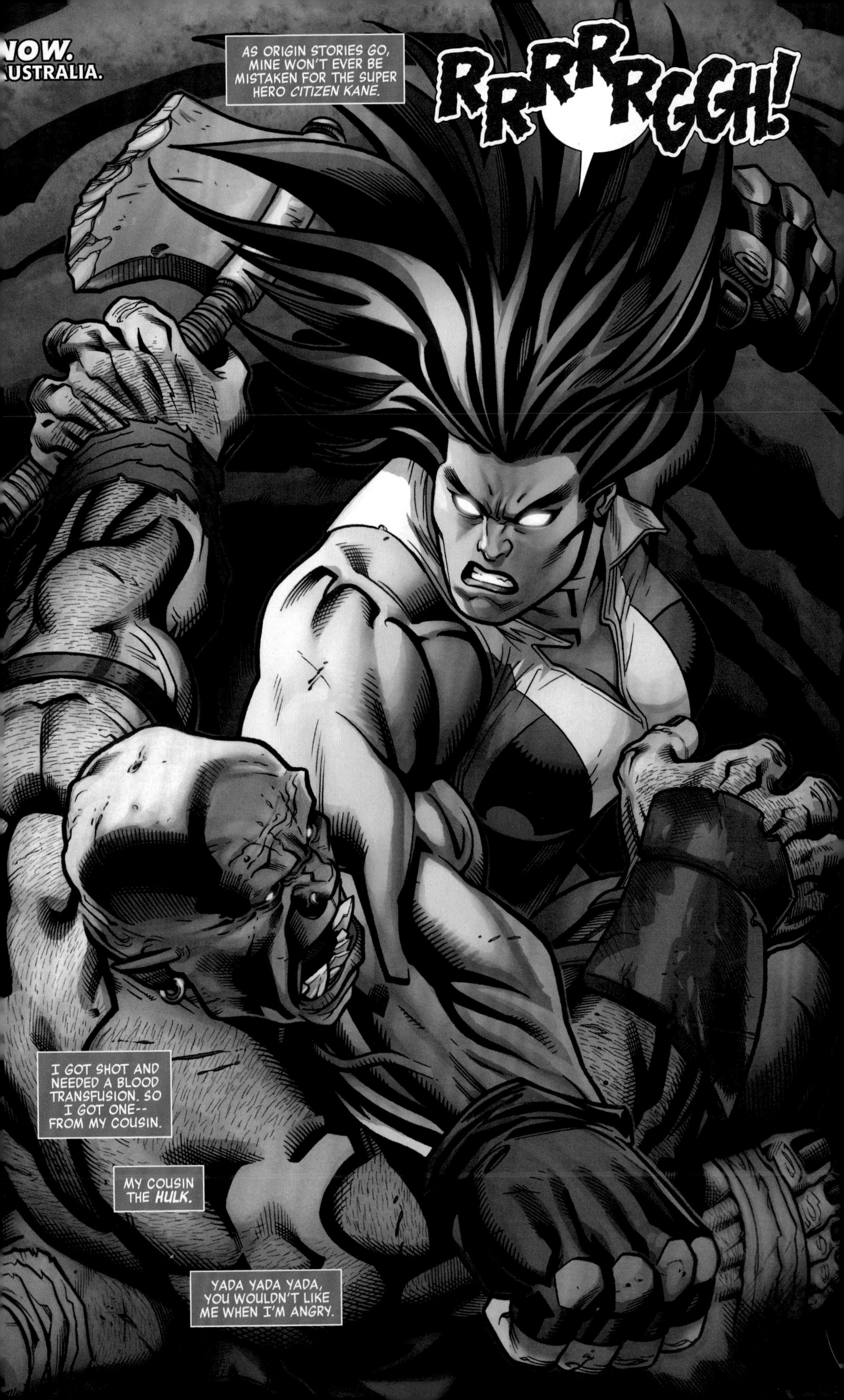
NOW.
USTRALIA.
AS ORIGIN STORIES GO, MINE WON'T EVER BE MISTAKEN FOR THE SUPER HERO *CITIZEN KANE.*
RRRRRRGGH!
I GOT SHOT AND NEEDED A BLOOD TRANSFUSION. SO I GOT ONE-- FROM MY COUSIN.
MY COUSIN THE *HULK.*
YADA YADA YADA, YOU WOULDN'T LIKE ME WHEN I'M ANGRY.

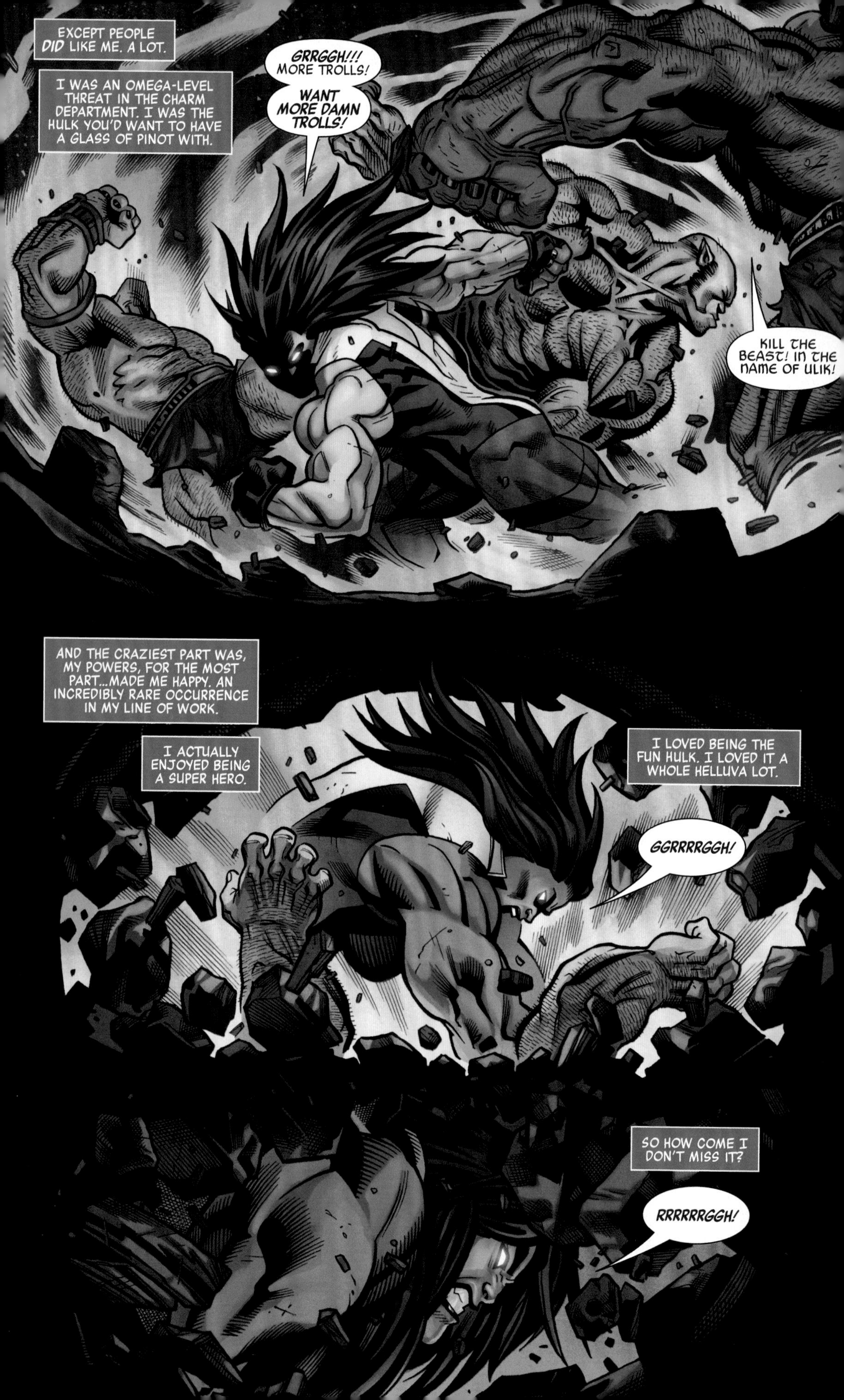
EXCEPT PEOPLE *DID* LIKE ME. A LOT.
I WAS AN OMEGA-LEVEL THREAT IN THE CHARM DEPARTMENT. I WAS THE HULK YOU'D WANT TO HAVE A GLASS OF PINOT WITH.
GRRGGH!!! MORE TROLLS!
WANT MORE DAMN TROLLS!
KILL THE BEAST! IN THE NAME OF ULIK!
AND THE CRAZIEST PART WAS, MY POWERS, FOR THE MOST PART...MADE ME HAPPY. AN INCREDIBLY RARE OCCURRENCE IN MY LINE OF WORK.
I ACTUALLY ENJOYED BEING A SUPER HERO.
I LOVED BEING THE FUN HULK. I LOVED IT A WHOLE HELLUVA LOT.
GGRRRRGGH!
SO HOW COME I DON'T MISS IT?
RRRRRRGGH!

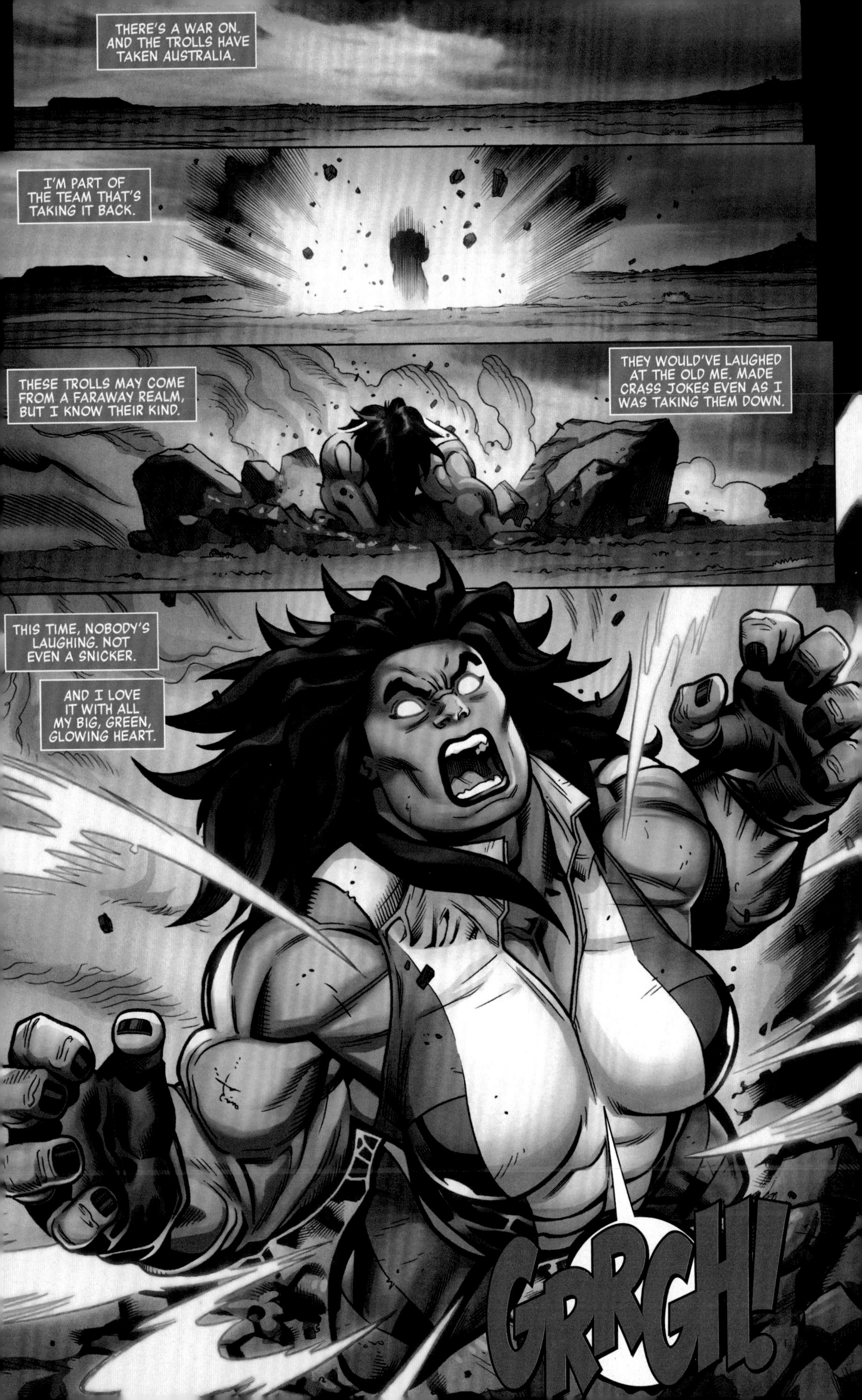
THERE'S A WAR ON. AND THE TROLLS HAVE TAKEN AUSTRALIA.
I'M PART OF THE TEAM THAT'S TAKING IT BACK.
THESE TROLLS MAY COME FROM A FARAWAY REALM, BUT I KNOW THEIR KIND.
THEY WOULD'VE LAUGHED AT THE OLD ME. MADE CRASS JOKES EVEN AS I WAS TAKING THEM DOWN.
THIS TIME, NOBODY'S LAUGHING. NOT EVEN A SNICKER.
AND I LOVE IT WITH ALL MY BIG, GREEN, GLOWING HEART.
GRRGH!

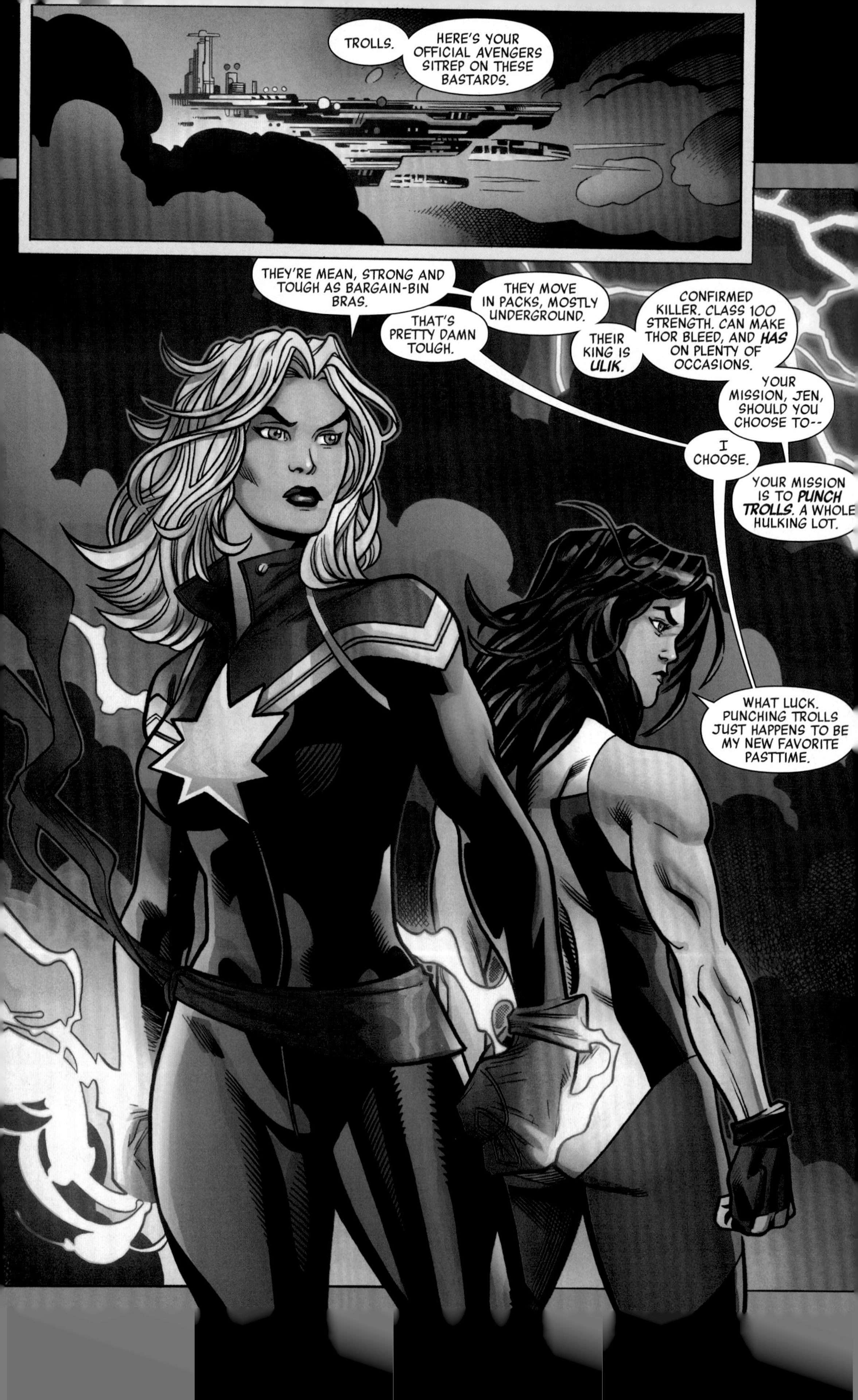
TROLLS.
HERE'S YOUR OFFICIAL AVENGERS SITREP ON THESE BASTARDS.
THEY'RE MEAN, STRONG AND TOUGH AS BARGAIN-BIN BRAS.
THEY MOVE IN PACKS, MOSTLY UNDERGROUND.
THAT'S PRETTY DAMN TOUGH.
THEIR KING IS ULIK.
CONFIRMED KILLER. CLASS 100 STRENGTH. CAN MAKE THOR BLEED, AND HAS ON PLENTY OF OCCASIONS.
YOUR MISSION, JEN, SHOULD YOU CHOOSE TO--
I CHOOSE.
YOUR MISSION IS TO PUNCH TROLLS. A WHOLE HULKING LOT.
WHAT LUCK. PUNCHING TROLLS JUST HAPPENS TO BE MY NEW FAVORITE PASTTIME.

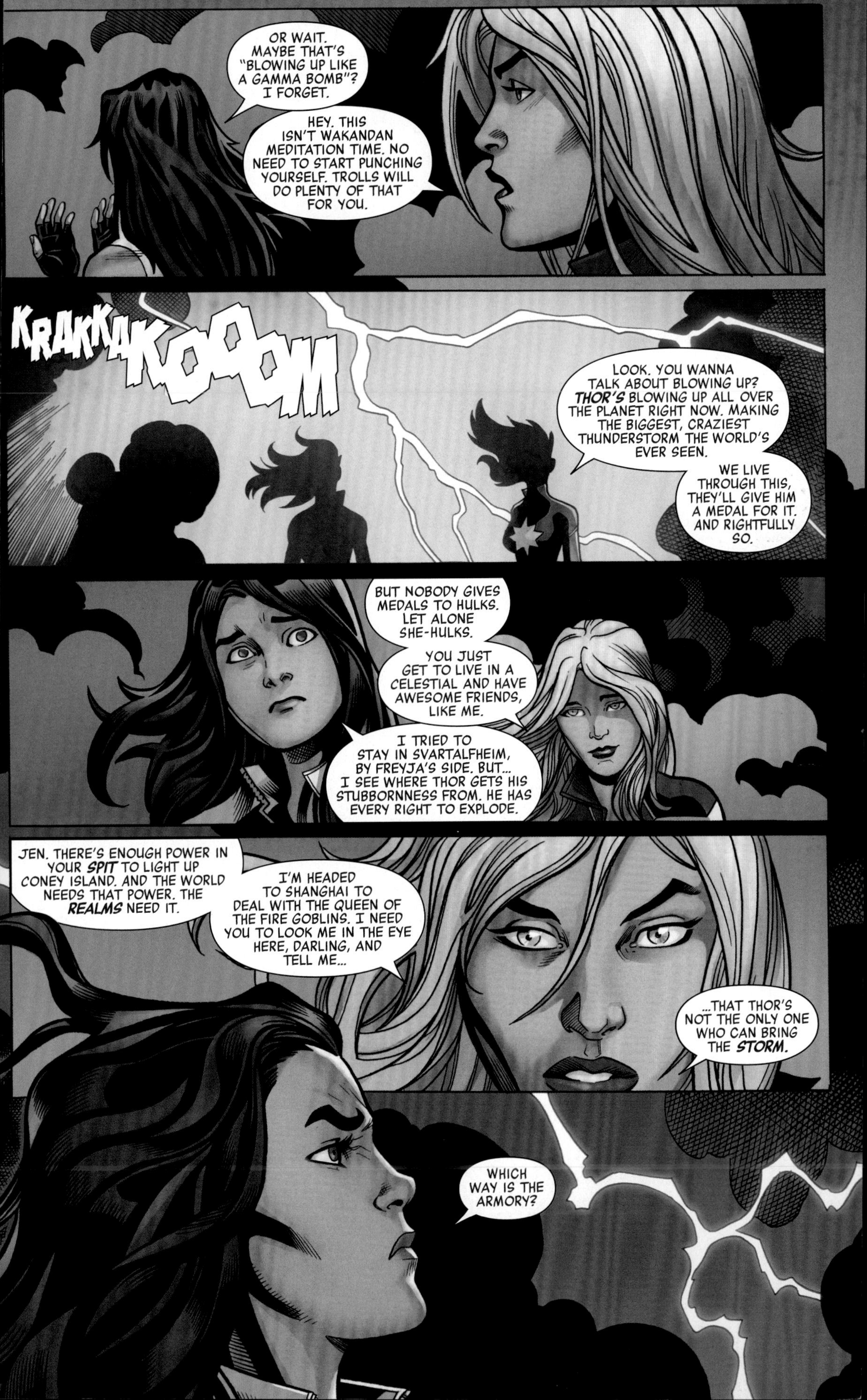
OR WAIT. MAYBE THAT'S "BLOWING UP LIKE A GAMMA BOMB"? I FORGET.
HEY. THIS ISN'T WAKANDAN MEDITATION TIME. NO NEED TO START PUNCHING YOURSELF. TROLLS WILL DO PLENTY OF THAT FOR YOU.
KRAKKAKOOOOM
LOOK. YOU WANNA TALK ABOUT BLOWING UP? THOR'S BLOWING UP ALL OVER THE PLANET RIGHT NOW. MAKING THE BIGGEST, CRAZIEST THUNDERSTORM THE WORLD'S EVER SEEN.
WE LIVE THROUGH THIS, THEY'LL GIVE HIM A MEDAL FOR IT. AND RIGHTFULLY SO.
BUT NOBODY GIVES MEDALS TO HULKS. LET ALONE SHE-HULKS.
YOU JUST GET TO LIVE IN A CELESTIAL AND HAVE AWESOME FRIENDS, LIKE ME.
I TRIED TO STAY IN SVARTALFHEIM, BY FREYJA'S SIDE. BUT... I SEE WHERE THOR GETS HIS STUBBORNNESS FROM. HE HAS EVERY RIGHT TO EXPLODE.
JEN. THERE'S ENOUGH POWER IN YOUR SPIT TO LIGHT UP CONEY ISLAND. AND THE WORLD NEEDS THAT POWER. THE REALMS NEED IT.
I'M HEADED TO SHANGHAI TO DEAL WITH THE QUEEN OF THE FIRE GOBLINS. I NEED YOU TO LOOK ME IN THE EYE HERE, DARLING, AND TELL ME...
...THAT THOR'S NOT THE ONLY ONE WHO CAN BRING THE STORM.
WHICH WAY IS THE ARMORY?

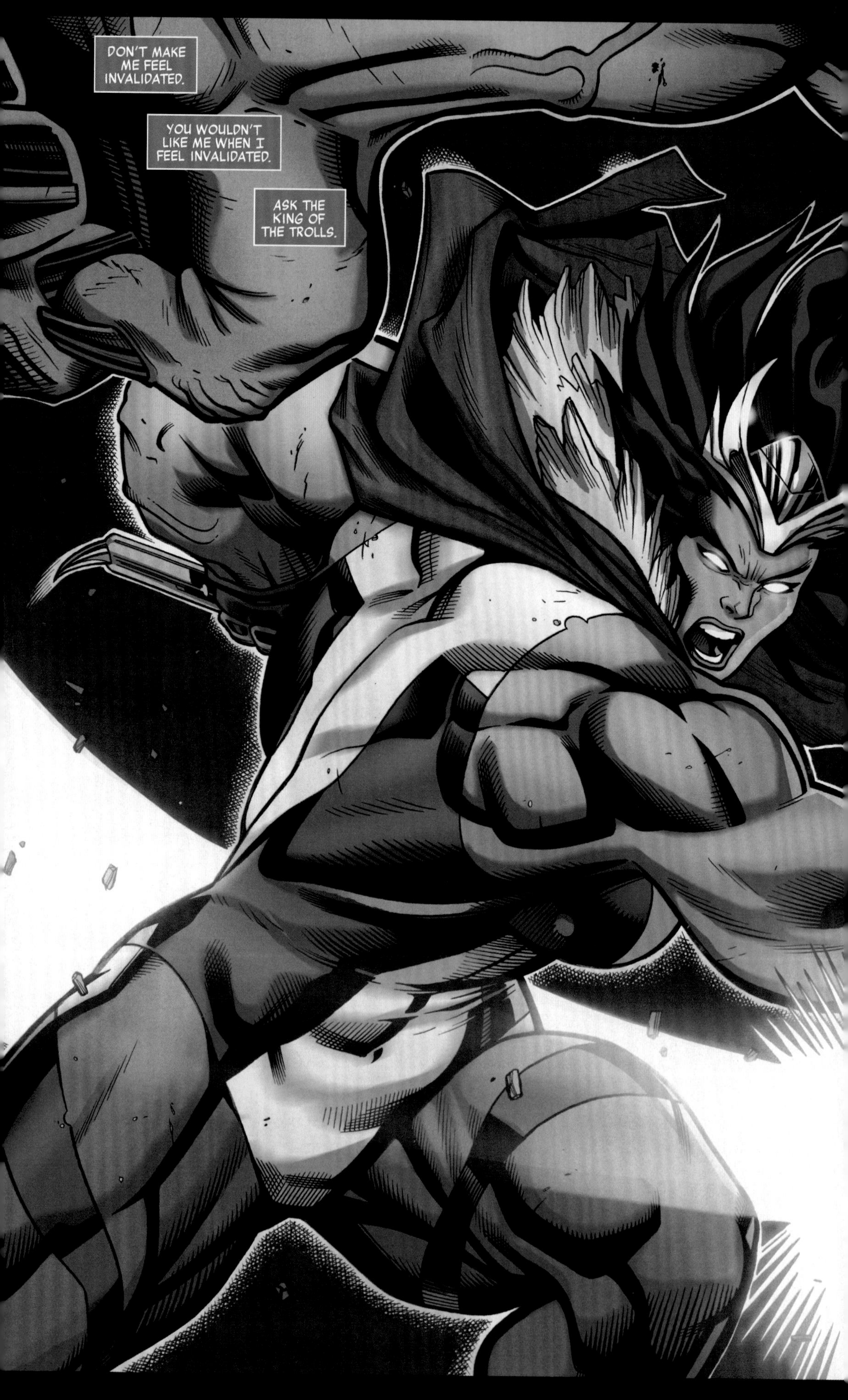
DON'T MAKE ME FEEL INVALIDATED.
YOU WOULDN'T LIKE ME WHEN I FEEL INVALIDATED.
ASK THE KING OF THE TROLLS.

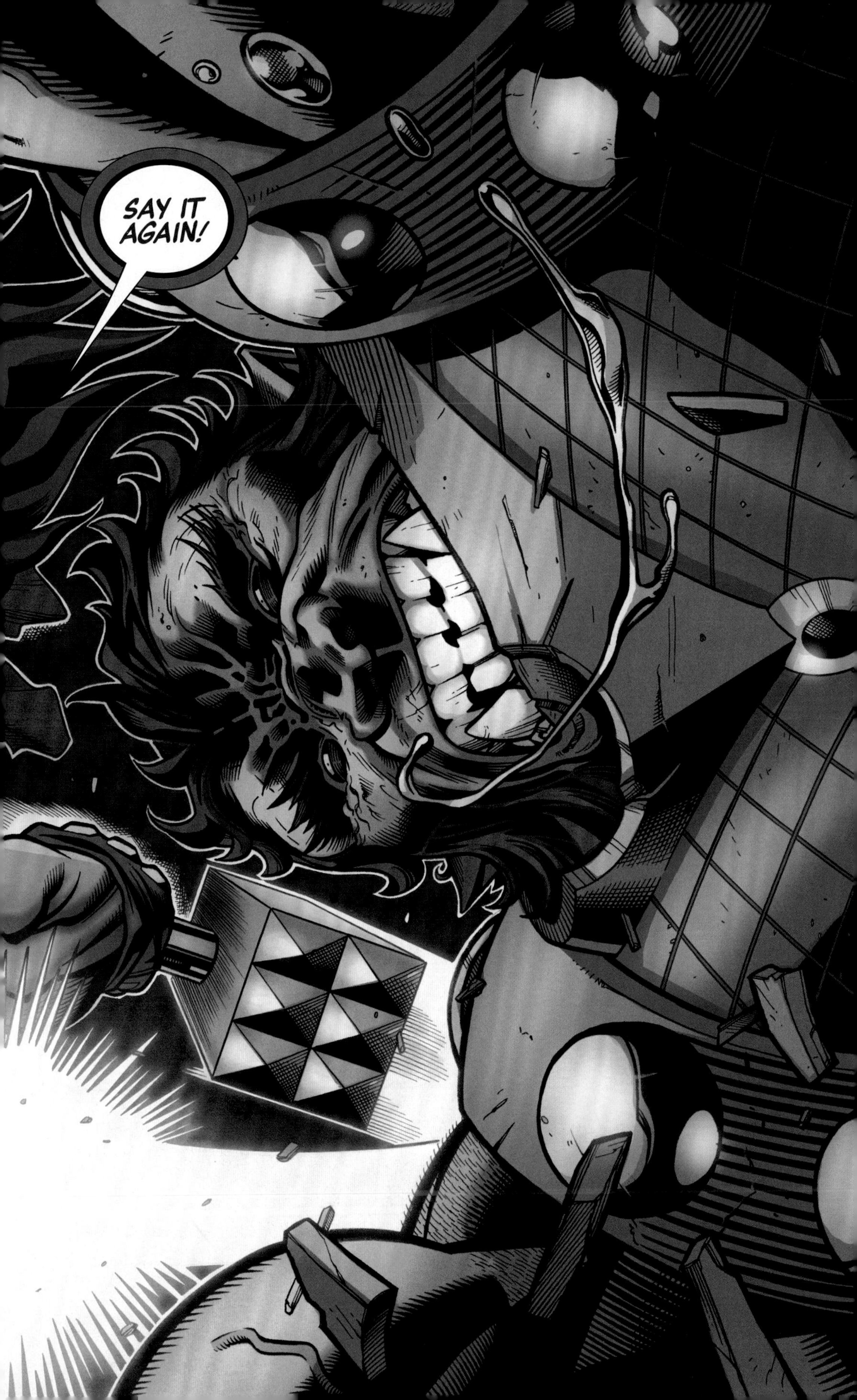
SAY IT AGAIN!

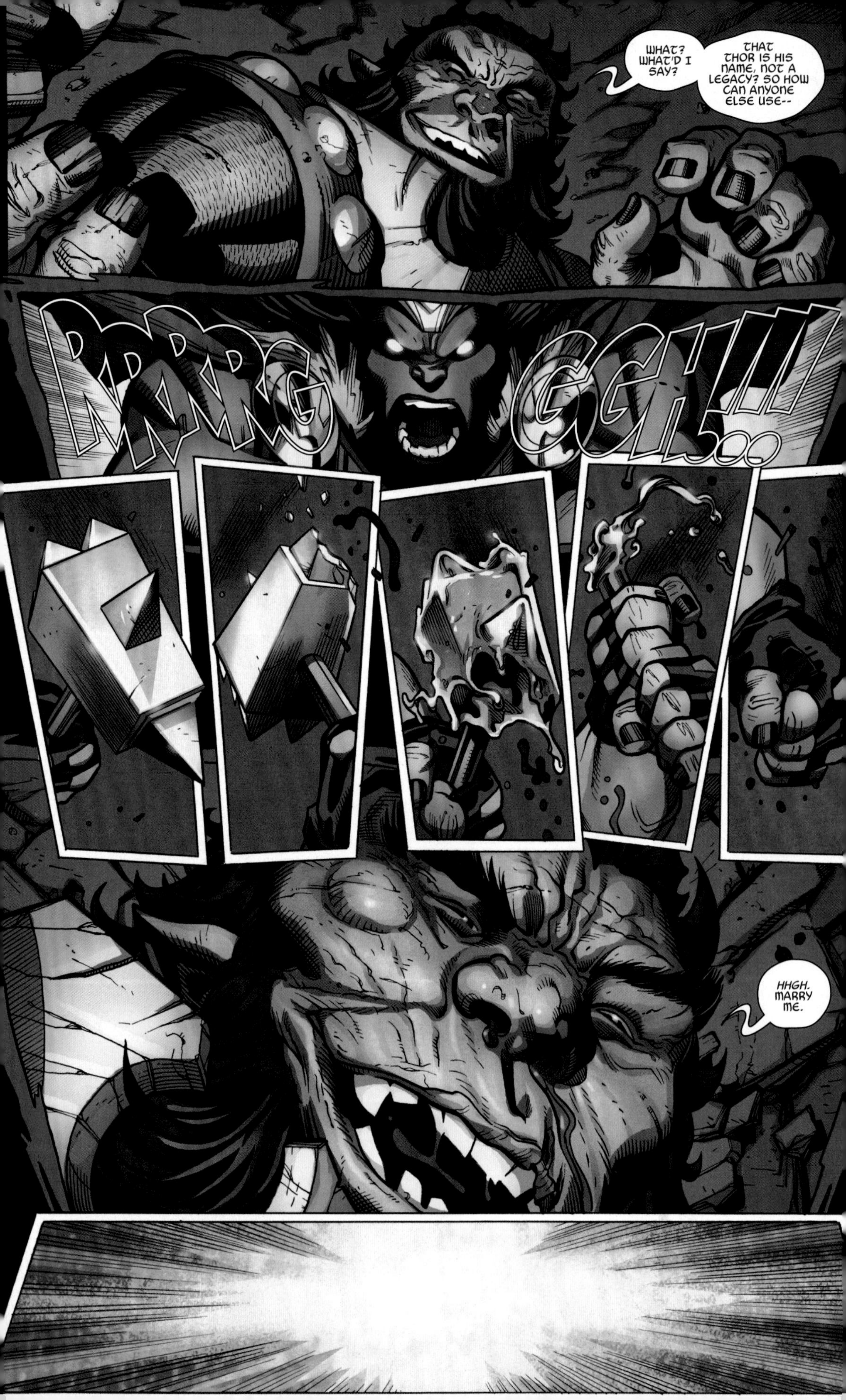
WHAT? WHAT'D I SAY?
THAT THOR IS HIS NAME, NOT A LEGACY? SO HOW CAN ANYONE ELSE USE--
RRRRRG GGHHH...
HHGH. MARRY ME.

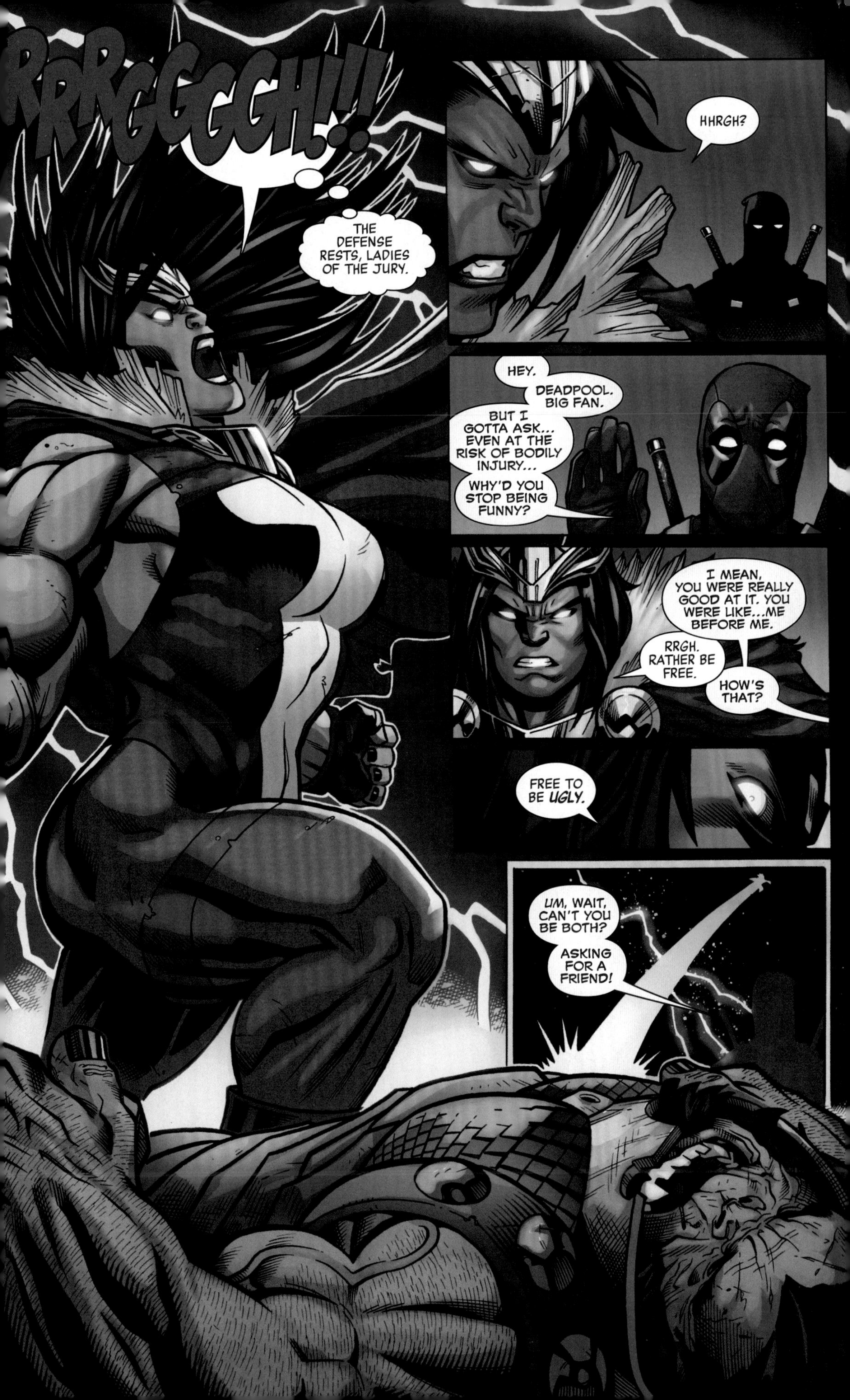
RRRGGGGH!!!
THE DEFENSE RESTS, LADIES OF THE JURY.
HHRGH?
HEY.
DEADPOOL. BIG FAN.
BUT I GOTTA ASK... EVEN AT THE RISK OF BODILY INJURY...
WHY'D YOU STOP BEING FUNNY?
I MEAN, YOU WERE REALLY GOOD AT IT. YOU WERE LIKE...ME BEFORE ME.
RRGH. RATHER BE FREE.
HOW'S THAT?
FREE TO BE UGLY.
UM, WAIT, CAN'T YOU BE BOTH?
ASKING FOR A FRIEND!

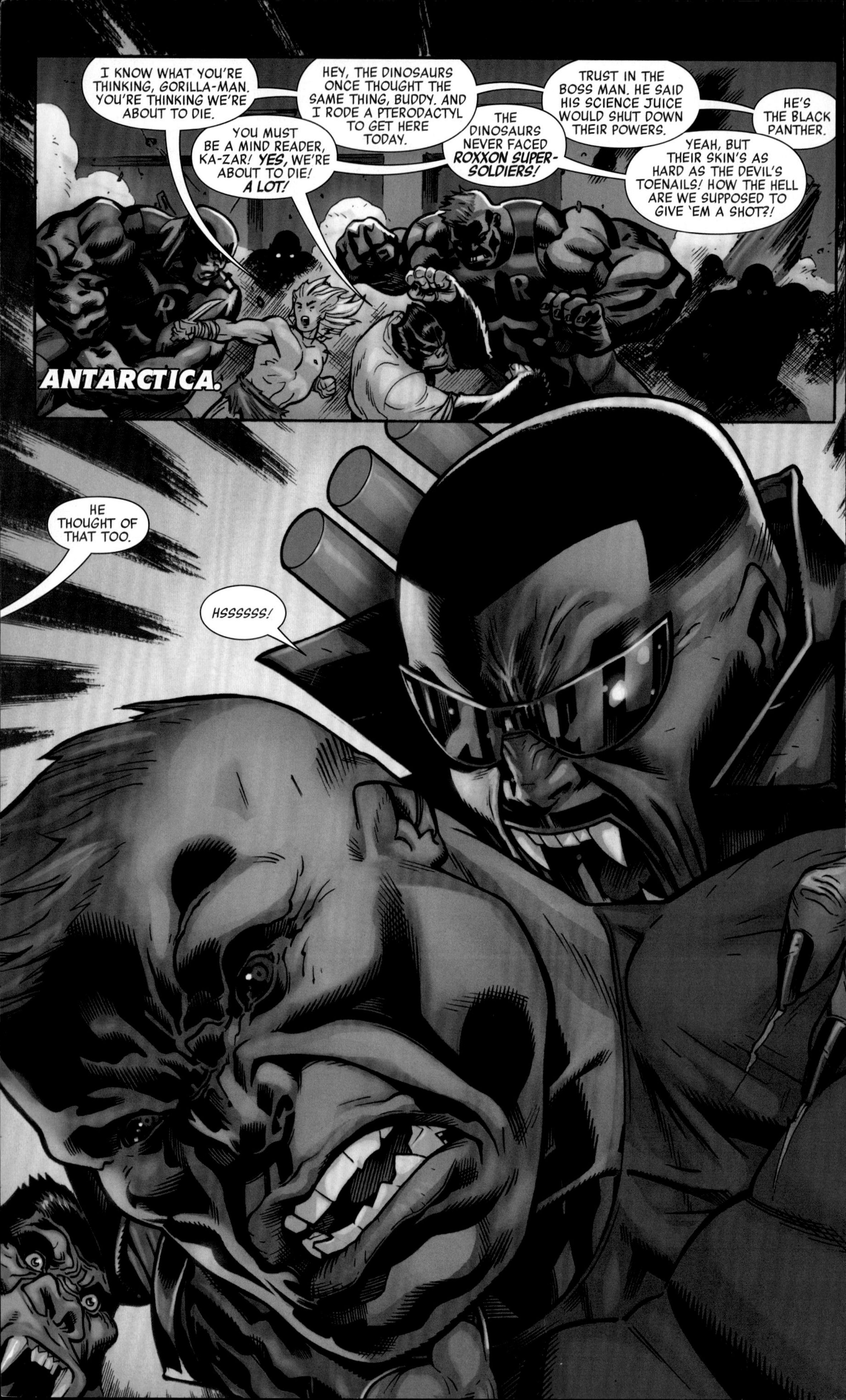
ANTARCTICA.
I KNOW WHAT YOU'RE THINKING, GORILLA-MAN. YOU'RE THINKING WE'RE ABOUT TO DIE.
YOU MUST BE A MIND READER, KA-ZAR! YES, WE'RE ABOUT TO DIE! A LOT!
HEY, THE DINOSAURS ONCE THOUGHT THE SAME THING, BUDDY. AND I RODE A PTERODACTYL TO GET HERE TODAY.
THE DINOSAURS NEVER FACED ROXXON SUPER-SOLDIERS!
TRUST IN THE BOSS MAN. HE SAID HIS SCIENCE JUICE WOULD SHUT DOWN THEIR POWERS.
HE'S THE BLACK PANTHER.
YEAH, BUT THEIR SKIN'S AS HARD AS THE DEVIL'S TOENAILS! HOW THE HELL ARE WE SUPPOSED TO GIVE 'EM A SHOT?!
HE THOUGHT OF THAT TOO.
HSSSSSS!

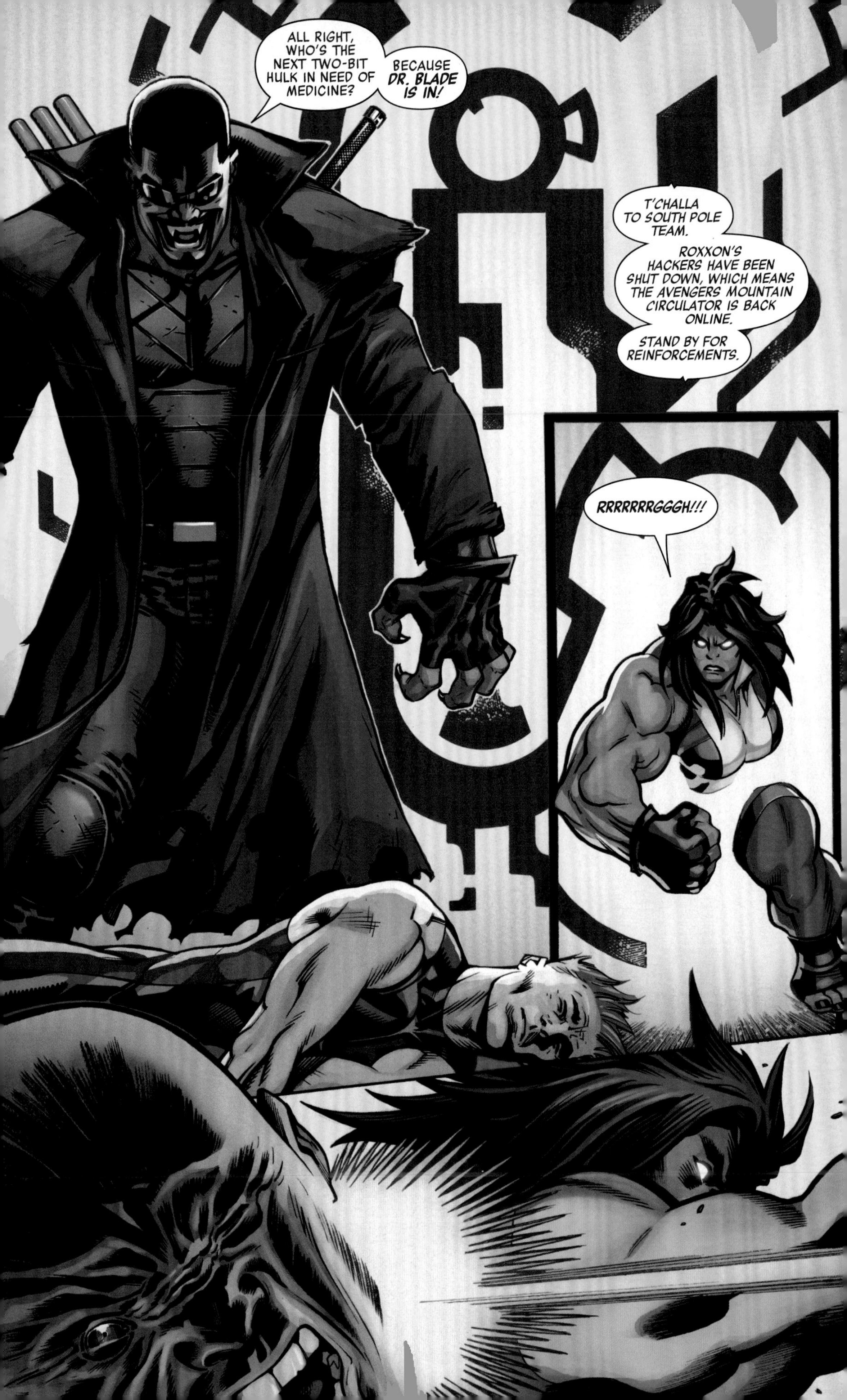
ALL RIGHT, WHO'S THE NEXT TWO-BIT HULK IN NEED OF MEDICINE?
BECAUSE DR. BLADE IS IN!
T'CHALLA TO SOUTH POLE TEAM.
ROXXON'S HACKERS HAVE BEEN SHUT DOWN, WHICH MEANS THE AVENGERS MOUNTAIN CIRCULATOR IS BACK ONLINE.
STAND BY FOR REINFORCEMENTS.
RRRRRRRGGGH!!!

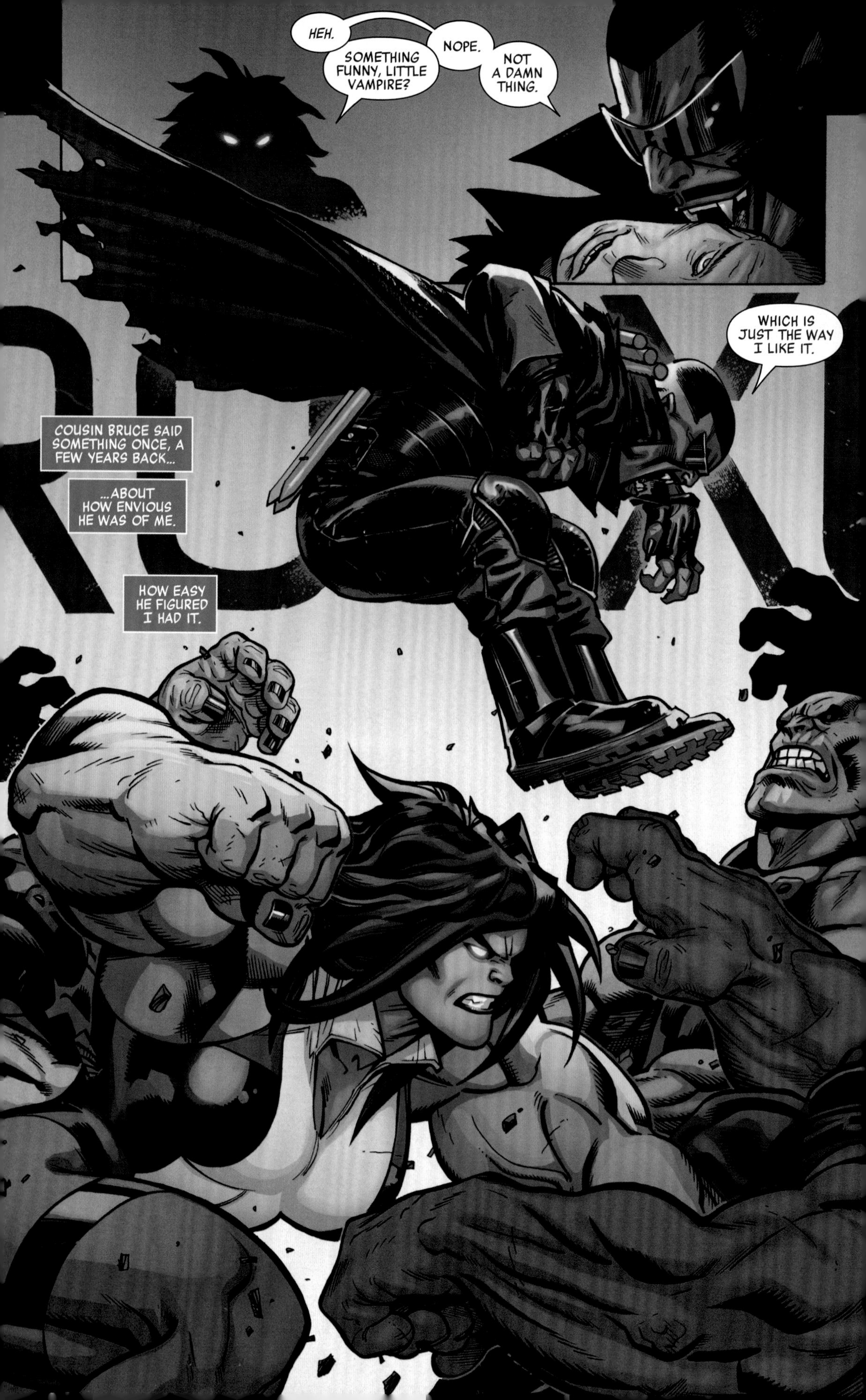
HEH.
SOMETHING FUNNY, LITTLE VAMPIRE?
NOPE.
NOT A DAMN THING.
WHICH IS JUST THE WAY I LIKE IT.
COUSIN BRUCE SAID SOMETHING ONCE, A FEW YEARS BACK...
...ABOUT HOW ENVIOUS HE WAS OF ME.
HOW EASY HE FIGURED I HAD IT.

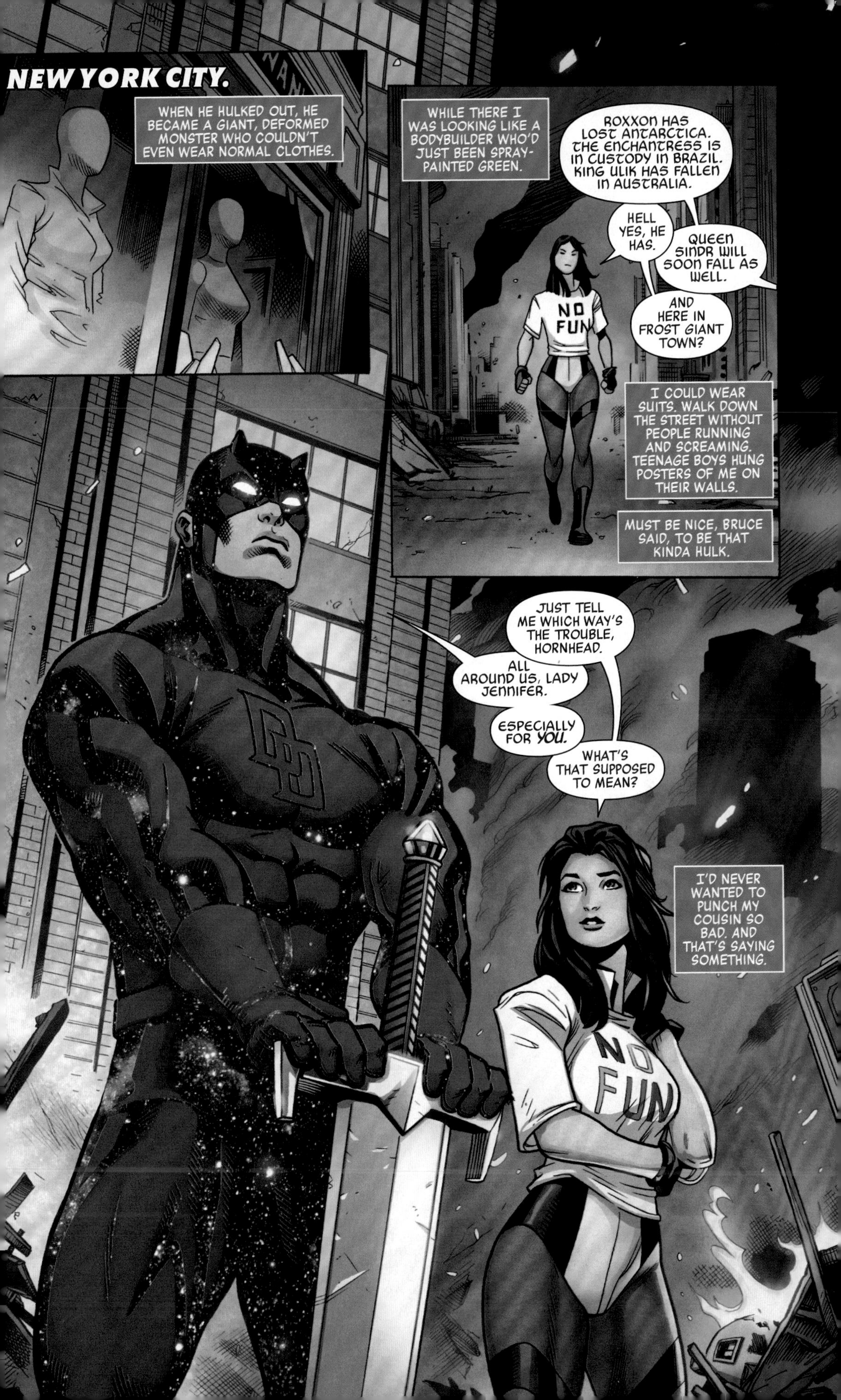

NEW YORK CITY.
WHEN HE HULKED OUT, HE BECAME A GIANT, DEFORMED MONSTER WHO COULDN'T EVEN WEAR NORMAL CLOTHES.
WHILE THERE I WAS LOOKING LIKE A BODYBUILDER WHO'D JUST BEEN SPRAY-PAINTED GREEN.
ROXXON HAS LOST ANTARCTICA. THE ENCHANTRESS IS IN CUSTODY IN BRAZIL. KING ULIK HAS FALLEN IN AUSTRALIA.
HELL YES, HE HAS.
QUEEN SINDR WILL SOON FALL AS WELL.
AND HERE IN FROST GIANT TOWN?
I COULD WEAR SUITS. WALK DOWN THE STREET WITHOUT PEOPLE RUNNING AND SCREAMING. TEENAGE BOYS HUNG POSTERS OF ME ON THEIR WALLS.
MUST BE NICE, BRUCE SAID, TO BE THAT KINDA HULK.
JUST TELL ME WHICH WAY'S THE TROUBLE, HORNHEAD.
ALL AROUND US, LADY JENNIFER.
ESPECIALLY FOR YOU.
WHAT'S THAT SUPPOSED TO MEAN?
I'D NEVER WANTED TO PUNCH MY COUSIN SO BAD. AND THAT'S SAYING SOMETHING.
NO FUN

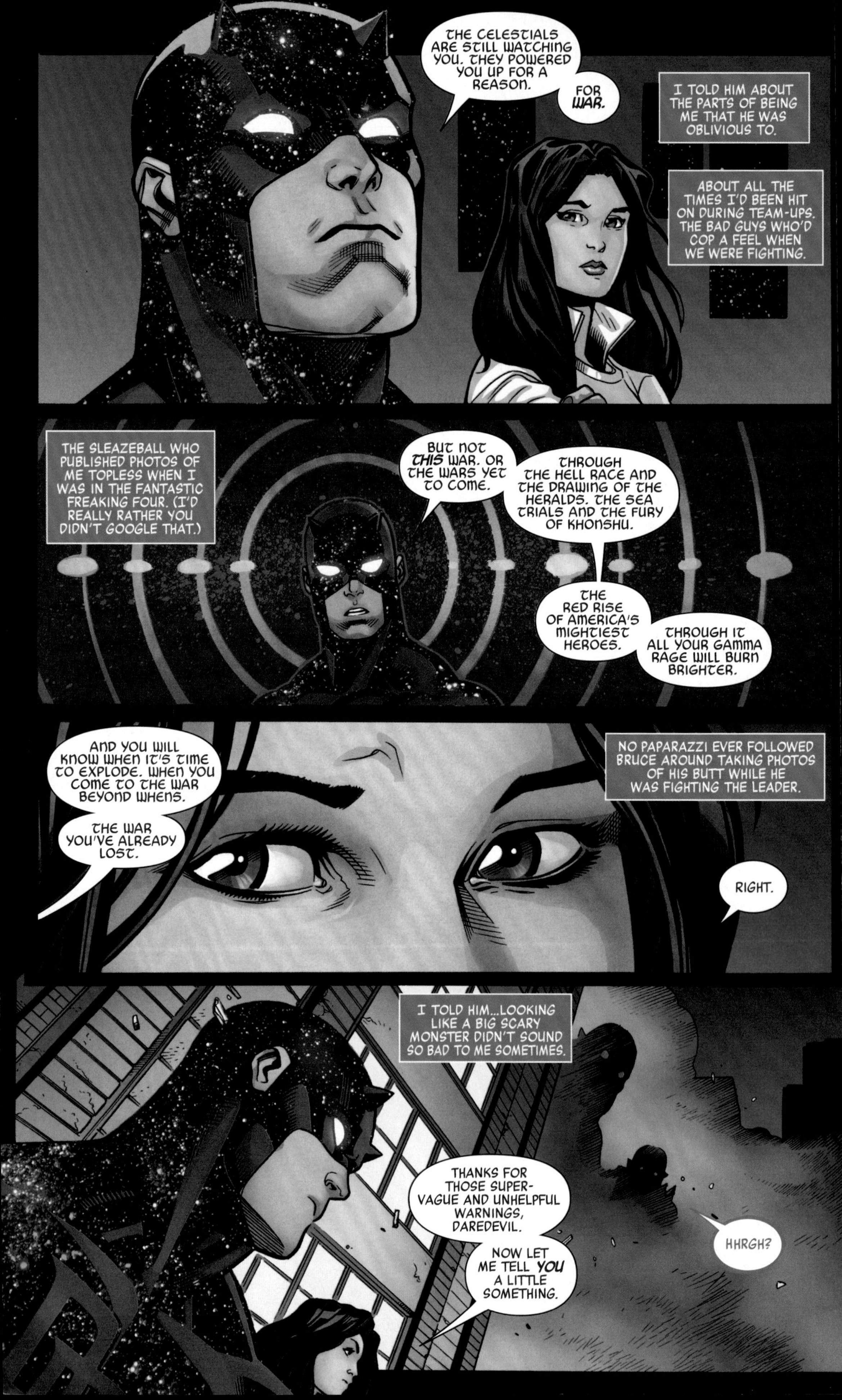
THE CELESTIALS ARE STILL WATCHING YOU. THEY POWERED YOU UP FOR A REASON.
FOR WAR.
I TOLD HIM ABOUT THE PARTS OF BEING ME THAT HE WAS OBLIVIOUS TO.
ABOUT ALL THE TIMES I'D BEEN HIT ON DURING TEAM-UPS. THE BAD GUYS WHO'D COP A FEEL WHEN WE WERE FIGHTING.
THE SLEAZEBALL WHO PUBLISHED PHOTOS OF ME TOPLESS WHEN I WAS IN THE FANTASTIC FREAKING FOUR. (I'D REALLY RATHER YOU DIDN'T GOOGLE THAT.)
BUT NOT THIS WAR. OR THE WARS YET TO COME.
THROUGH THE HELL RACE AND THE DRAWING OF THE HERALDS. THE SEA TRIALS AND THE FURY OF KHONSHU.
THE RED RISE OF AMERICA'S MIGHTIEST HEROES.
THROUGH IT ALL YOUR GAMMA RAGE WILL BURN BRIGHTER.
AND YOU WILL KNOW WHEN IT'S TIME TO EXPLODE. WHEN YOU COME TO THE WAR BEYOND WHENS.
THE WAR YOU'VE ALREADY LOST.
NO PAPARAZZI EVER FOLLOWED BRUCE AROUND TAKING PHOTOS OF HIS BUTT WHILE HE WAS FIGHTING THE LEADER.
RIGHT.
I TOLD HIM...LOOKING LIKE A BIG SCARY MONSTER DIDN'T SOUND SO BAD TO ME SOMETIMES.
THANKS FOR THOSE SUPER-VAGUE AND UNHELPFUL WARNINGS, DAREDEVIL.
NOW LET ME TELL YOU A LITTLE SOMETHING.
HHRGH?

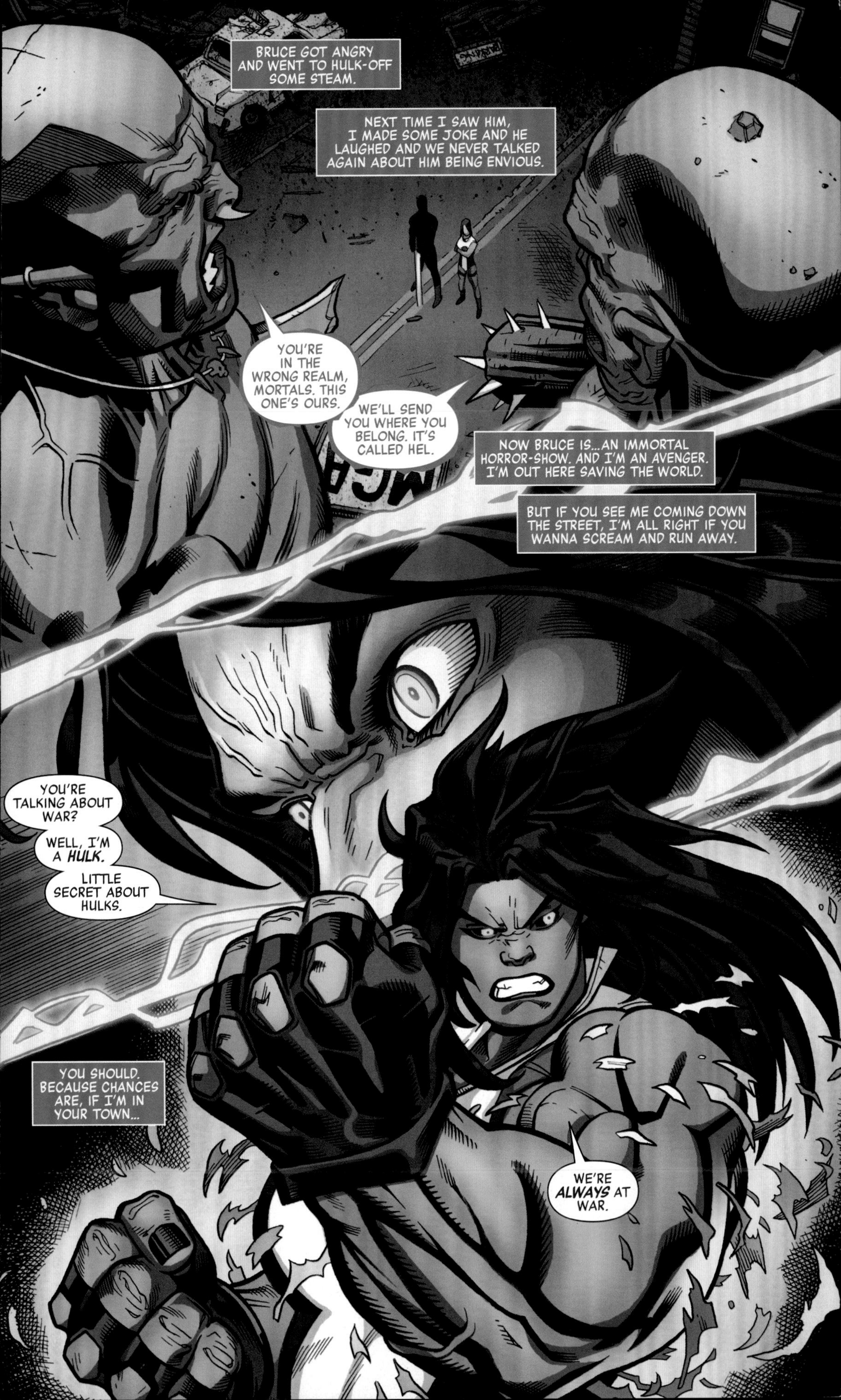
BRUCE GOT ANGRY AND WENT TO HULK-OFF SOME STEAM.
NEXT TIME I SAW HIM, I MADE SOME JOKE AND HE LAUGHED AND WE NEVER TALKED AGAIN ABOUT HIM BEING ENVIOUS.
YOU'RE IN THE WRONG REALM, MORTALS. THIS ONE'S OURS.
WE'LL SEND YOU WHERE YOU BELONG. IT'S CALLED HEL.
NOW BRUCE IS...AN IMMORTAL HORROR-SHOW. AND I'M AN AVENGER. I'M OUT HERE SAVING THE WORLD.
BUT IF YOU SEE ME COMING DOWN THE STREET, I'M ALL RIGHT IF YOU WANNA SCREAM AND RUN AWAY.
YOU'RE TALKING ABOUT WAR?
WELL, I'M A *HULK.*
LITTLE SECRET ABOUT HULKS.
YOU SHOULD. BECAUSE CHANCES ARE, IF I'M IN YOUR TOWN...
WE'RE *ALWAYS* AT WAR.

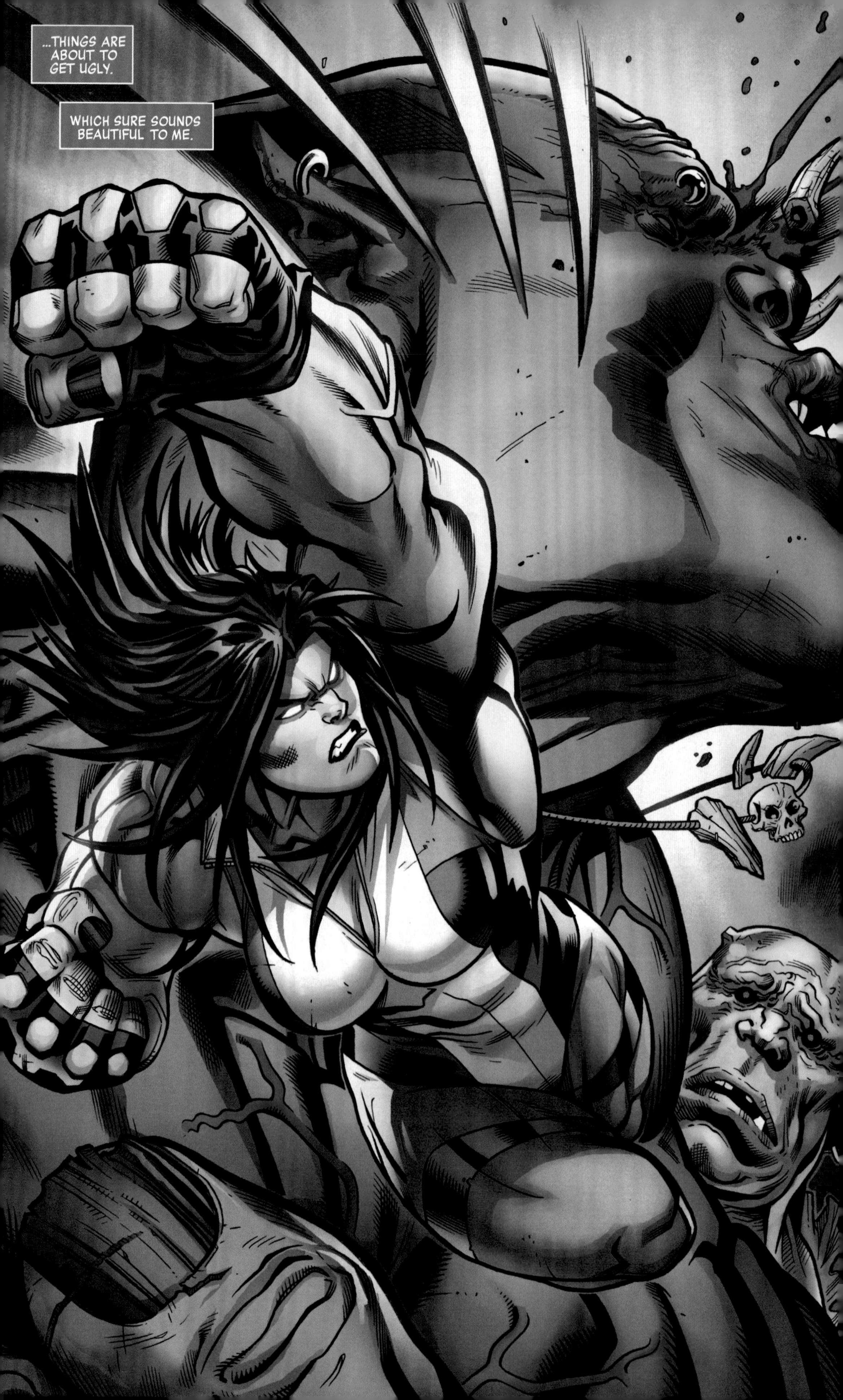
...THINGS ARE ABOUT TO GET UGLY.
WHICH SURE SOUNDS BEAUTIFUL TO ME.

21 THE DAY AFTER A DAY UNLIKE ANY OTHER

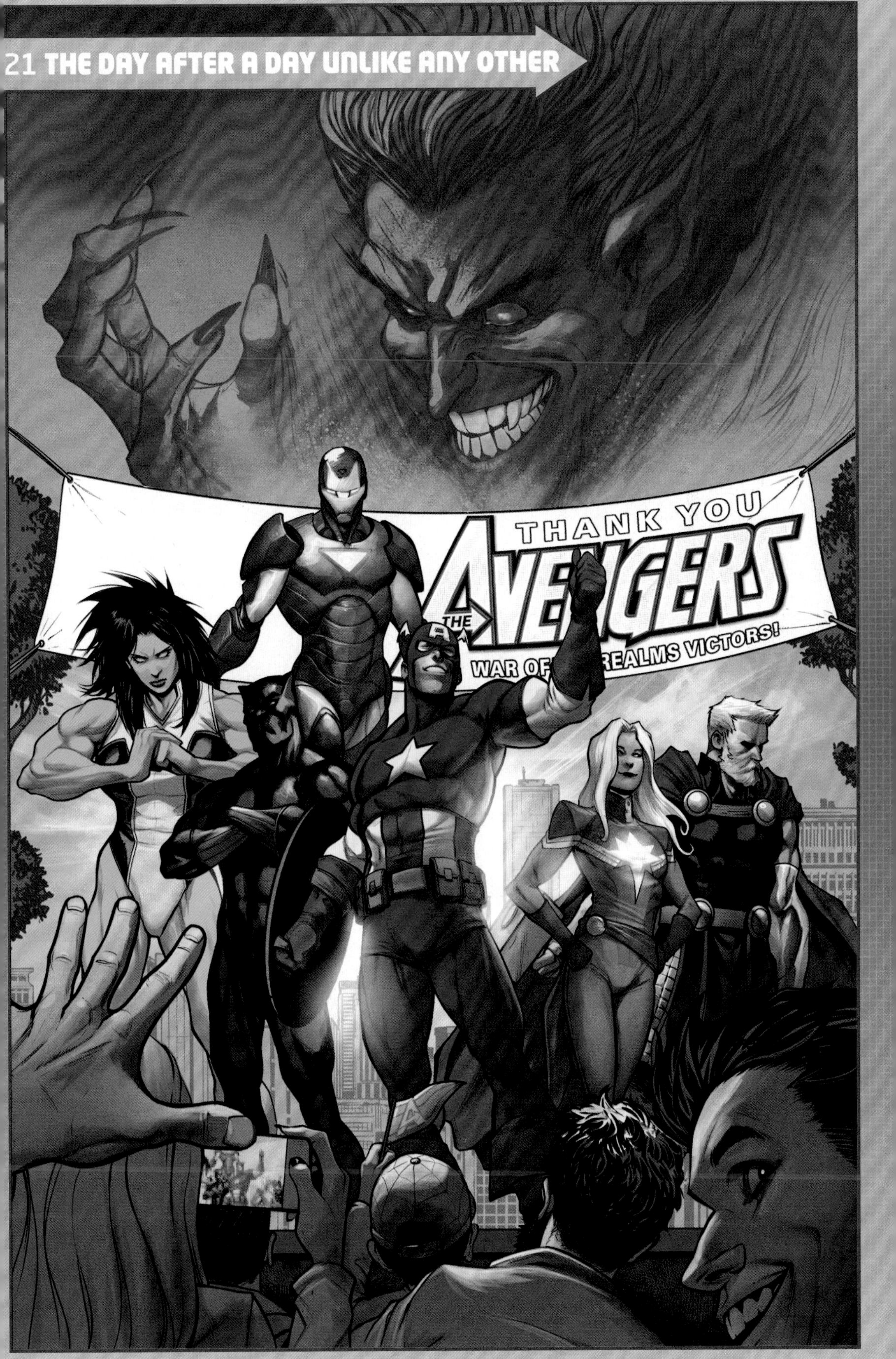

THANK YOU
THE AVENGERS
WAR OF
REALMS VICTORS!

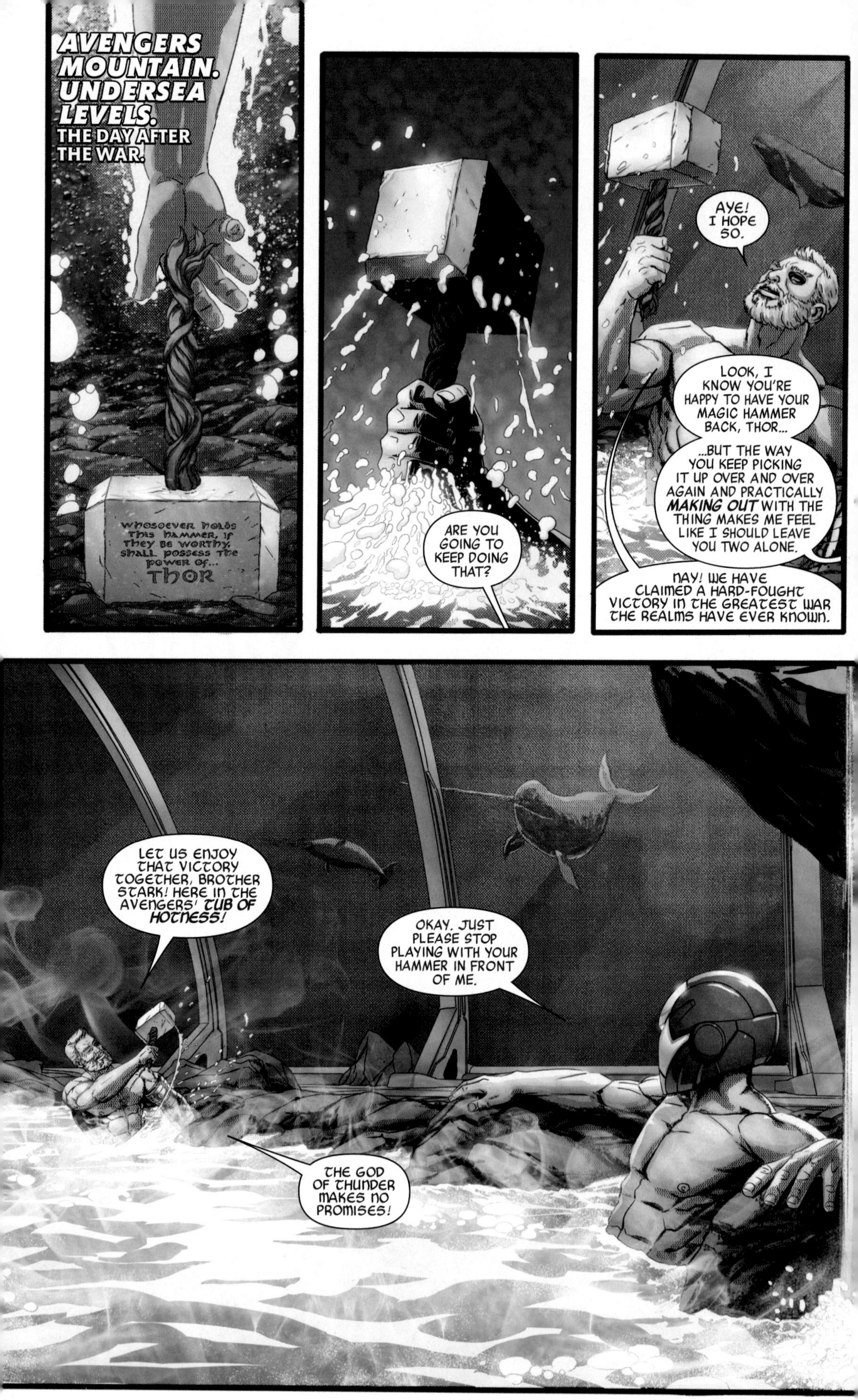
AVENGERS MOUNTAIN. UNDERSEA LEVELS.
THE DAY AFTER THE WAR.
Whosoever holds this hammer, if they be worthy, shall possess the power of... THOR
ARE YOU GOING TO KEEP DOING THAT?
AYE! I HOPE SO.
LOOK, I KNOW YOU'RE HAPPY TO HAVE YOUR MAGIC HAMMER BACK, THOR...
...BUT THE WAY YOU KEEP PICKING IT UP OVER AND OVER AGAIN AND PRACTICALLY MAKING OUT WITH THE THING MAKES ME FEEL LIKE I SHOULD LEAVE YOU TWO ALONE.
NAY! WE HAVE CLAIMED A HARD-FOUGHT VICTORY IN THE GREATEST WAR THE REALMS HAVE EVER KNOWN.
LET US ENJOY THAT VICTORY TOGETHER, BROTHER STARK! HERE IN THE AVENGERS' TUB OF HOTNESS!
OKAY. JUST PLEASE STOP PLAYING WITH YOUR HAMMER IN FRONT OF ME.
THE GOD OF THUNDER MAKES NO PROMISES!

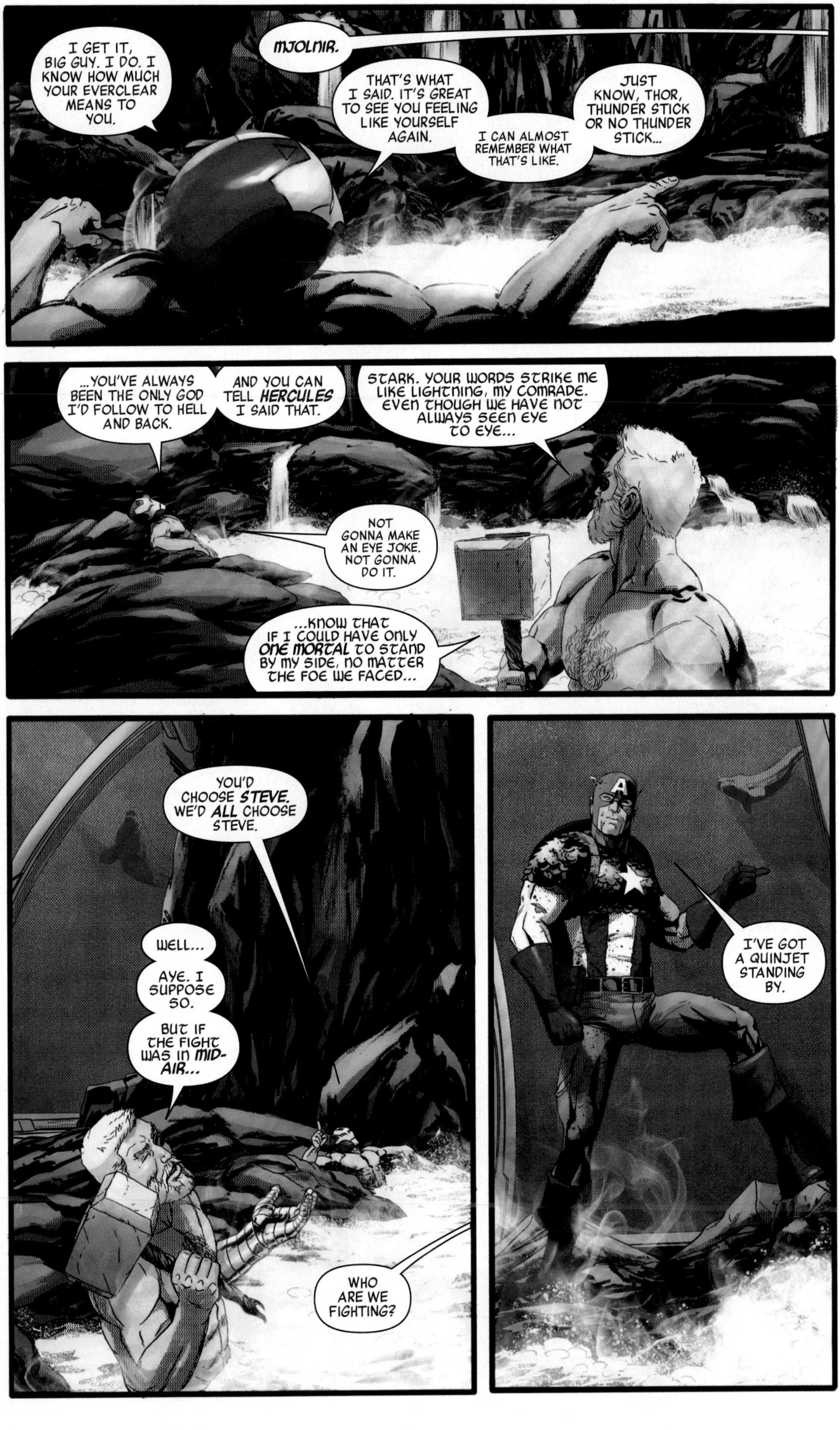
MJOLNIR.
I GET IT, BIG GUY. I DO. I KNOW HOW MUCH YOUR EVERCLEAR MEANS TO YOU.
THAT'S WHAT I SAID. IT'S GREAT TO SEE YOU FEELING LIKE YOURSELF AGAIN.
I CAN ALMOST REMEMBER WHAT THAT'S LIKE.
JUST KNOW, THOR, THUNDER STICK OR NO THUNDER STICK...
...YOU'VE ALWAYS BEEN THE ONLY GOD I'D FOLLOW TO HELL AND BACK.
AND YOU CAN TELL HERCULES I SAID THAT.
STARK. YOUR WORDS STRIKE ME LIKE LIGHTNING, MY COMRADE. EVEN THOUGH WE HAVE NOT ALWAYS SEEN EYE TO EYE...
NOT GONNA MAKE AN EYE JOKE. NOT GONNA DO IT.
...KNOW THAT IF I COULD HAVE ONLY ONE MORTAL TO STAND BY MY SIDE, NO MATTER THE FOE WE FACED...
YOU'D CHOOSE STEVE. WE'D ALL CHOOSE STEVE.
WELL...
AYE. I SUPPOSE SO.
BUT IF THE FIGHT WAS IN MID-AIR...
WHO ARE WE FIGHTING?
I'VE GOT A QUINJET STANDING BY.

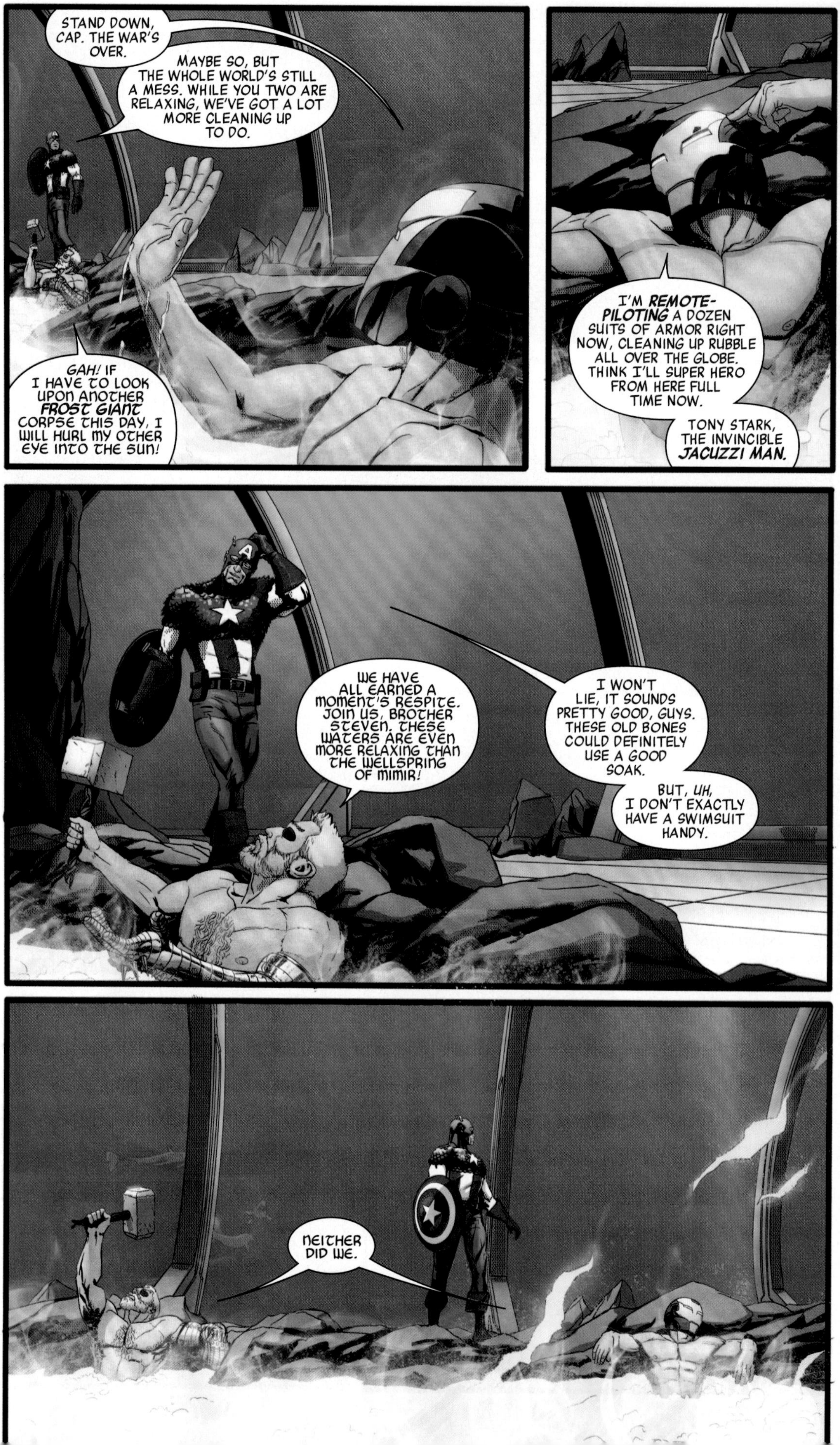
STAND DOWN, CAP. THE WAR'S OVER.
MAYBE SO, BUT THE WHOLE WORLD'S STILL A MESS. WHILE YOU TWO ARE RELAXING, WE'VE GOT A LOT MORE CLEANING UP TO DO.
GAH! IF I HAVE TO LOOK UPON ANOTHER FROST GIANT CORPSE THIS DAY, I WILL HURL MY OTHER EYE INTO THE SUN!
I'M REMOTE-PILOTING A DOZEN SUITS OF ARMOR RIGHT NOW, CLEANING UP RUBBLE ALL OVER THE GLOBE. THINK I'LL SUPER HERO FROM HERE FULL TIME NOW.
TONY STARK, THE INVINCIBLE JACUZZI MAN.
WE HAVE ALL EARNED A MOMENT'S RESPITE. JOIN US, BROTHER STEVEN. THESE WATERS ARE EVEN MORE RELAXING THAN THE WELLSPRING OF MIMIR!
I WON'T LIE, IT SOUNDS PRETTY GOOD, GUYS. THESE OLD BONES COULD DEFINITELY USE A GOOD SOAK.
BUT, UH, I DON'T EXACTLY HAVE A SWIMSUIT HANDY.
NEITHER DID WE.

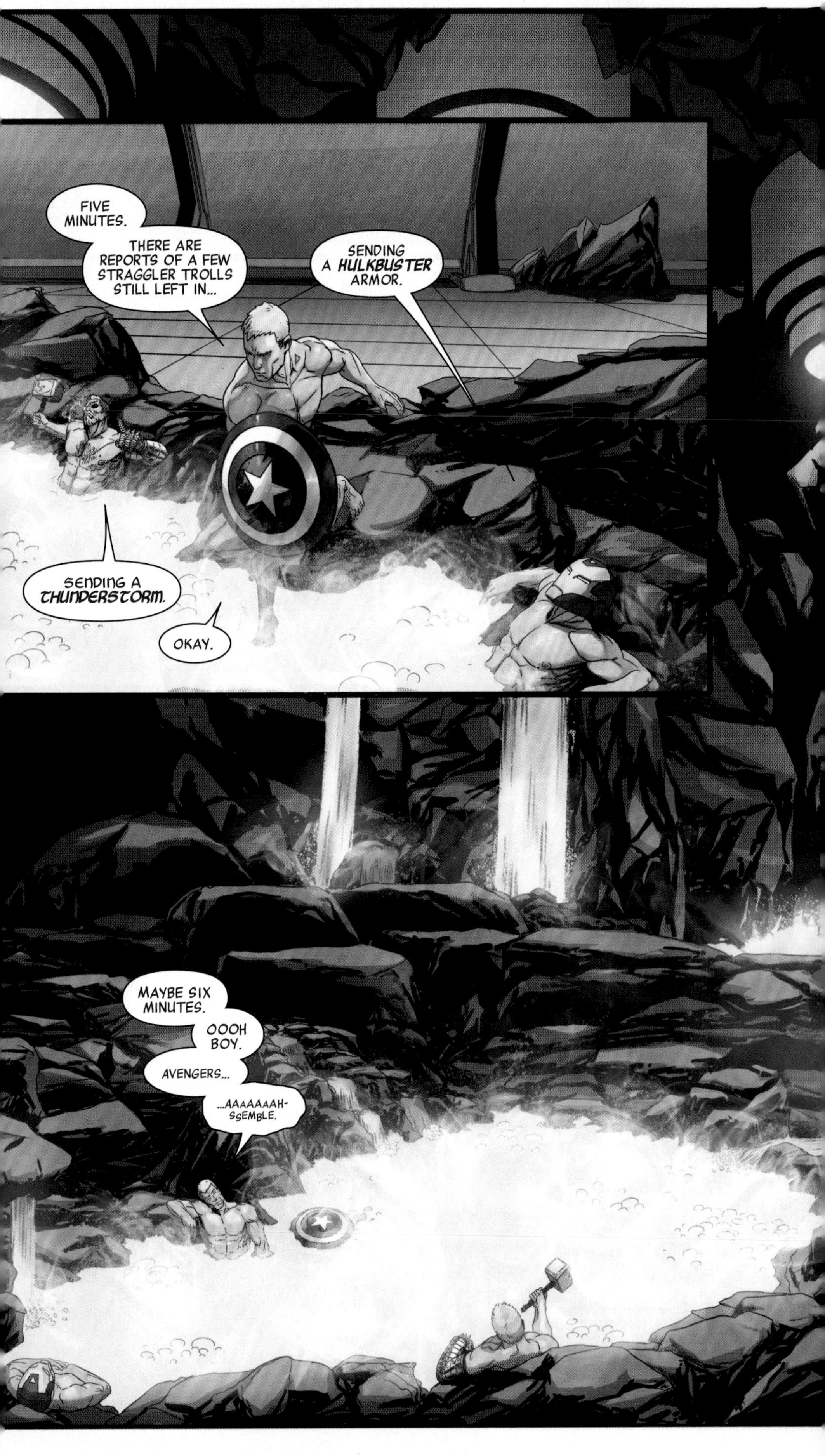
FIVE MINUTES.
THERE ARE REPORTS OF A FEW STRAGGLER TROLLS STILL LEFT IN...
SENDING A HULKBUSTER ARMOR.
SENDING A THUNDERSTORM.
OKAY.
MAYBE SIX MINUTES.
OOOH BOY.
AVENGERS...
...AAAAAAAH-SSEMBLE.

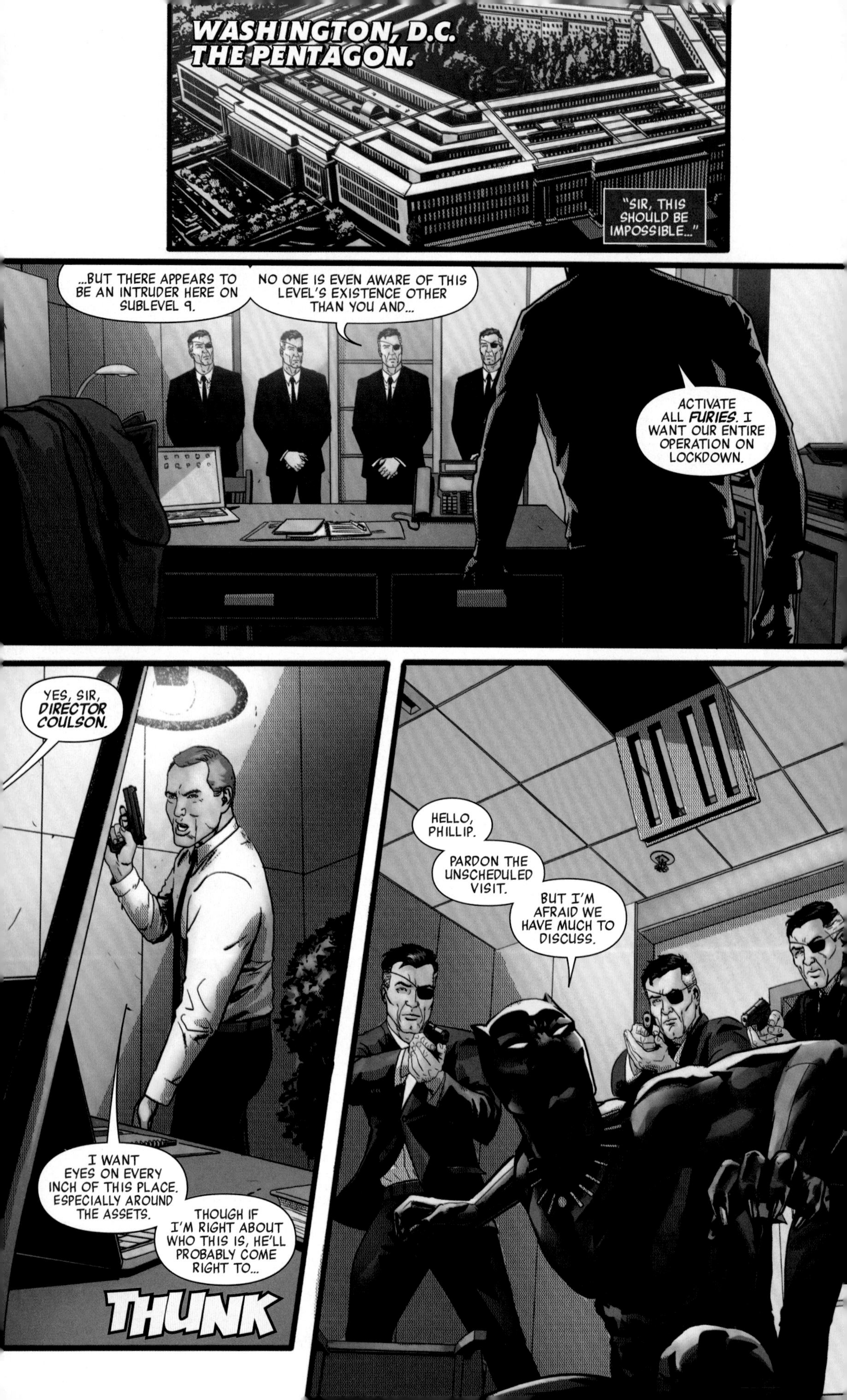
WASHINGTON, D.C. THE PENTAGON.
"SIR, THIS SHOULD BE IMPOSSIBLE..."
...BUT THERE APPEARS TO BE AN INTRUDER HERE ON SUBLEVEL 9.
NO ONE IS EVEN AWARE OF THIS LEVEL'S EXISTENCE OTHER THAN YOU AND...
ACTIVATE ALL FURIES. I WANT OUR ENTIRE OPERATION ON LOCKDOWN.
YES, SIR, DIRECTOR COULSON.
I WANT EYES ON EVERY INCH OF THIS PLACE. ESPECIALLY AROUND THE ASSETS.
THOUGH IF I'M RIGHT ABOUT WHO THIS IS, HE'LL PROBABLY COME RIGHT TO...
THUNK
HELLO, PHILLIP.
PARDON THE UNSCHEDULED VISIT.
BUT I'M AFRAID WE HAVE MUCH TO DISCUSS.

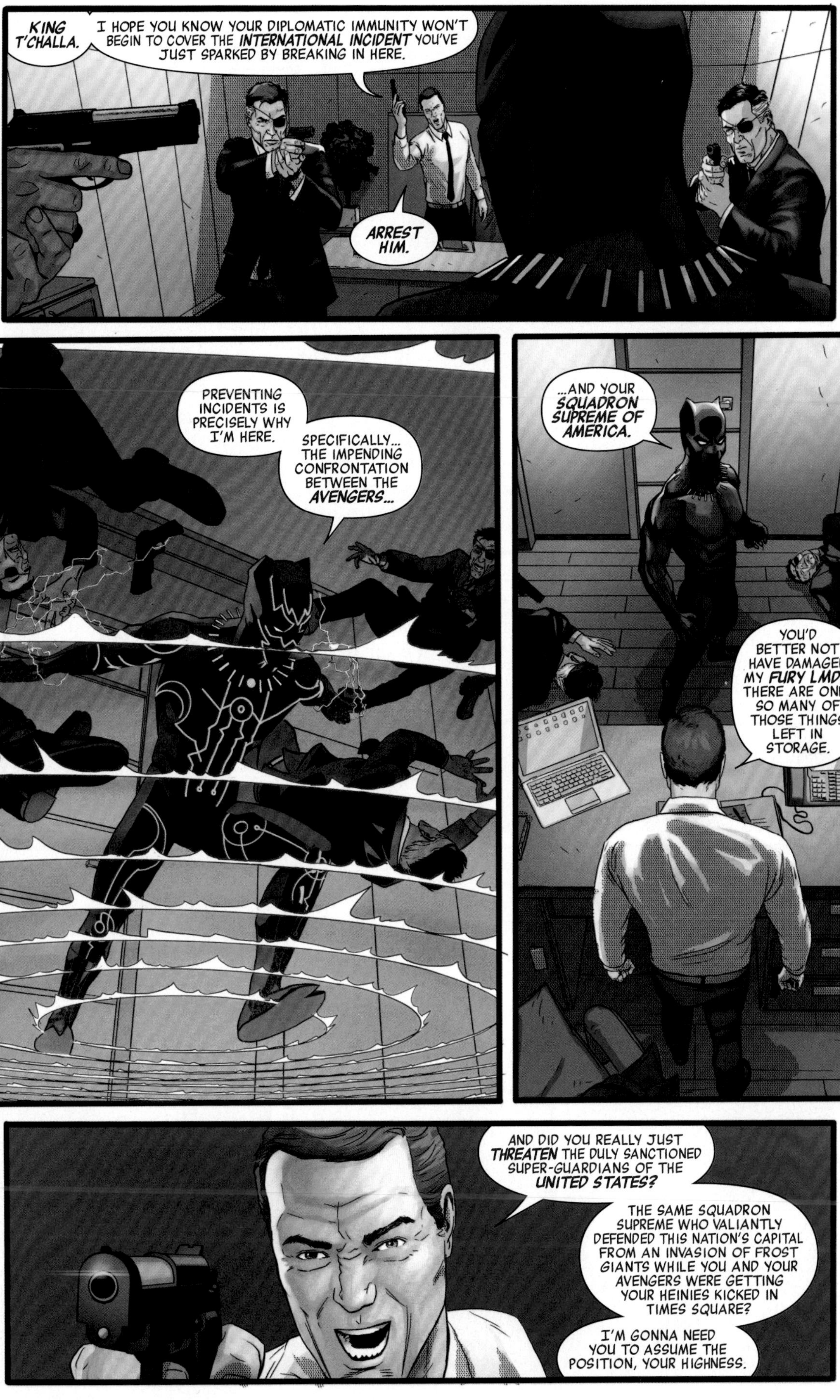
KING T'CHALLA.
I HOPE YOU KNOW YOUR DIPLOMATIC IMMUNITY WON'T BEGIN TO COVER THE INTERNATIONAL INCIDENT YOU'VE JUST SPARKED BY BREAKING IN HERE.
ARREST HIM.
PREVENTING INCIDENTS IS PRECISELY WHY I'M HERE.
SPECIFICALLY... THE IMPENDING CONFRONTATION BETWEEN THE AVENGERS...
...AND YOUR SQUADRON SUPREME OF AMERICA.
YOU'D BETTER NOT HAVE DAMAGED MY FURY LMDs. THERE ARE ONLY SO MANY OF THOSE THINGS LEFT IN STORAGE.
AND DID YOU REALLY JUST THREATEN THE DULY SANCTIONED SUPER-GUARDIANS OF THE UNITED STATES?
THE SAME SQUADRON SUPREME WHO VALIANTLY DEFENDED THIS NATION'S CAPITAL FROM AN INVASION OF FROST GIANTS WHILE YOU AND YOUR AVENGERS WERE GETTING YOUR HEINIES KICKED IN TIMES SQUARE?
I'M GONNA NEED YOU TO ASSUME THE POSITION, YOUR HIGHNESS.

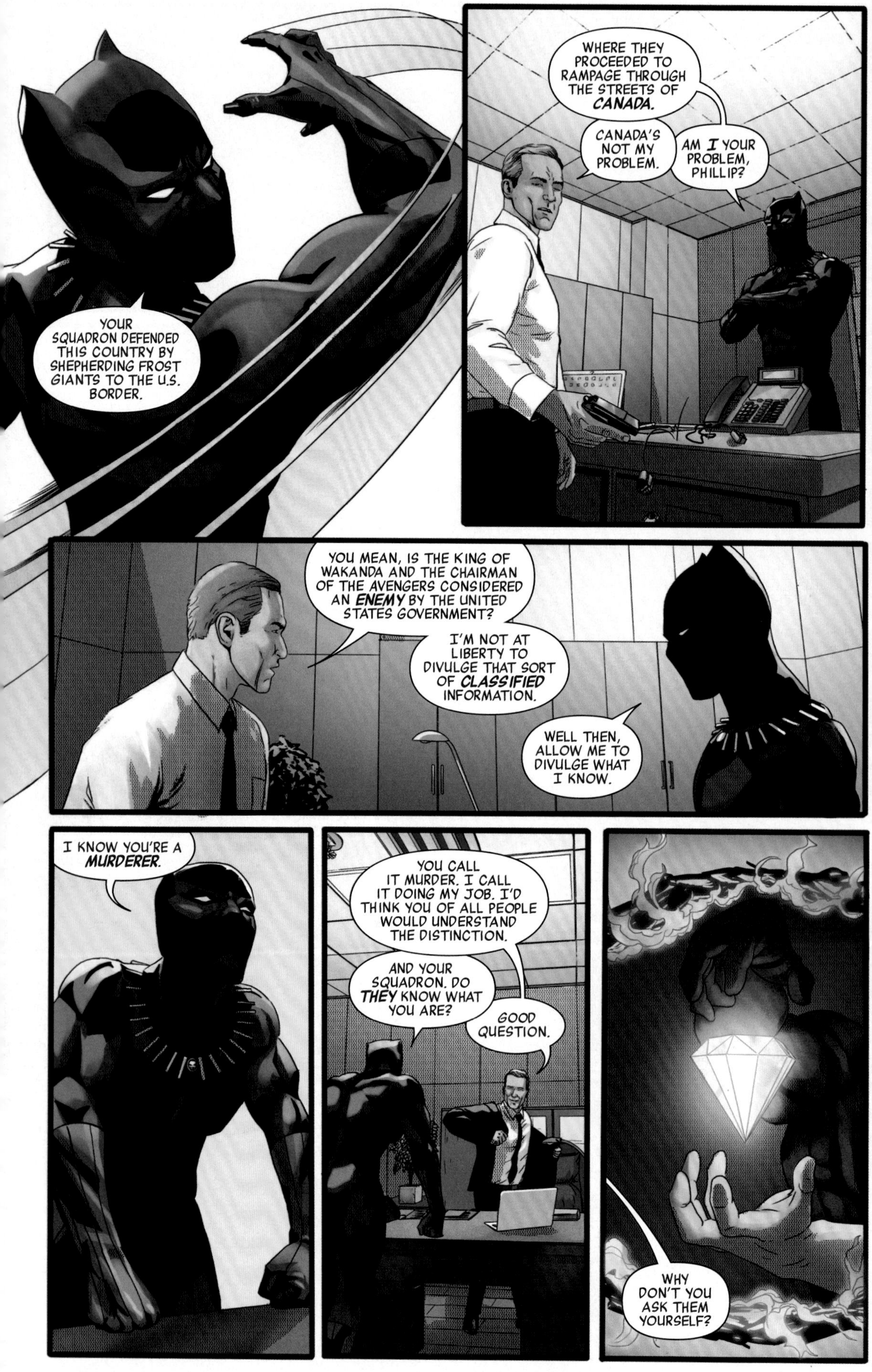

YOUR SQUADRON DEFENDED THIS COUNTRY BY SHEPHERDING FROST GIANTS TO THE U.S. BORDER.
WHERE THEY PROCEEDED TO RAMPAGE THROUGH THE STREETS OF CANADA.
CANADA'S NOT MY PROBLEM.
AM I YOUR PROBLEM, PHILLIP?
YOU MEAN, IS THE KING OF WAKANDA AND THE CHAIRMAN OF THE AVENGERS CONSIDERED AN ENEMY BY THE UNITED STATES GOVERNMENT?
I'M NOT AT LIBERTY TO DIVULGE THAT SORT OF CLASSIFIED INFORMATION.
WELL THEN, ALLOW ME TO DIVULGE WHAT I KNOW.
I KNOW YOU'RE A MURDERER.
YOU CALL IT MURDER. I CALL IT DOING MY JOB. I'D THINK YOU OF ALL PEOPLE WOULD UNDERSTAND THE DISTINCTION.
AND YOUR SQUADRON. DO THEY KNOW WHAT YOU ARE?
GOOD QUESTION.
WHY DON'T YOU ASK THEM YOURSELF?

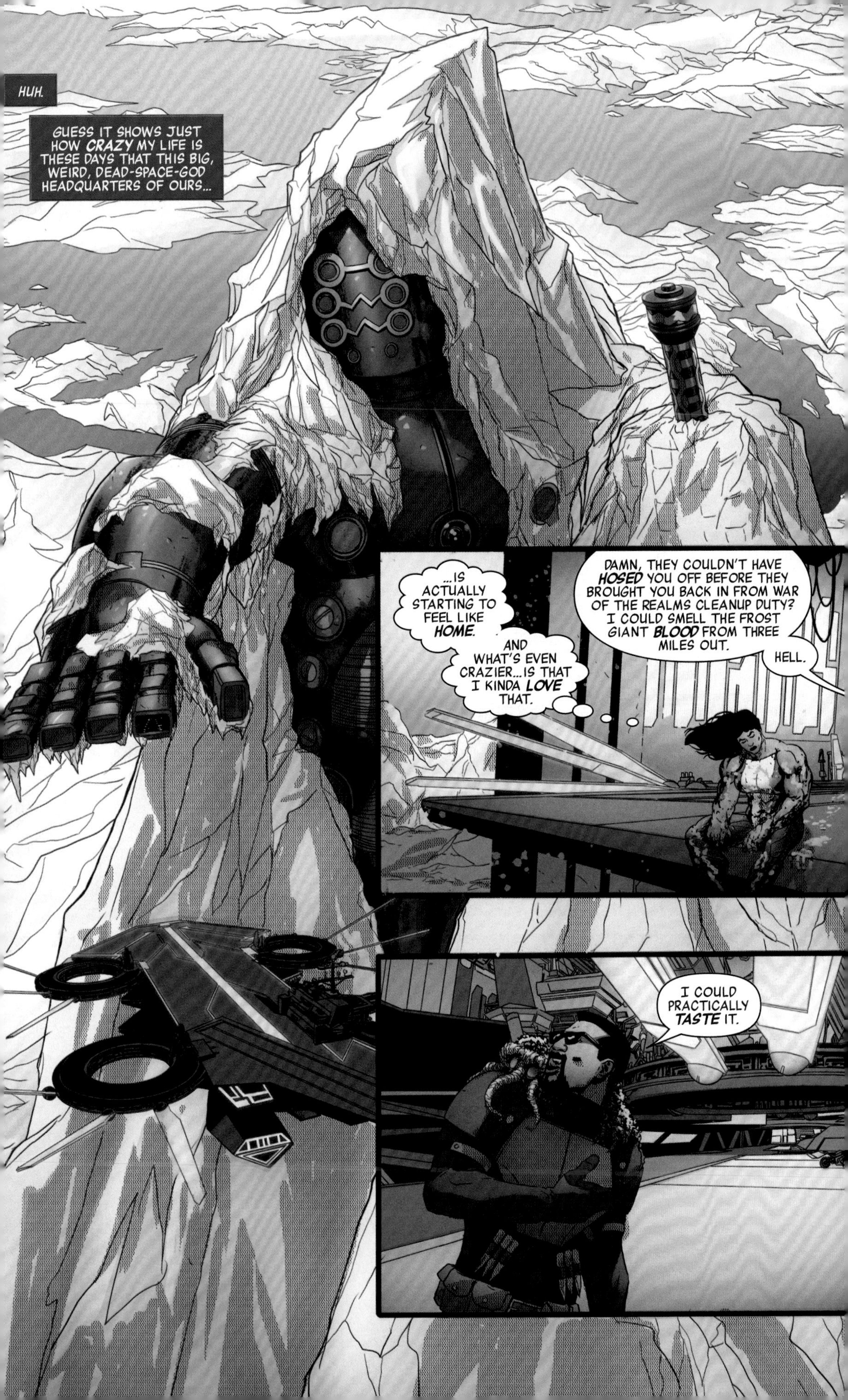
HUH.
GUESS IT SHOWS JUST HOW CRAZY MY LIFE IS THESE DAYS THAT THIS BIG, WEIRD, DEAD-SPACE-GOD HEADQUARTERS OF OURS...
...IS ACTUALLY STARTING TO FEEL LIKE HOME.
AND WHAT'S EVEN CRAZIER...IS THAT I KINDA LOVE THAT.
DAMN, THEY COULDN'T HAVE HOSED YOU OFF BEFORE THEY BROUGHT YOU BACK IN FROM WAR OF THE REALMS CLEANUP DUTY? I COULD SMELL THE FROST GIANT BLOOD FROM THREE MILES OUT.
HELL.
I COULD PRACTICALLY TASTE IT.

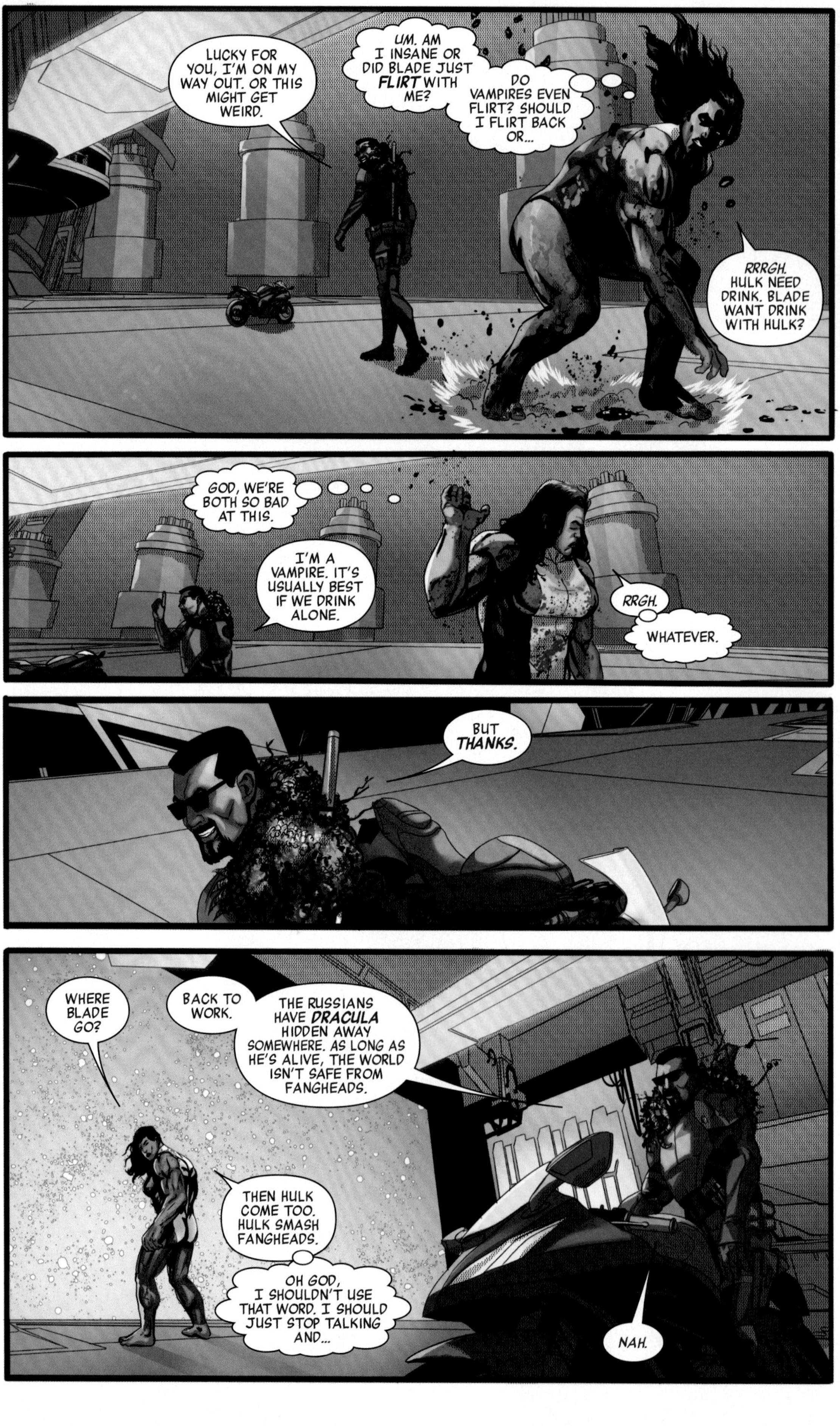
LUCKY FOR YOU, I'M ON MY WAY OUT. OR THIS MIGHT GET WEIRD.
UM. AM I INSANE OR DID BLADE JUST *FLIRT* WITH ME?
DO VAMPIRES EVEN FLIRT? SHOULD I FLIRT BACK OR...
RRRGH. HULK NEED DRINK. BLADE WANT DRINK WITH HULK?
GOD, WE'RE BOTH SO BAD AT THIS.
I'M A VAMPIRE. IT'S USUALLY BEST IF WE DRINK ALONE.
RRGH.
WHATEVER.
BUT *THANKS.*
WHERE BLADE GO?
BACK TO WORK.
THE RUSSIANS HAVE *DRACULA* HIDDEN AWAY SOMEWHERE. AS LONG AS HE'S ALIVE, THE WORLD ISN'T SAFE FROM FANGHEADS.
THEN HULK COME TOO. HULK SMASH FANGHEADS.
OH GOD, I SHOULDN'T USE THAT WORD. I SHOULD JUST STOP TALKING AND...
NAH.

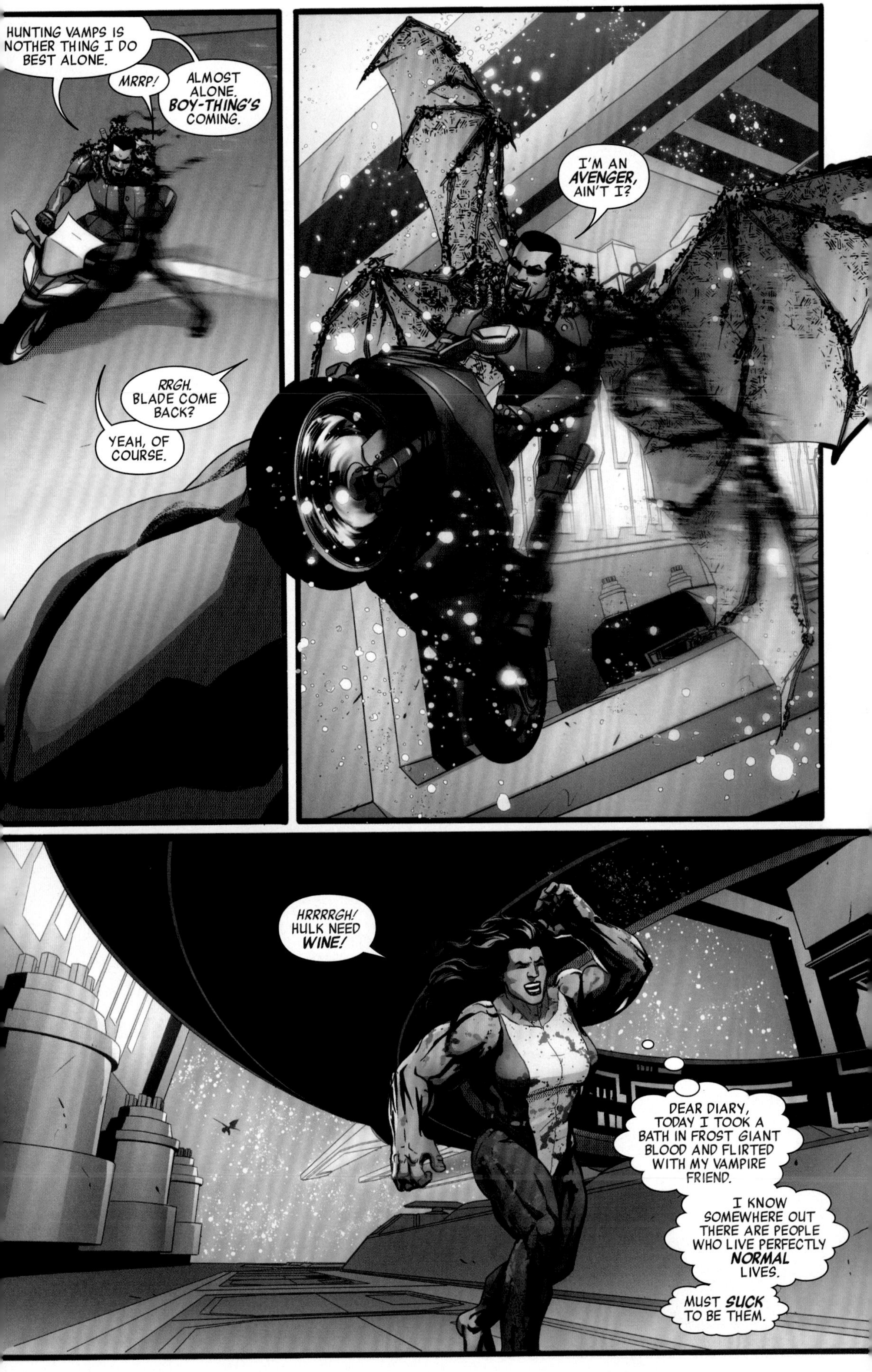
HUNTING VAMPS IS NOTHER THING I DO BEST ALONE.
MRRP!
ALMOST ALONE. BOY-THING'S COMING.
I'M AN AVENGER, AIN'T I?
RRGH. BLADE COME BACK?
YEAH, OF COURSE.
HRRRRGH! HULK NEED WINE!
DEAR DIARY, TODAY I TOOK A BATH IN FROST GIANT BLOOD AND FLIRTED WITH MY VAMPIRE FRIEND.
I KNOW SOMEWHERE OUT THERE ARE PEOPLE WHO LIVE PERFECTLY NORMAL LIVES.
MUST SUCK TO BE THEM.

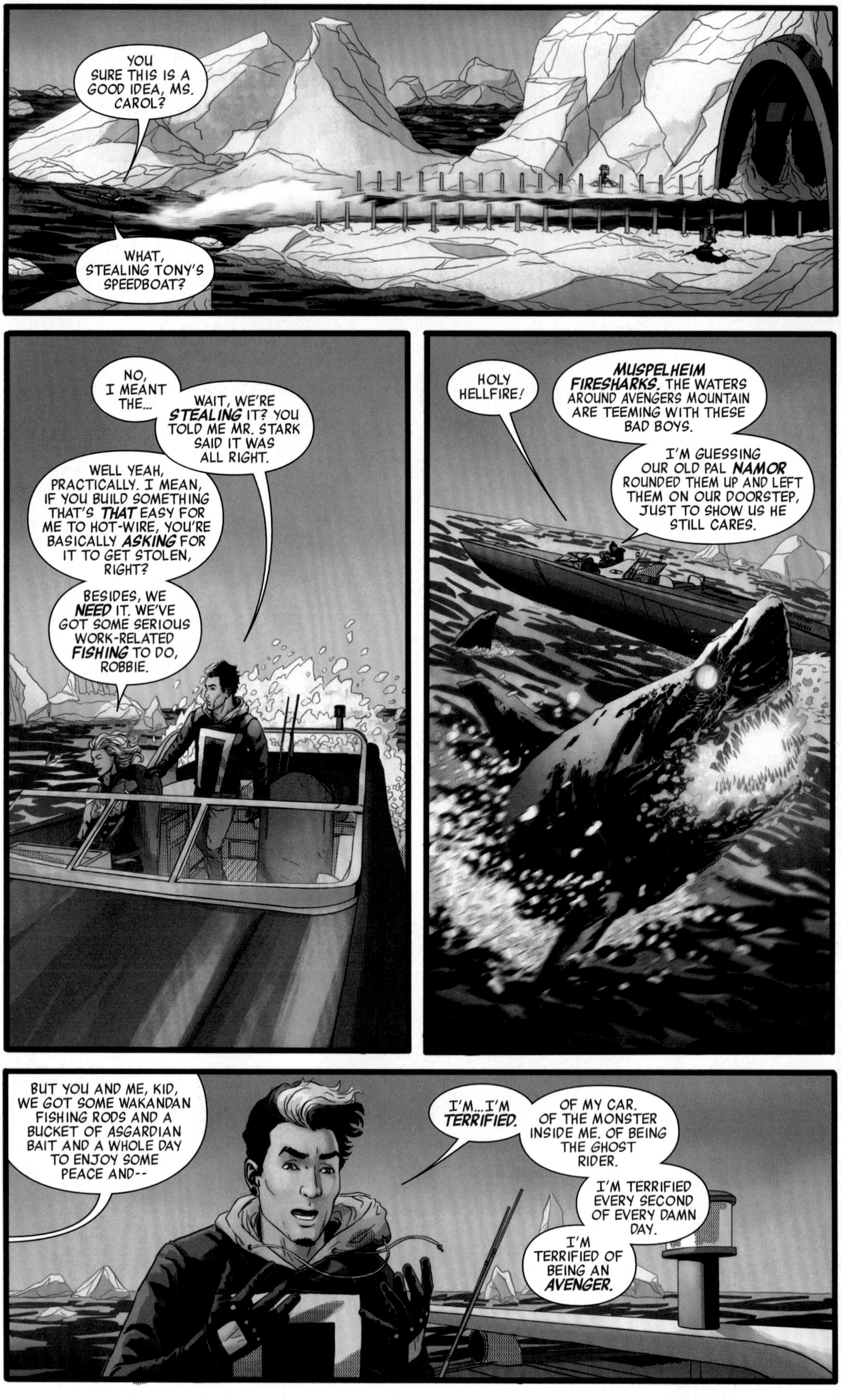
YOU SURE THIS IS A GOOD IDEA, MS. CAROL?
WHAT, STEALING TONY'S SPEEDBOAT?
NO, I MEANT THE...
WAIT, WE'RE STEALING IT? YOU TOLD ME MR. STARK SAID IT WAS ALL RIGHT.
WELL YEAH, PRACTICALLY. I MEAN, IF YOU BUILD SOMETHING THAT'S THAT EASY FOR ME TO HOT-WIRE, YOU'RE BASICALLY ASKING FOR IT TO GET STOLEN, RIGHT?
BESIDES, WE NEED IT. WE'VE GOT SOME SERIOUS WORK-RELATED FISHING TO DO, ROBBIE.
HOLY HELLFIRE!
MUSPELHEIM FIRESHARKS. THE WATERS AROUND AVENGERS MOUNTAIN ARE TEEMING WITH THESE BAD BOYS.
I'M GUESSING OUR OLD PAL NAMOR ROUNDED THEM UP AND LEFT THEM ON OUR DOORSTEP, JUST TO SHOW US HE STILL CARES.
BUT YOU AND ME, KID, WE GOT SOME WAKANDAN FISHING RODS AND A BUCKET OF ASGARDIAN BAIT AND A WHOLE DAY TO ENJOY SOME PEACE AND--
I'M...I'M TERRIFIED.
OF MY CAR. OF THE MONSTER INSIDE ME. OF BEING THE GHOST RIDER.
I'M TERRIFIED EVERY SECOND OF EVERY DAMN DAY.
I'M TERRIFIED OF BEING AN AVENGER.

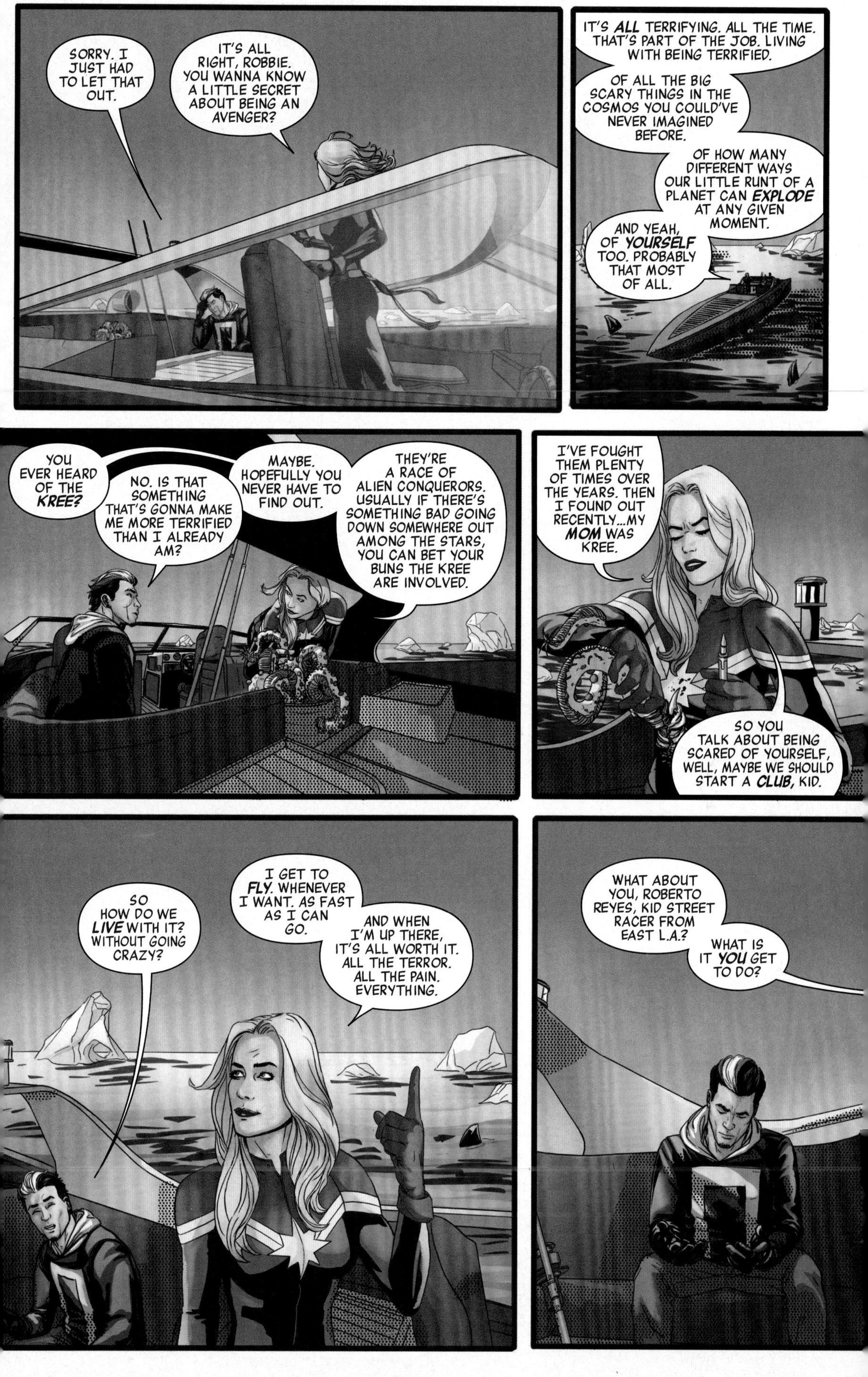
SORRY. I JUST HAD TO LET THAT OUT.
IT'S ALL RIGHT, ROBBIE. YOU WANNA KNOW A LITTLE SECRET ABOUT BEING AN AVENGER?
IT'S ALL TERRIFYING. ALL THE TIME. THAT'S PART OF THE JOB. LIVING WITH BEING TERRIFIED.
OF ALL THE BIG SCARY THINGS IN THE COSMOS YOU COULD'VE NEVER IMAGINED BEFORE.
OF HOW MANY DIFFERENT WAYS OUR LITTLE RUNT OF A PLANET CAN EXPLODE AT ANY GIVEN MOMENT.
AND YEAH, OF YOURSELF TOO. PROBABLY THAT MOST OF ALL.
YOU EVER HEARD OF THE KREE?
NO. IS THAT SOMETHING THAT'S GONNA MAKE ME MORE TERRIFIED THAN I ALREADY AM?
MAYBE. HOPEFULLY YOU NEVER HAVE TO FIND OUT.
THEY'RE A RACE OF ALIEN CONQUERORS. USUALLY IF THERE'S SOMETHING BAD GOING DOWN SOMEWHERE OUT AMONG THE STARS, YOU CAN BET YOUR BUNS THE KREE ARE INVOLVED.
I'VE FOUGHT THEM PLENTY OF TIMES OVER THE YEARS. THEN I FOUND OUT RECENTLY...MY MOM WAS KREE.
SO YOU TALK ABOUT BEING SCARED OF YOURSELF, WELL, MAYBE WE SHOULD START A CLUB, KID.
SO HOW DO WE LIVE WITH IT? WITHOUT GOING CRAZY?
I GET TO FLY. WHENEVER I WANT. AS FAST AS I CAN GO.
AND WHEN I'M UP THERE, IT'S ALL WORTH IT. ALL THE TERROR. ALL THE PAIN. EVERYTHING.
WHAT ABOUT YOU, ROBERTO REYES, KID STREET RACER FROM EAST L.A.?
WHAT IS IT YOU GET TO DO?

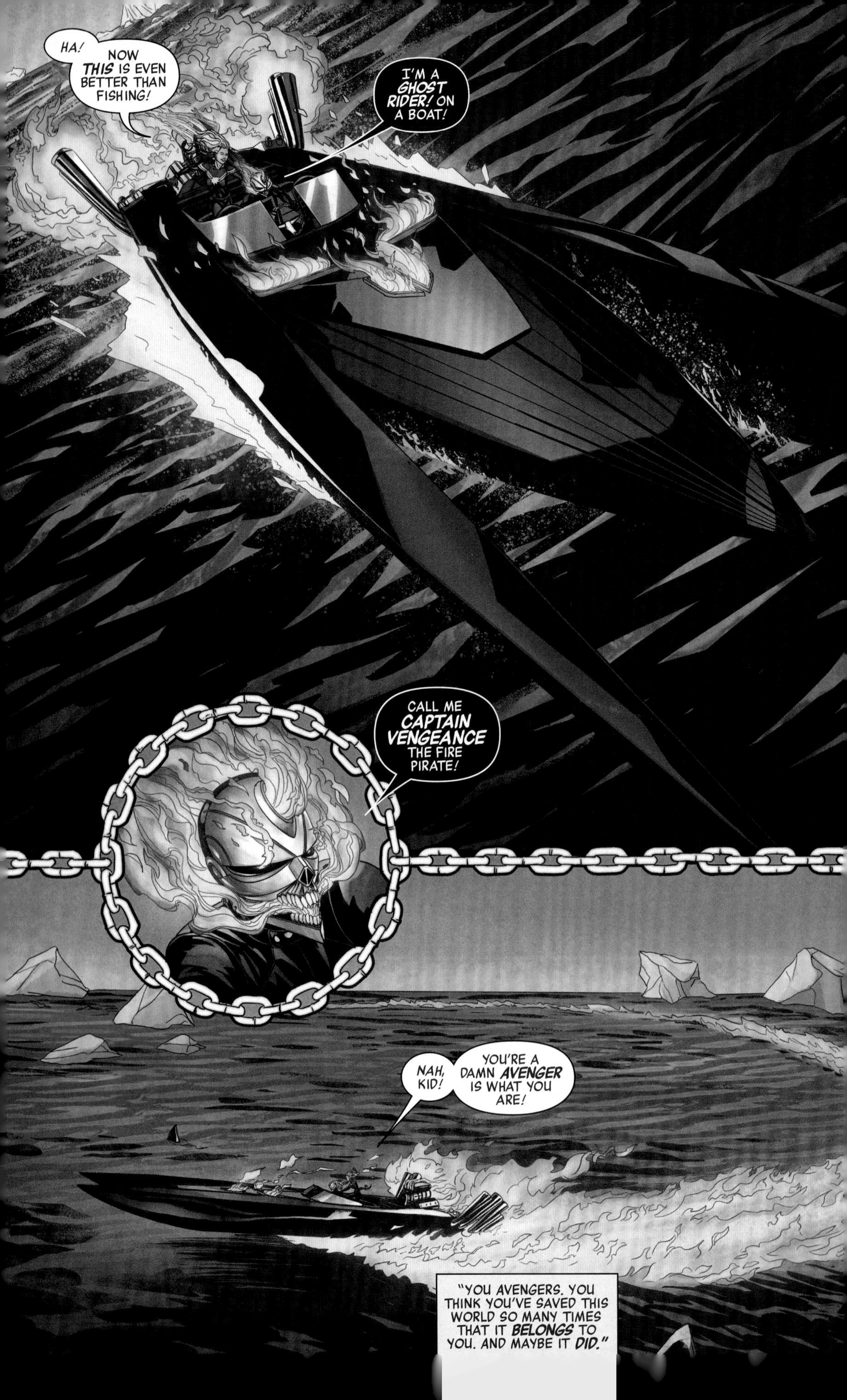
HA! NOW THIS IS EVEN BETTER THAN FISHING!
I'M A GHOST RIDER! ON A BOAT!
CALL ME CAPTAIN VENGEANCE THE FIRE PIRATE!
NAH, KID!
YOU'RE A DAMN AVENGER IS WHAT YOU ARE!
"YOU AVENGERS. YOU THINK YOU'VE SAVED THIS WORLD SO MANY TIMES THAT IT BELONGS TO YOU. AND MAYBE IT DID."

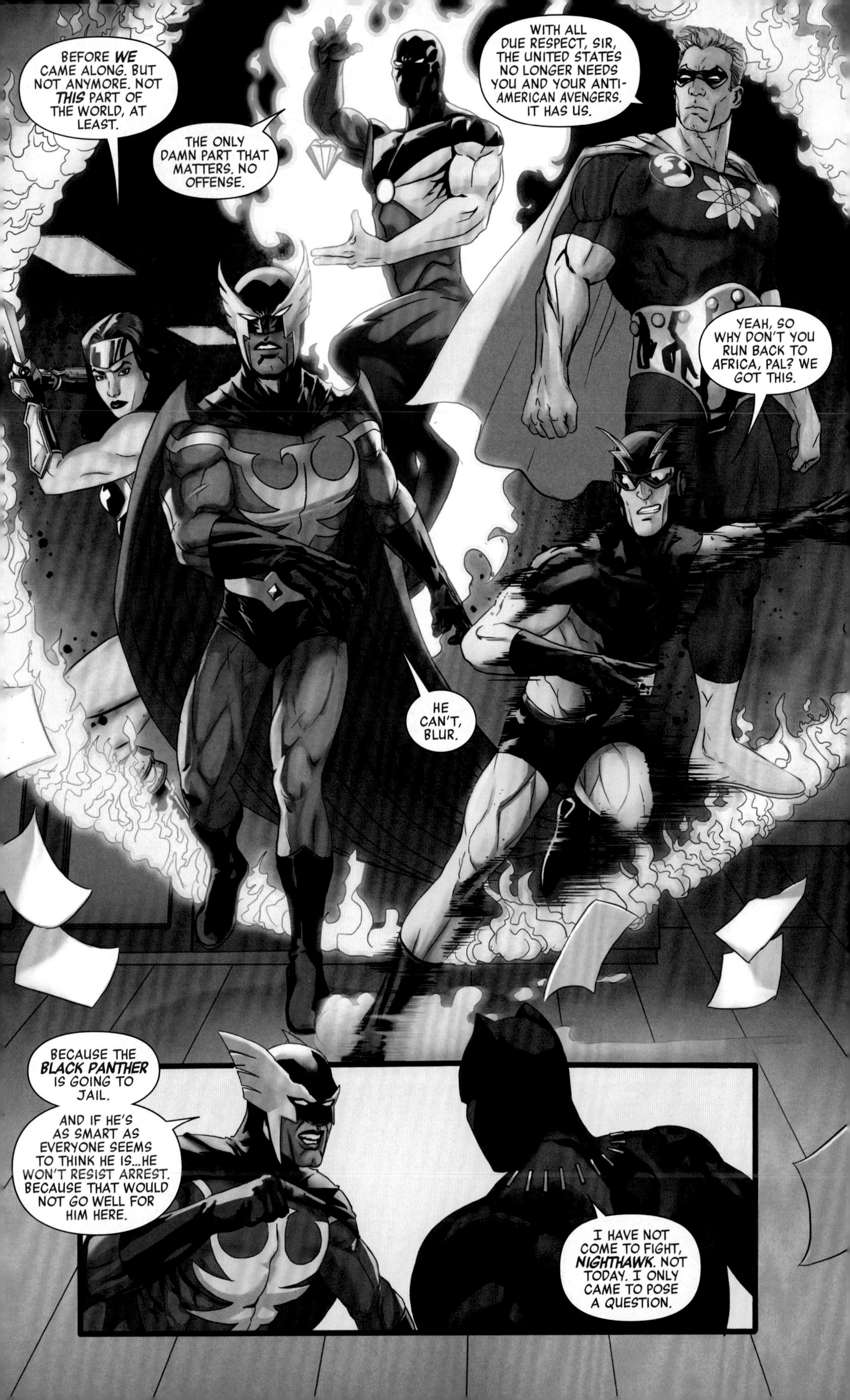
BEFORE WE CAME ALONG. BUT NOT ANYMORE. NOT THIS PART OF THE WORLD, AT LEAST.
THE ONLY DAMN PART THAT MATTERS. NO OFFENSE.
WITH ALL DUE RESPECT, SIR, THE UNITED STATES NO LONGER NEEDS YOU AND YOUR ANTI-AMERICAN AVENGERS. IT HAS US.
YEAH, SO WHY DON'T YOU RUN BACK TO AFRICA, PAL? WE GOT THIS.
HE CAN'T, BLUR.
BECAUSE THE BLACK PANTHER IS GOING TO JAIL.
AND IF HE'S AS SMART AS EVERYONE SEEMS TO THINK HE IS...HE WON'T RESIST ARREST. BECAUSE THAT WOULD NOT GO WELL FOR HIM HERE.
I HAVE NOT COME TO FIGHT, NIGHTHAWK. NOT TODAY. I ONLY CAME TO POSE A QUESTION.

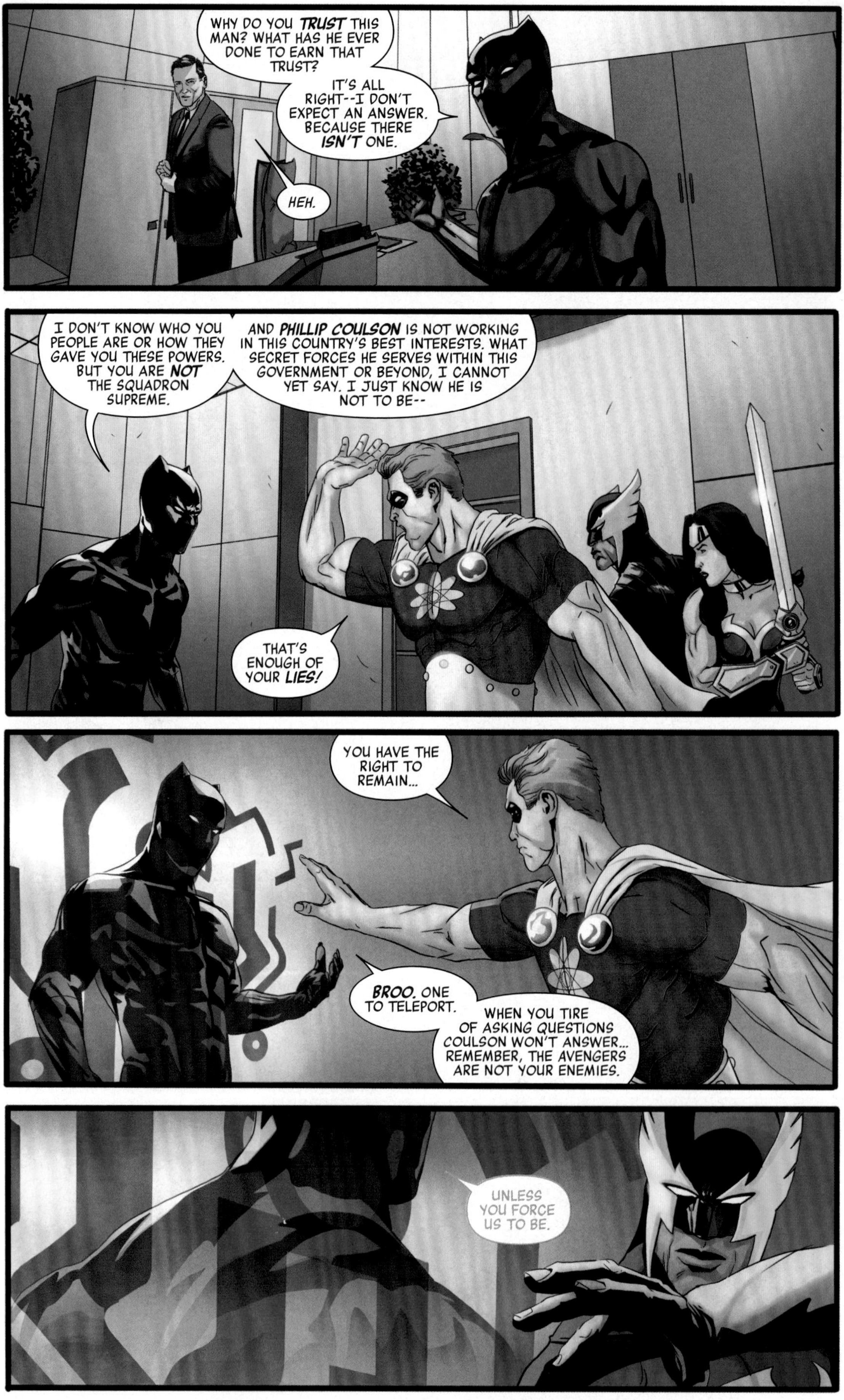
WHY DO YOU TRUST THIS MAN? WHAT HAS HE EVER DONE TO EARN THAT TRUST?
IT'S ALL RIGHT--I DON'T EXPECT AN ANSWER. BECAUSE THERE ISN'T ONE.
HEH.
I DON'T KNOW WHO YOU PEOPLE ARE OR HOW THEY GAVE YOU THESE POWERS. BUT YOU ARE NOT THE SQUADRON SUPREME.
AND PHILLIP COULSON IS NOT WORKING IN THIS COUNTRY'S BEST INTERESTS. WHAT SECRET FORCES HE SERVES WITHIN THIS GOVERNMENT OR BEYOND, I CANNOT YET SAY. I JUST KNOW HE IS NOT TO BE--
THAT'S ENOUGH OF YOUR LIES!
YOU HAVE THE RIGHT TO REMAIN...
BROO. ONE TO TELEPORT.
WHEN YOU TIRE OF ASKING QUESTIONS COULSON WON'T ANSWER... REMEMBER, THE AVENGERS ARE NOT YOUR ENEMIES.
UNLESS YOU FORCE US TO BE.

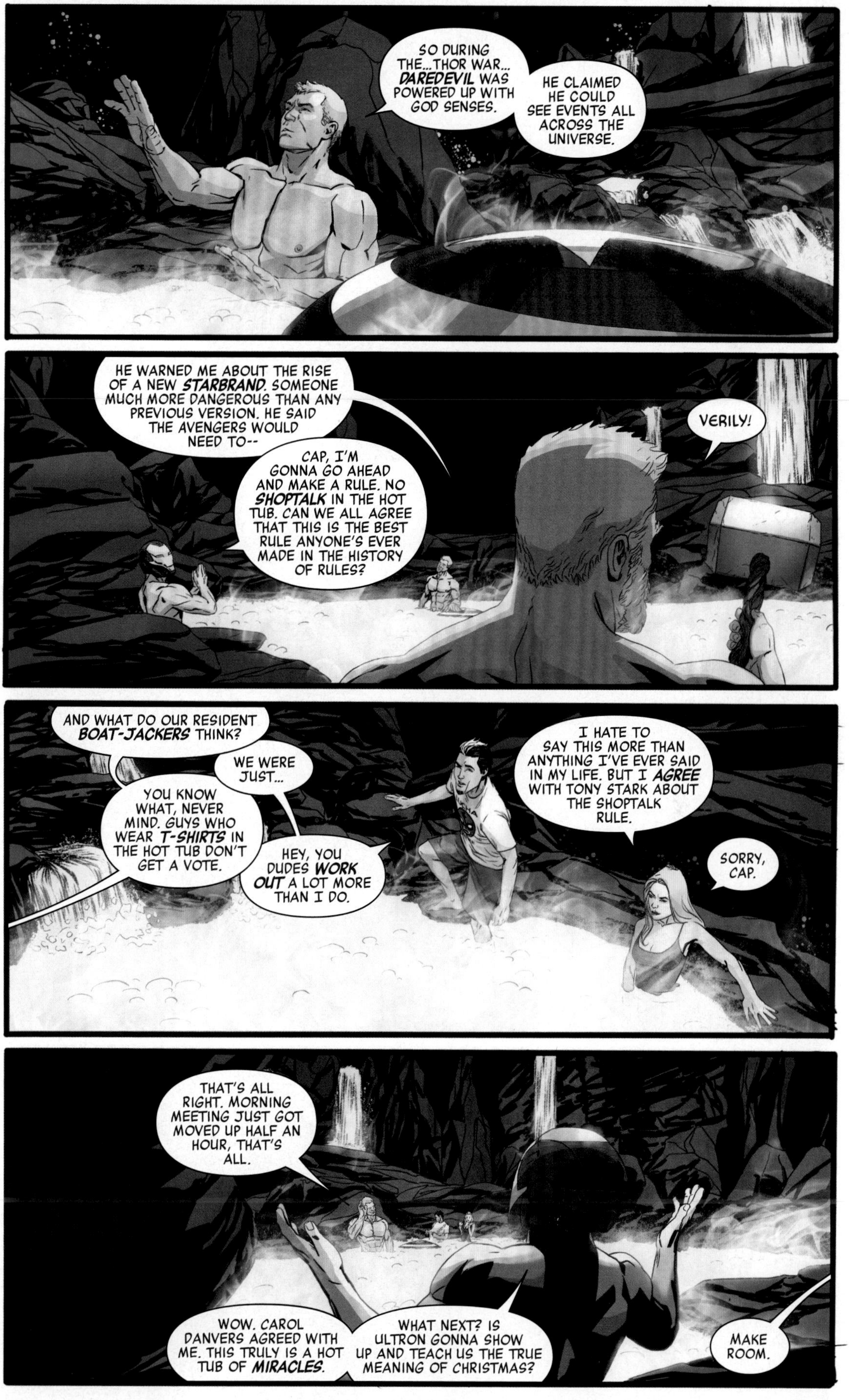
SO DURING THE... THOR WAR... DAREDEVIL WAS POWERED UP WITH GOD SENSES.
HE CLAIMED HE COULD SEE EVENTS ALL ACROSS THE UNIVERSE.
HE WARNED ME ABOUT THE RISE OF A NEW STARBRAND. SOMEONE MUCH MORE DANGEROUS THAN ANY PREVIOUS VERSION. HE SAID THE AVENGERS WOULD NEED TO--
CAP, I'M GONNA GO AHEAD AND MAKE A RULE. NO SHOPTALK IN THE HOT TUB. CAN WE ALL AGREE THAT THIS IS THE BEST RULE ANYONE'S EVER MADE IN THE HISTORY OF RULES?
VERILY!
AND WHAT DO OUR RESIDENT BOAT-JACKERS THINK?
WE WERE JUST...
YOU KNOW WHAT, NEVER MIND. GUYS WHO WEAR T-SHIRTS IN THE HOT TUB DON'T GET A VOTE.
HEY, YOU DUDES WORK OUT A LOT MORE THAN I DO.
I HATE TO SAY THIS MORE THAN ANYTHING I'VE EVER SAID IN MY LIFE. BUT I AGREE WITH TONY STARK ABOUT THE SHOPTALK RULE.
SORRY, CAP.
THAT'S ALL RIGHT. MORNING MEETING JUST GOT MOVED UP HALF AN HOUR, THAT'S ALL.
WOW. CAROL DANVERS AGREED WITH ME. THIS TRULY IS A HOT TUB OF MIRACLES.
WHAT NEXT? IS ULTRON GONNA SHOW UP AND TEACH US THE TRUE MEANING OF CHRISTMAS?
MAKE ROOM.

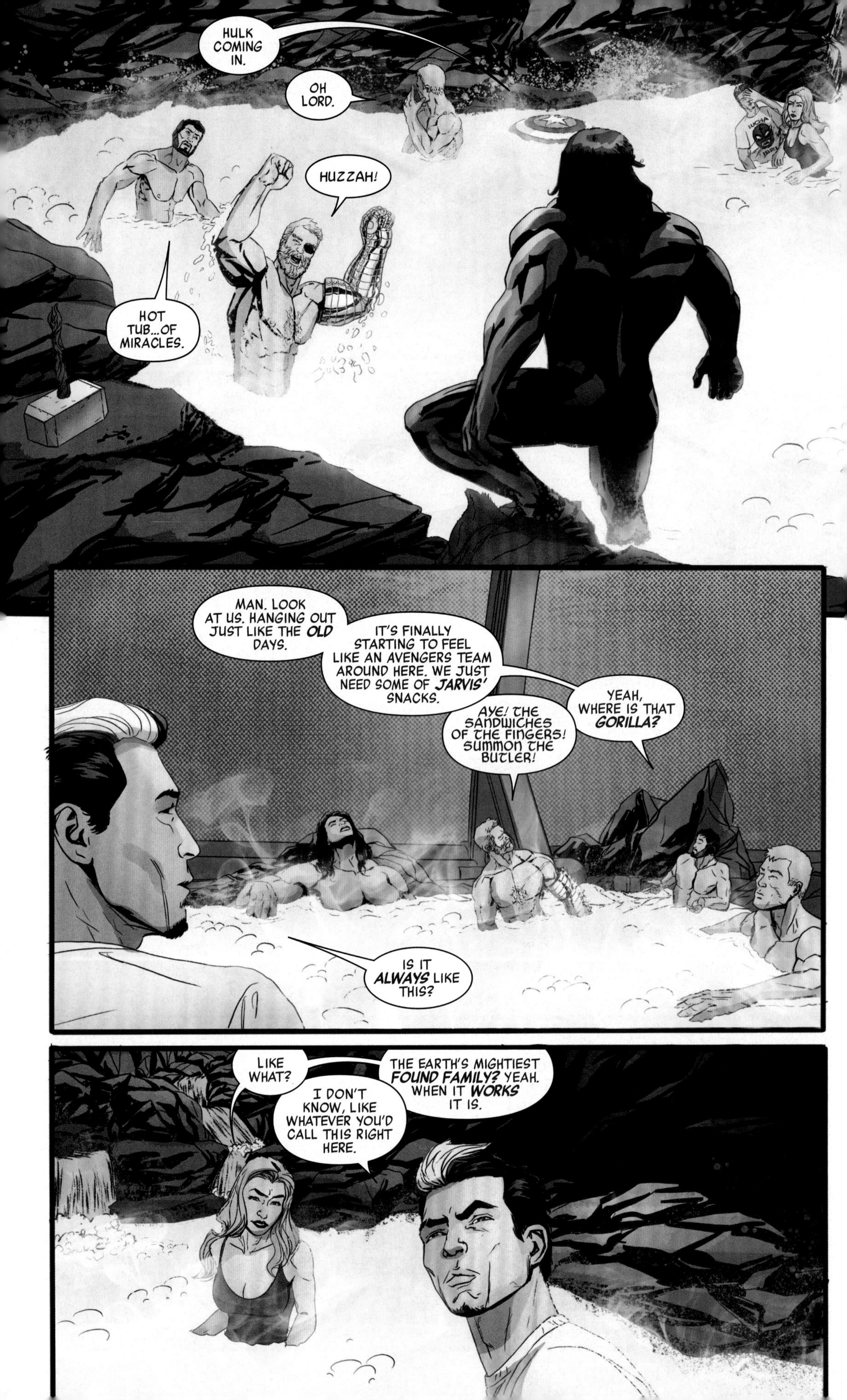
HULK COMING IN.
OH LORD.
HUZZAH!
HOT TUB...OF MIRACLES.
MAN. LOOK AT US. HANGING OUT JUST LIKE THE OLD DAYS.
IT'S FINALLY STARTING TO FEEL LIKE AN AVENGERS TEAM AROUND HERE. WE JUST NEED SOME OF JARVIS' SNACKS.
YEAH, WHERE IS THAT GORILLA?
AYE! THE SANDWICHES OF THE FINGERS! SUMMON THE BUTLER!
IS IT ALWAYS LIKE THIS?
LIKE WHAT?
I DON'T KNOW, LIKE WHATEVER YOU'D CALL THIS RIGHT HERE.
THE EARTH'S MIGHTIEST FOUND FAMILY? YEAH. WHEN IT WORKS IT IS.

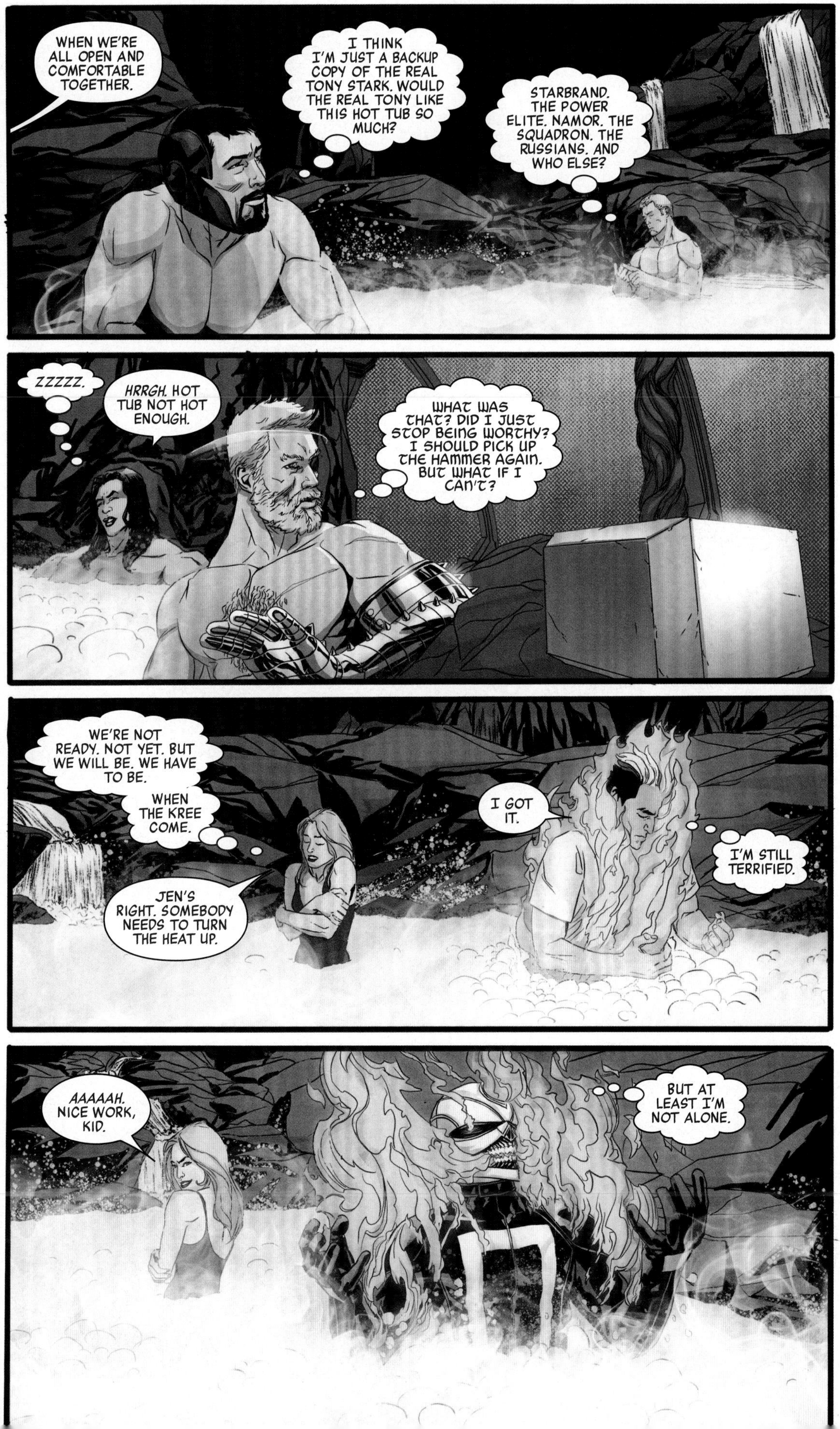
WHEN WE'RE ALL OPEN AND COMFORTABLE TOGETHER.
I THINK I'M JUST A BACKUP COPY OF THE REAL TONY STARK. WOULD THE REAL TONY LIKE THIS HOT TUB SO MUCH?
STARBRAND. THE POWER ELITE. NAMOR. THE SQUADRON. THE RUSSIANS. AND WHO ELSE?
ZZZZZ.
HRRGH. HOT TUB NOT HOT ENOUGH.
WHAT WAS THAT? DID I JUST STOP BEING WORTHY? I SHOULD PICK UP THE HAMMER AGAIN. BUT WHAT IF I CAN'T?
WE'RE NOT READY. NOT YET. BUT WE WILL BE. WE HAVE TO BE.
WHEN THE KREE COME.
JEN'S RIGHT. SOMEBODY NEEDS TO TURN THE HEAT UP.
I GOT IT.
I'M STILL TERRIFIED.
AAAAAH. NICE WORK, KID.
BUT AT LEAST I'M NOT ALONE.

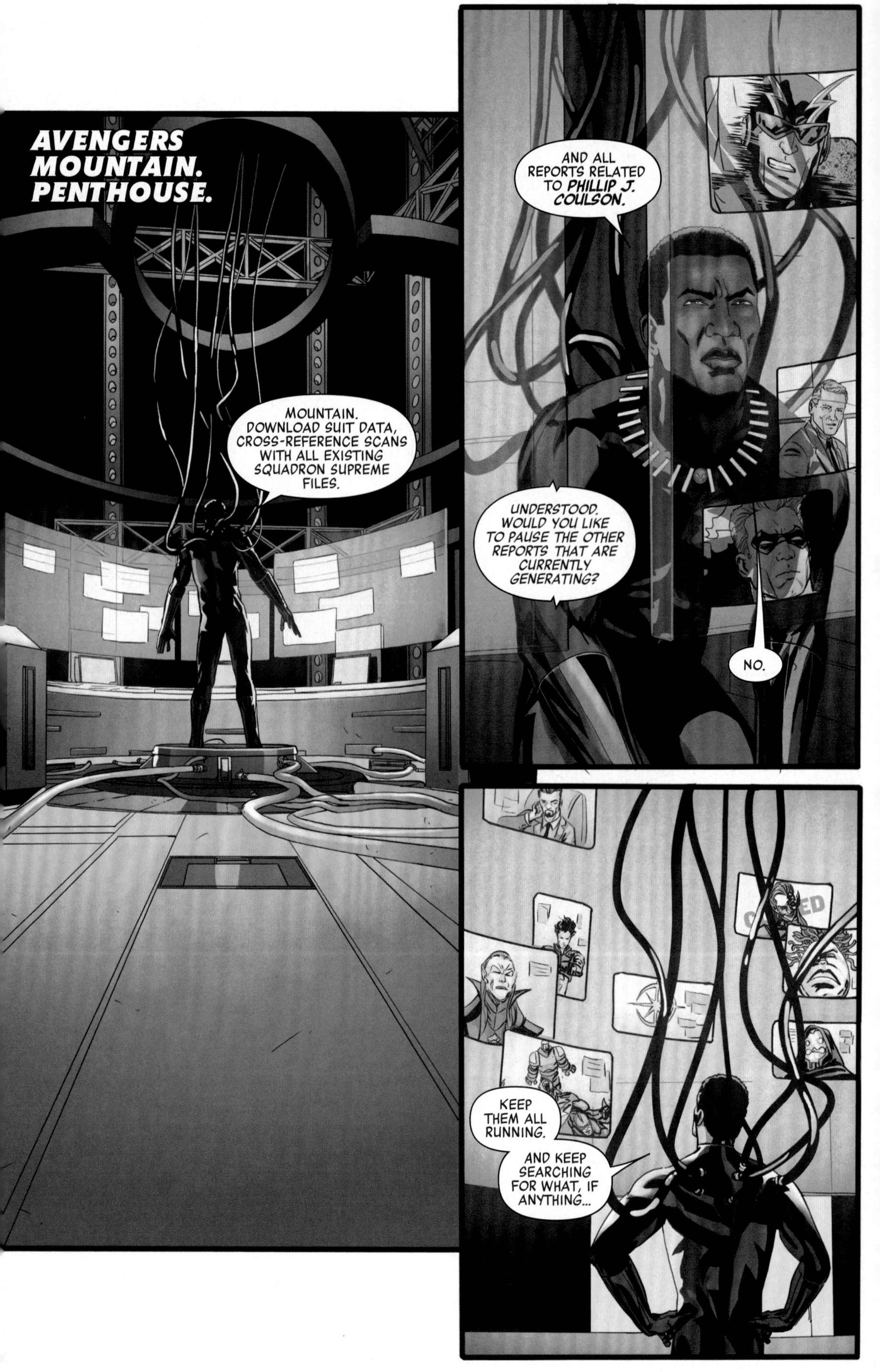
AVENGERS MOUNTAIN. PENTHOUSE.
MOUNTAIN. DOWNLOAD SUIT DATA, CROSS-REFERENCE SCANS WITH ALL EXISTING SQUADRON SUPREME FILES.
AND ALL REPORTS RELATED TO PHILLIP J. COULSON.
UNDERSTOOD. WOULD YOU LIKE TO PAUSE THE OTHER REPORTS THAT ARE CURRENTLY GENERATING?
NO.
KEEP THEM ALL RUNNING.
AND KEEP SEARCHING FOR WHAT, IF ANYTHING...

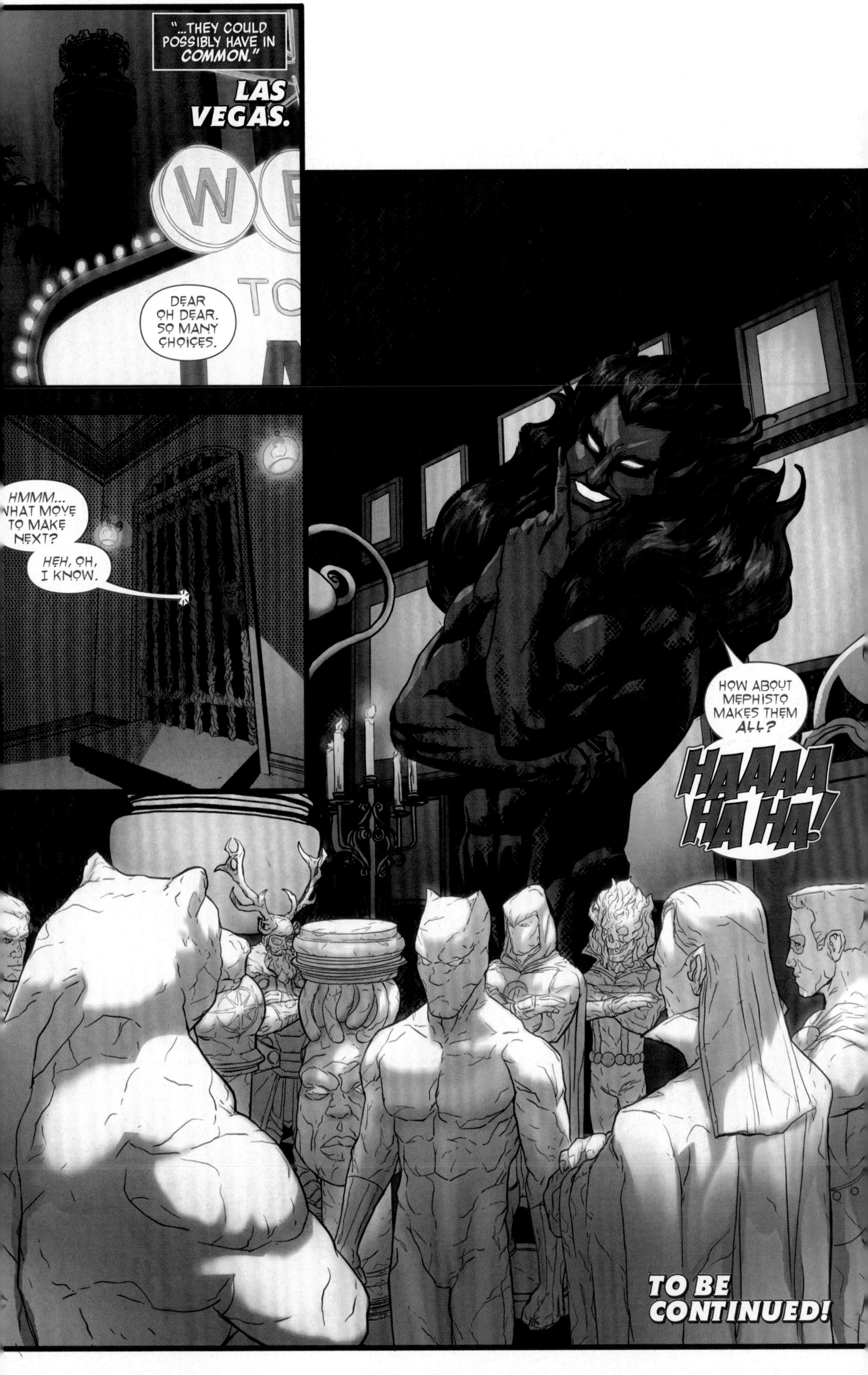
"...THEY COULD POSSIBLY HAVE IN COMMON."
LAS VEGAS.
DEAR OH DEAR. SO MANY CHOICES.
HMMM... HAT MOVE TO MAKE NEXT?
HEH, OH, I KNOW.
HOW ABOUT MEPHISTO MAKES THEM ALL?
HAAAA HA HA!
TO BE CONTINUED!

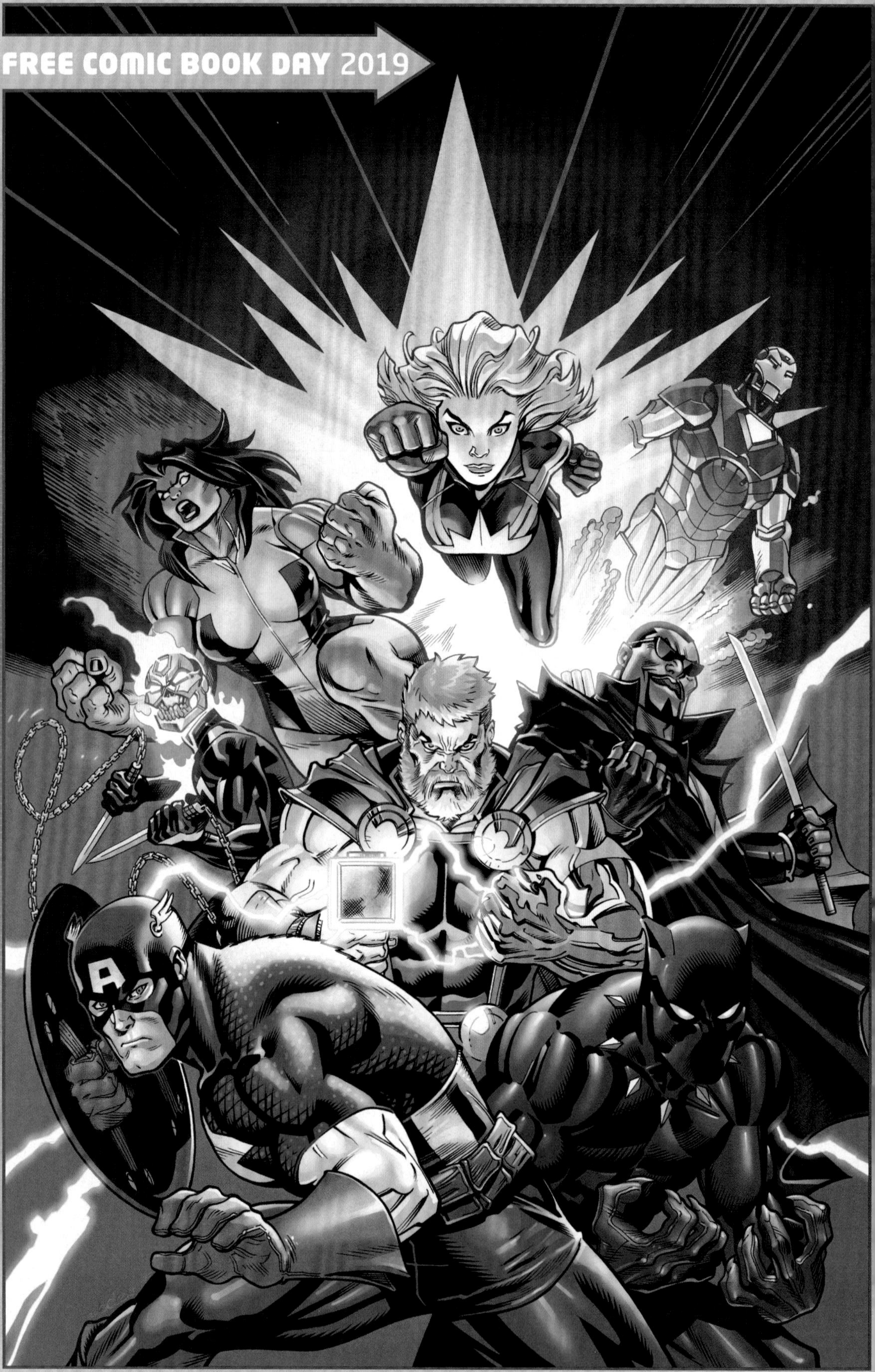
FREE COMIC BOOK DAY 2019

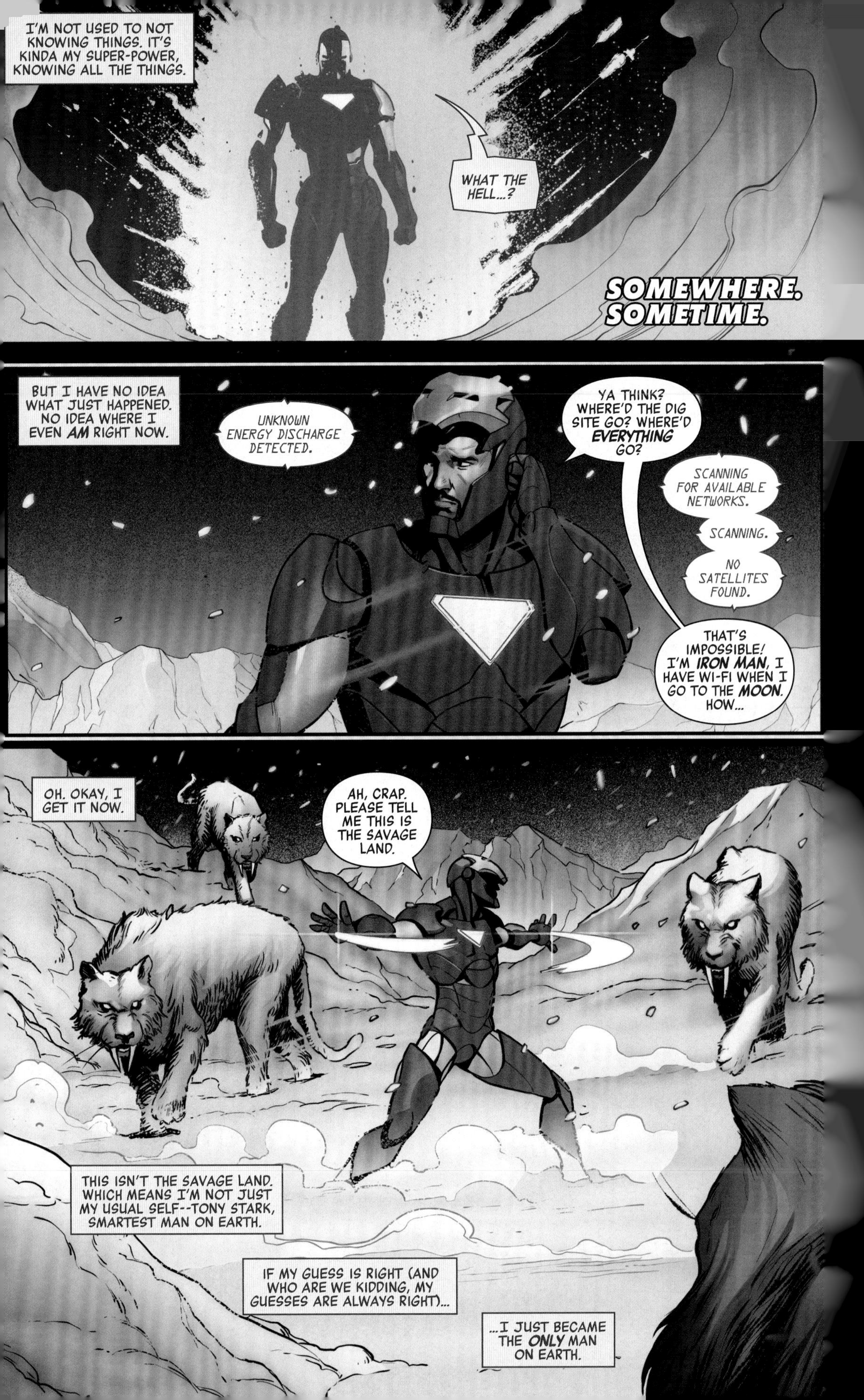
I'M NOT USED TO NOT KNOWING THINGS. IT'S KINDA MY SUPER-POWER, KNOWING ALL THE THINGS.
WHAT THE HELL...?
SOMEWHERE. SOMETIME.
BUT I HAVE NO IDEA WHAT JUST HAPPENED. NO IDEA WHERE I EVEN AM RIGHT NOW.
UNKNOWN ENERGY DISCHARGE DETECTED.
YA THINK? WHERE'D THE DIG SITE GO? WHERE'D EVERYTHING GO?
SCANNING FOR AVAILABLE NETWORKS.
SCANNING.
NO SATELLITES FOUND.
THAT'S IMPOSSIBLE! I'M IRON MAN, I HAVE WI-FI WHEN I GO TO THE MOON. HOW...
OH. OKAY, I GET IT NOW.
AH, CRAP. PLEASE TELL ME THIS IS THE SAVAGE LAND.
THIS ISN'T THE SAVAGE LAND. WHICH MEANS I'M NOT JUST MY USUAL SELF--TONY STARK, SMARTEST MAN ON EARTH.
IF MY GUESS IS RIGHT (AND WHO ARE WE KIDDING, MY GUESSES ARE ALWAYS RIGHT)...
...I JUST BECAME THE ONLY MAN ON EARTH.

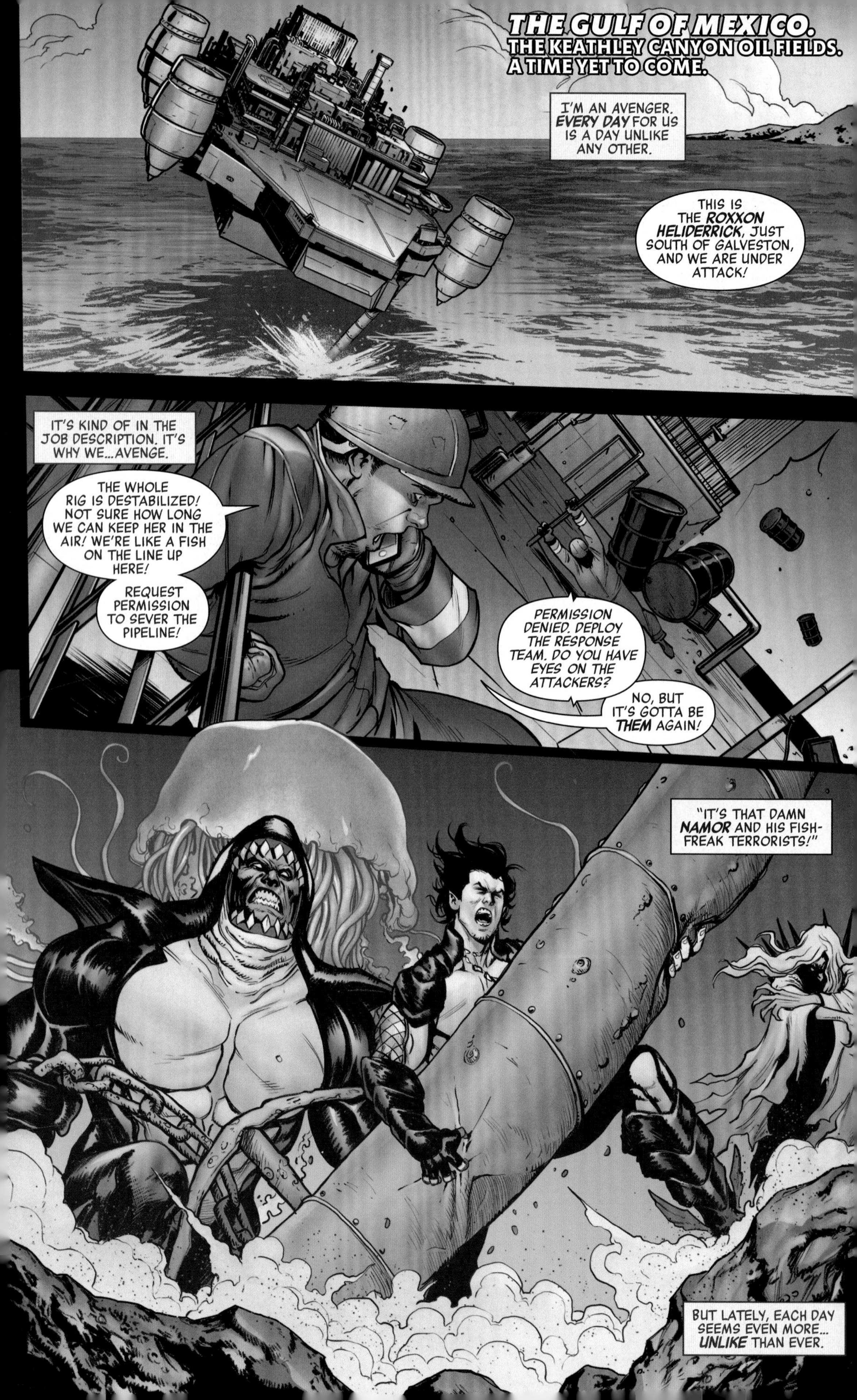
THE GULF OF MEXICO.
THE KEATHLEY CANYON OIL FIELDS.
A TIME YET TO COME.
I'M AN AVENGER. EVERY DAY FOR US IS A DAY UNLIKE ANY OTHER.
THIS IS THE ROXXON HELIDERRICK, JUST SOUTH OF GALVESTON, AND WE ARE UNDER ATTACK!
IT'S KIND OF IN THE JOB DESCRIPTION. IT'S WHY WE...AVENGE.
THE WHOLE RIG IS DESTABILIZED! NOT SURE HOW LONG WE CAN KEEP HER IN THE AIR! WE'RE LIKE A FISH ON THE LINE UP HERE!
REQUEST PERMISSION TO SEVER THE PIPELINE!
PERMISSION DENIED. DEPLOY THE RESPONSE TEAM. DO YOU HAVE EYES ON THE ATTACKERS?
NO, BUT IT'S GOTTA BE THEM AGAIN!
"IT'S THAT DAMN NAMOR AND HIS FISH-FREAK TERRORISTS!"
BUT LATELY, EACH DAY SEEMS EVEN MORE... UNLIKE THAN EVER.

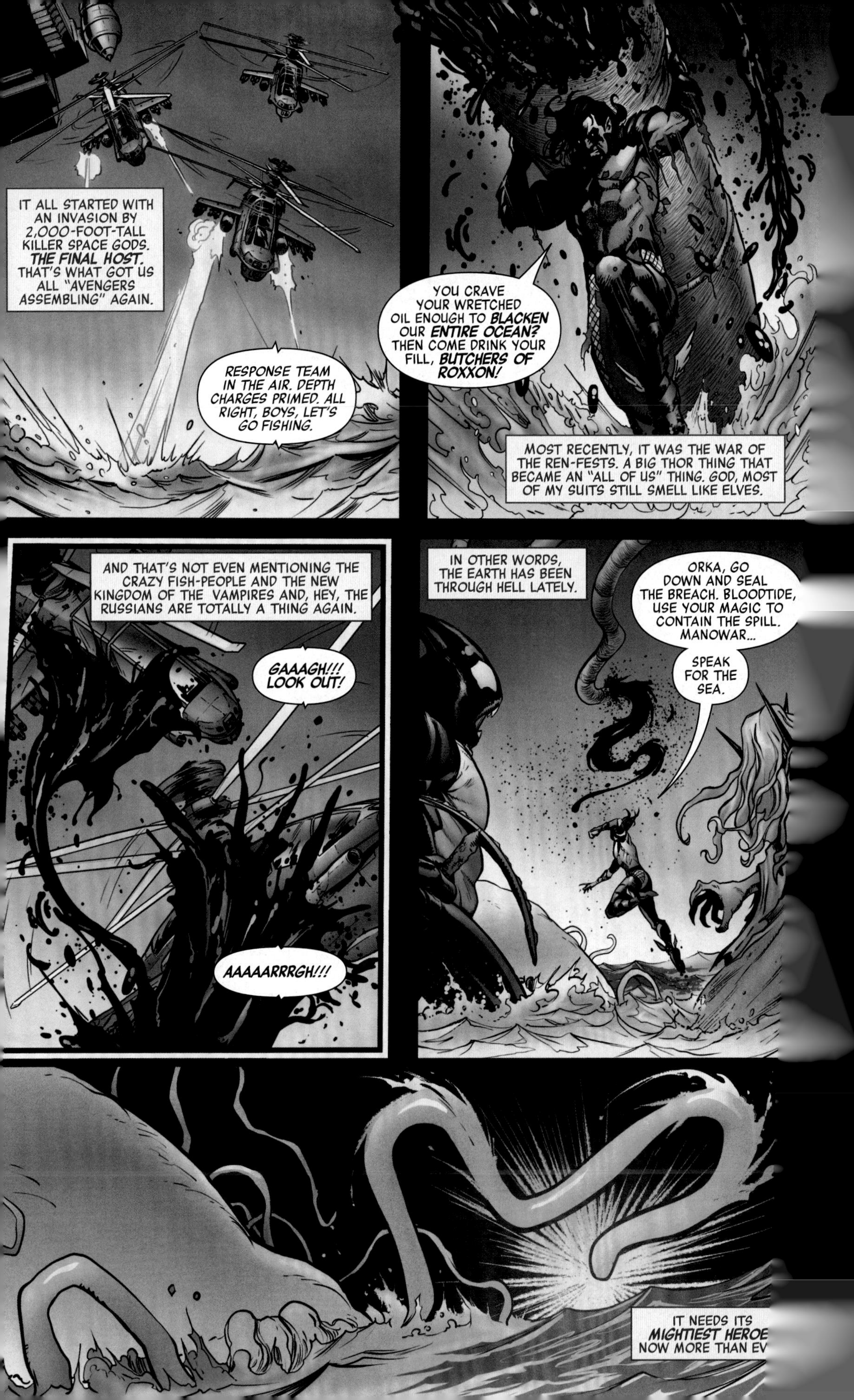
IT ALL STARTED WITH AN INVASION BY 2,000-FOOT-TALL KILLER SPACE GODS. THE FINAL HOST. THAT'S WHAT GOT US ALL "AVENGERS ASSEMBLING" AGAIN.
RESPONSE TEAM IN THE AIR. DEPTH CHARGES PRIMED. ALL RIGHT, BOYS, LET'S GO FISHING.
YOU CRAVE YOUR WRETCHED OIL ENOUGH TO BLACKEN OUR ENTIRE OCEAN? THEN COME DRINK YOUR FILL, BUTCHERS OF ROXXON!
MOST RECENTLY, IT WAS THE WAR OF THE REN-FESTS. A BIG THOR THING THAT BECAME AN "ALL OF US" THING. GOD, MOST OF MY SUITS STILL SMELL LIKE ELVES.
AND THAT'S NOT EVEN MENTIONING THE CRAZY FISH-PEOPLE AND THE NEW KINGDOM OF THE VAMPIRES AND, HEY, THE RUSSIANS ARE TOTALLY A THING AGAIN.
GAAAGH!!! LOOK OUT!
AAAAARRRGH!!!
IN OTHER WORDS, THE EARTH HAS BEEN THROUGH HELL LATELY.
ORKA, GO DOWN AND SEAL THE BREACH. BLOODTIDE, USE YOUR MAGIC TO CONTAIN THE SPILL. MANOWAR...
SPEAK FOR THE SEA.
IT NEEDS ITS MIGHTIEST HEROE
NOW MORE THAN EV

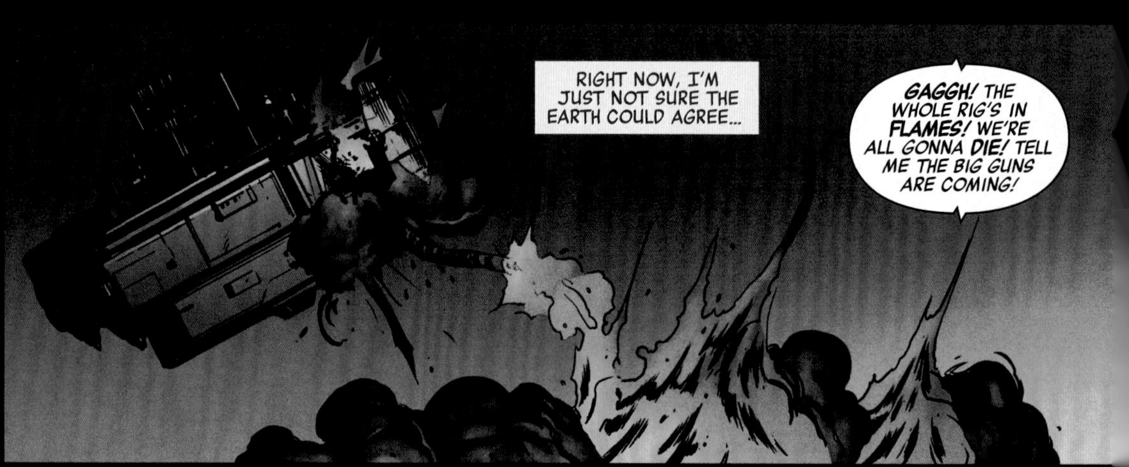
RIGHT NOW, I'M JUST NOT SURE THE EARTH COULD AGREE...
GAGGH! THE WHOLE RIG'S IN FLAMES! WE'RE ALL GONNA DIE! TELL ME THE BIG GUNS ARE COMING!

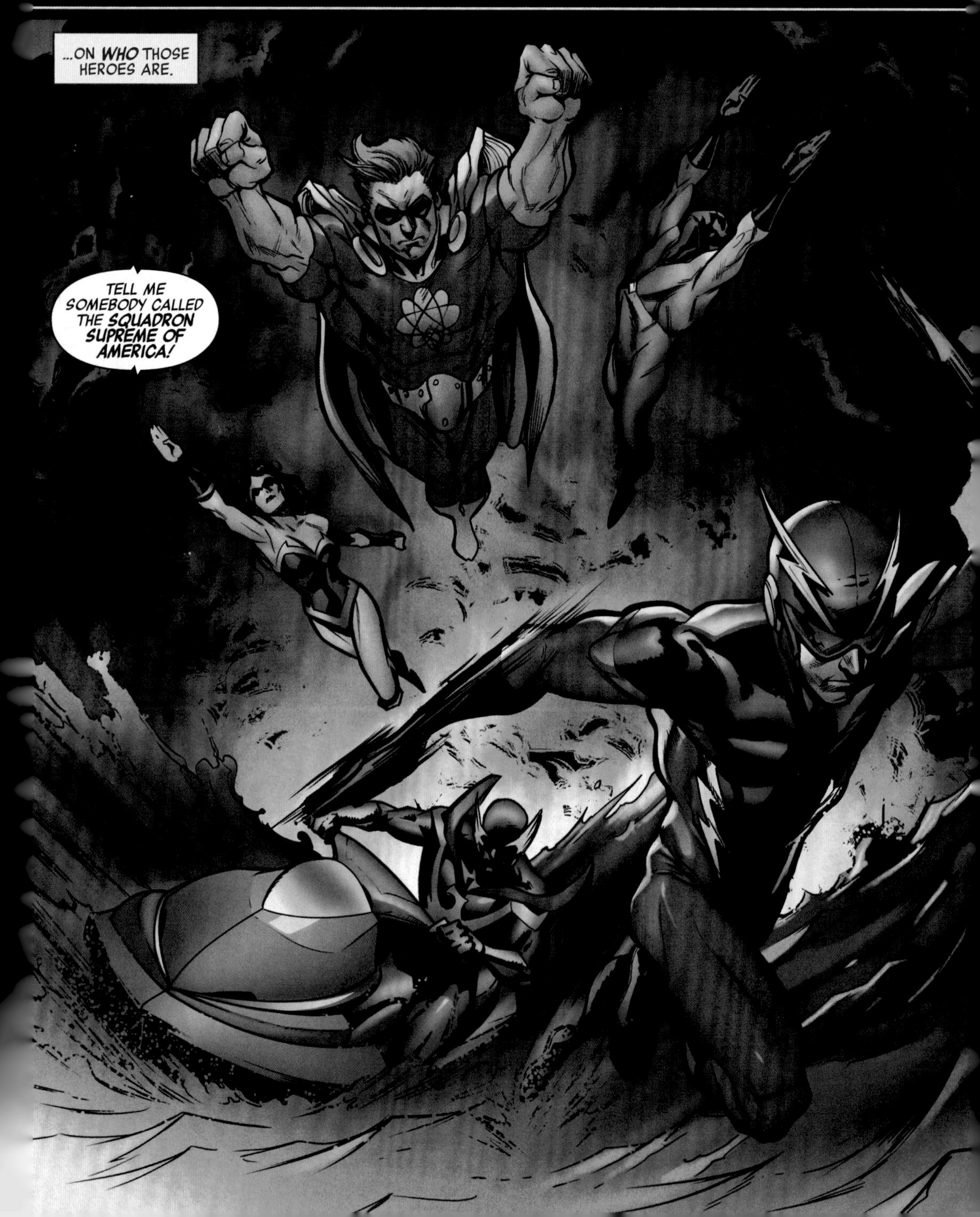
...ON WHO THOSE HEROES ARE.
TELL ME SOMEBODY CALLED THE SQUADRON SUPREME OF AMERICA!

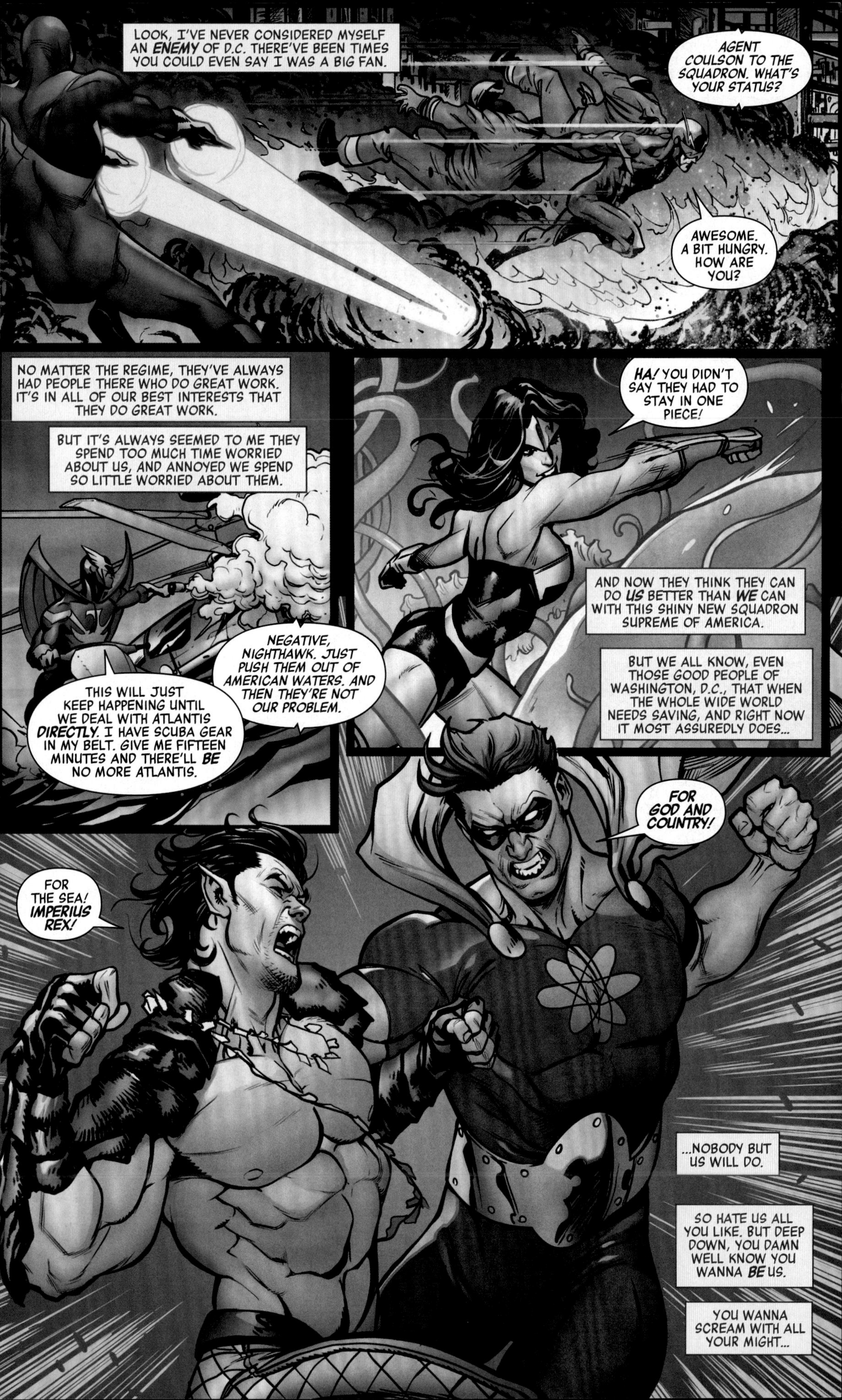
LOOK, I'VE NEVER CONSIDERED MYSELF AN ENEMY OF D.C. THERE'VE BEEN TIMES YOU COULD EVEN SAY I WAS A BIG FAN.
AGENT COULSON TO THE SQUADRON. WHAT'S YOUR STATUS?
AWESOME. A BIT HUNGRY. HOW ARE YOU?
NO MATTER THE REGIME, THEY'VE ALWAYS HAD PEOPLE THERE WHO DO GREAT WORK. IT'S IN ALL OF OUR BEST INTERESTS THAT THEY DO GREAT WORK.
BUT IT'S ALWAYS SEEMED TO ME THEY SPEND TOO MUCH TIME WORRIED ABOUT US, AND ANNOYED WE SPEND SO LITTLE WORRIED ABOUT THEM.
THIS WILL JUST KEEP HAPPENING UNTIL WE DEAL WITH ATLANTIS DIRECTLY. I HAVE SCUBA GEAR IN MY BELT. GIVE ME FIFTEEN MINUTES AND THERE'LL BE NO MORE ATLANTIS.
NEGATIVE, NIGHTHAWK. JUST PUSH THEM OUT OF AMERICAN WATERS. AND THEN THEY'RE NOT OUR PROBLEM.
HA! YOU DIDN'T SAY THEY HAD TO STAY IN ONE PIECE!
AND NOW THEY THINK THEY CAN DO US BETTER THAN WE CAN WITH THIS SHINY NEW SQUADRON SUPREME OF AMERICA.
BUT WE ALL KNOW, EVEN THOSE GOOD PEOPLE OF WASHINGTON, D.C., THAT WHEN THE WHOLE WIDE WORLD NEEDS SAVING, AND RIGHT NOW IT MOST ASSUREDLY DOES...
FOR GOD AND COUNTRY!
FOR THE SEA! IMPERIUS REX!
...NOBODY BUT US WILL DO.
SO HATE US ALL YOU LIKE. BUT DEEP DOWN, YOU DAMN WELL KNOW YOU WANNA BE US.
YOU WANNA SCREAM WITH ALL YOUR MIGHT...

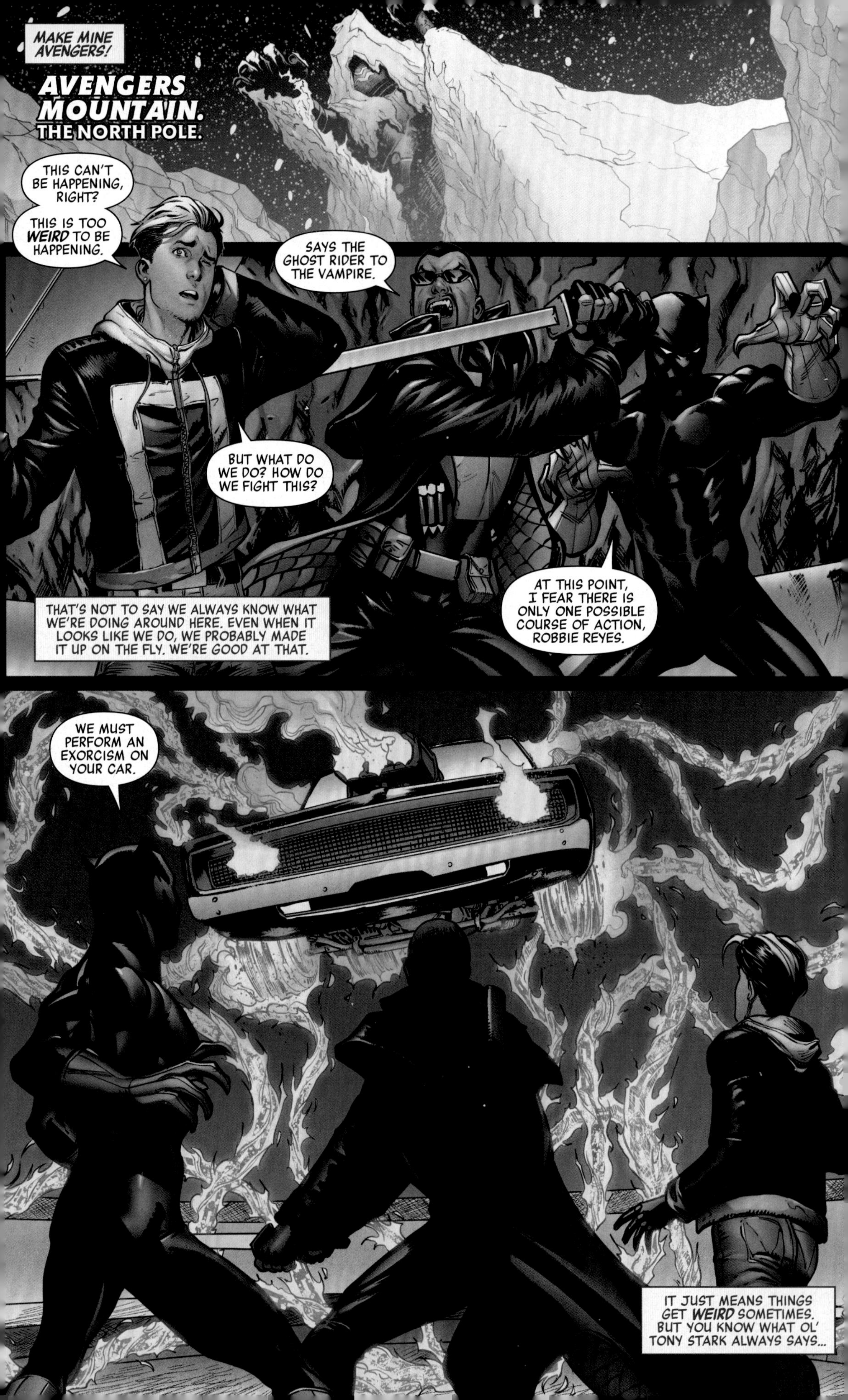
MAKE MINE AVENGERS!
AVENGERS MOUNTAIN. THE NORTH POLE.
THIS CAN'T BE HAPPENING, RIGHT?
THIS IS TOO WEIRD TO BE HAPPENING.
SAYS THE GHOST RIDER TO THE VAMPIRE.
BUT WHAT DO WE DO? HOW DO WE FIGHT THIS?
THAT'S NOT TO SAY WE ALWAYS KNOW WHAT WE'RE DOING AROUND HERE. EVEN WHEN IT LOOKS LIKE WE DO, WE PROBABLY MADE IT UP ON THE FLY. WE'RE GOOD AT THAT.
AT THIS POINT, I FEAR THERE IS ONLY ONE POSSIBLE COURSE OF ACTION, ROBBIE REYES.
WE MUST PERFORM AN EXORCISM ON YOUR CAR.
IT JUST MEANS THINGS GET WEIRD SOMETIMES. BUT YOU KNOW WHAT OL' TONY STARK ALWAYS SAYS...

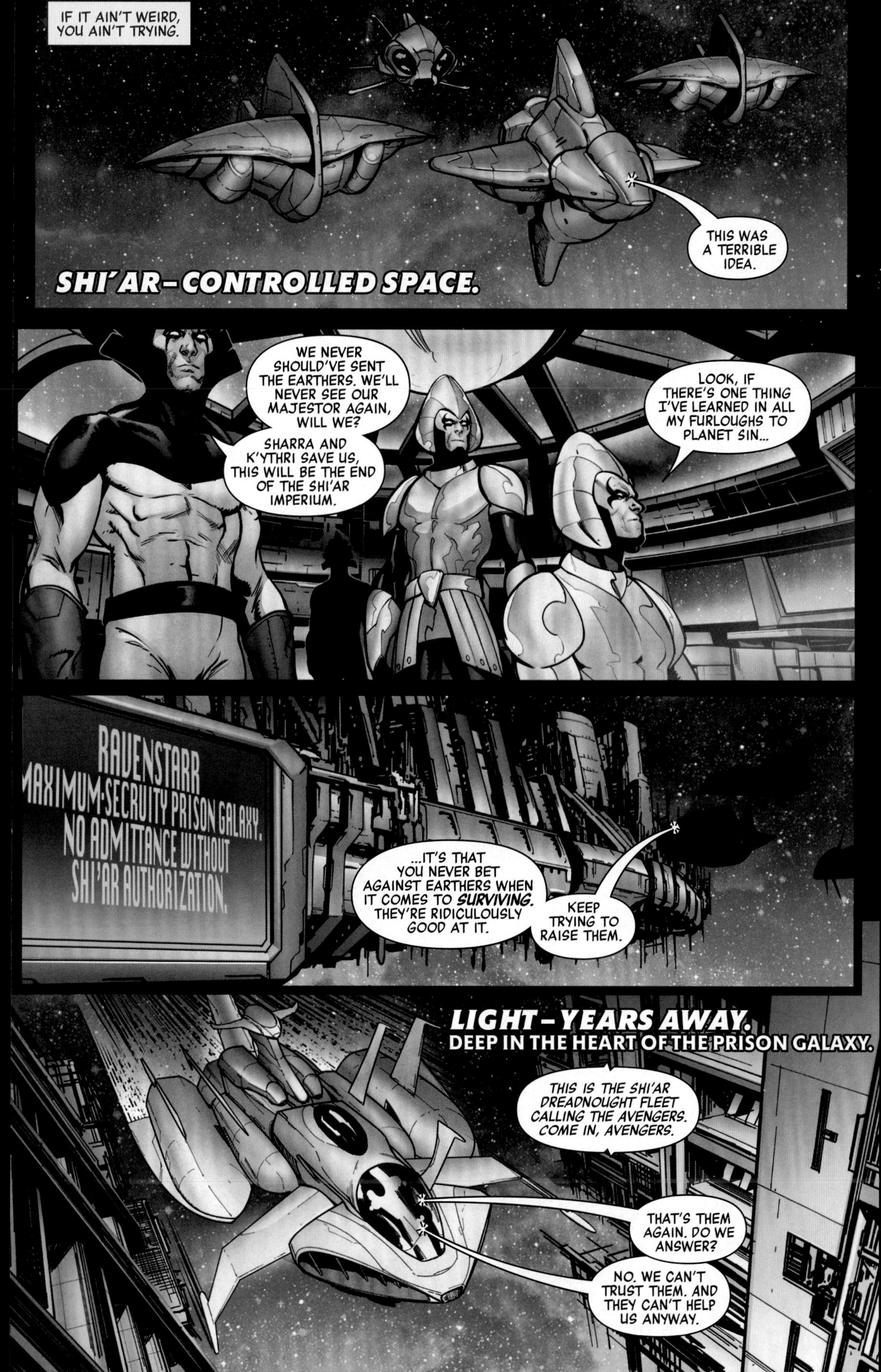
IF IT AIN'T WEIRD, YOU AIN'T TRYING.
THIS WAS A TERRIBLE IDEA.
SHI'AR–CONTROLLED SPACE.
WE NEVER SHOULD'VE SENT THE EARTHERS. WE'LL NEVER SEE OUR MAJESTOR AGAIN, WILL WE?
SHARRA AND K'YTHRI SAVE US, THIS WILL BE THE END OF THE SHI'AR IMPERIUM.
LOOK, IF THERE'S ONE THING I'VE LEARNED IN ALL MY FURLOUGHS TO PLANET SIN...
RAVENSTARR MAXIMUM-SECURITY PRISON GALAXY. NO ADMITTANCE WITHOUT SHI'AR AUTHORIZATION.
...IT'S THAT YOU NEVER BET AGAINST EARTHERS WHEN IT COMES TO SURVIVING. THEY'RE RIDICULOUSLY GOOD AT IT.
KEEP TRYING TO RAISE THEM.
LIGHT–YEARS AWAY.
DEEP IN THE HEART OF THE PRISON GALAXY.
THIS IS THE SHI'AR DREADNOUGHT FLEET CALLING THE AVENGERS. COME IN, AVENGERS.
THAT'S THEM AGAIN. DO WE ANSWER?
NO. WE CAN'T TRUST THEM. AND THEY CAN'T HELP US ANYWAY.

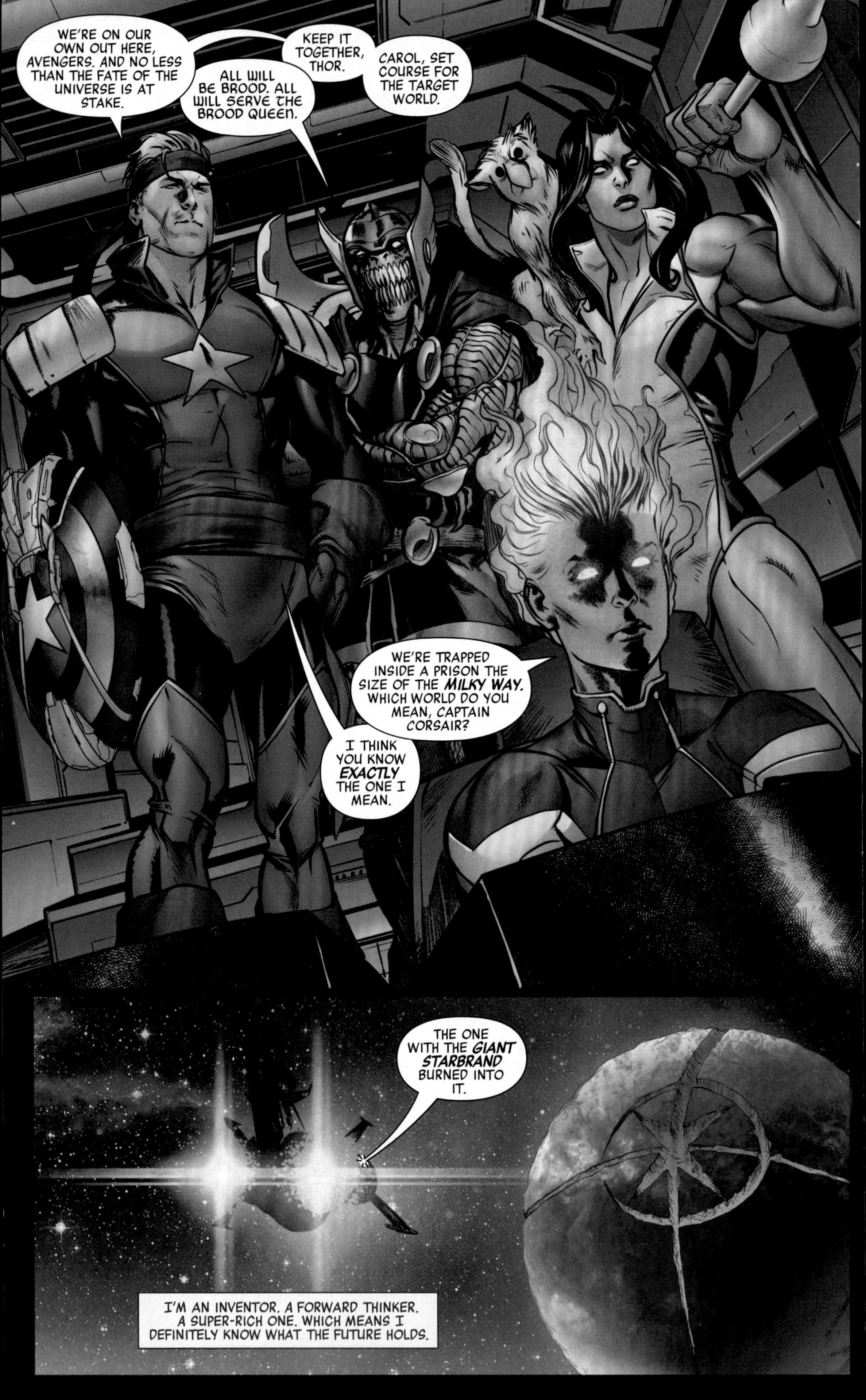
WE'RE ON OUR OWN OUT HERE, AVENGERS. AND NO LESS THAN THE FATE OF THE UNIVERSE IS AT STAKE.
KEEP IT TOGETHER, THOR.
ALL WILL BE BROOD. ALL WILL SERVE THE BROOD QUEEN.
CAROL, SET COURSE FOR THE TARGET WORLD.
WE'RE TRAPPED INSIDE A PRISON THE SIZE OF THE MILKY WAY. WHICH WORLD DO YOU MEAN, CAPTAIN CORSAIR?
I THINK YOU KNOW EXACTLY THE ONE I MEAN.
THE ONE WITH THE GIANT STARBRAND BURNED INTO IT.
I'M AN INVENTOR. A FORWARD THINKER. A SUPER-RICH ONE. WHICH MEANS I DEFINITELY KNOW WHAT THE FUTURE HOLDS.

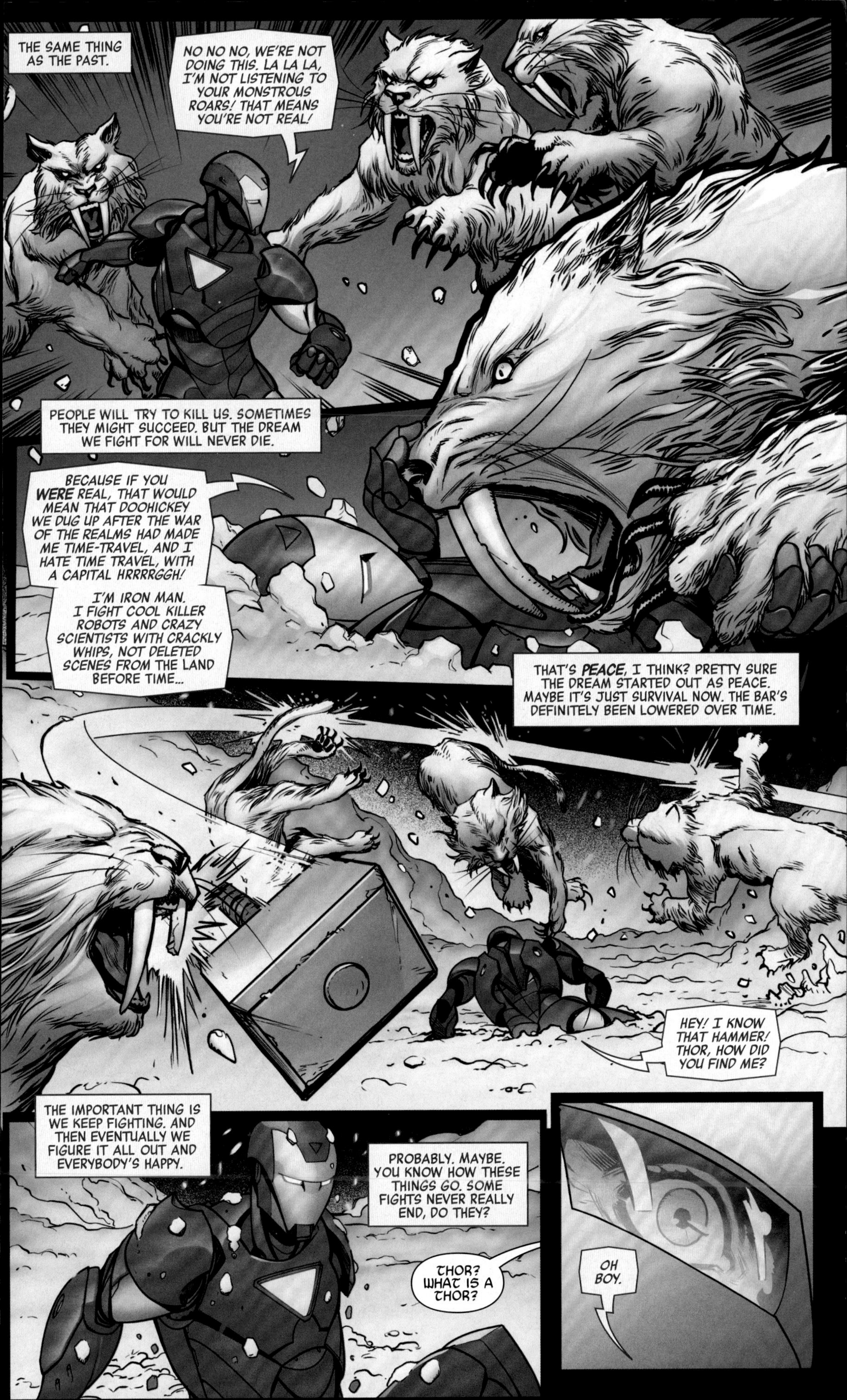

THE SAME THING AS THE PAST.
NO NO NO, WE'RE NOT DOING THIS. LA LA LA, I'M NOT LISTENING TO YOUR MONSTROUS ROARS! THAT MEANS YOU'RE NOT REAL!
PEOPLE WILL TRY TO KILL US. SOMETIMES THEY MIGHT SUCCEED. BUT THE DREAM WE FIGHT FOR WILL NEVER DIE.
BECAUSE IF YOU WERE REAL, THAT WOULD MEAN THAT DOOHICKEY WE DUG UP AFTER THE WAR OF THE REALMS HAD MADE ME TIME-TRAVEL, AND I HATE TIME TRAVEL, WITH A CAPITAL HRRRRGGH!
I'M IRON MAN. I FIGHT COOL KILLER ROBOTS AND CRAZY SCIENTISTS WITH CRACKLY WHIPS, NOT DELETED SCENES FROM THE LAND BEFORE TIME...
THAT'S PEACE, I THINK? PRETTY SURE THE DREAM STARTED OUT AS PEACE. MAYBE IT'S JUST SURVIVAL NOW. THE BAR'S DEFINITELY BEEN LOWERED OVER TIME.
HEY! I KNOW THAT HAMMER! THOR, HOW DID YOU FIND ME?
THE IMPORTANT THING IS WE KEEP FIGHTING. AND THEN EVENTUALLY WE FIGURE IT ALL OUT AND EVERYBODY'S HAPPY.
PROBABLY. MAYBE. YOU KNOW HOW THESE THINGS GO. SOME FIGHTS NEVER REALLY END, DO THEY?
THOR? WHAT IS A THOR?
OH BOY.

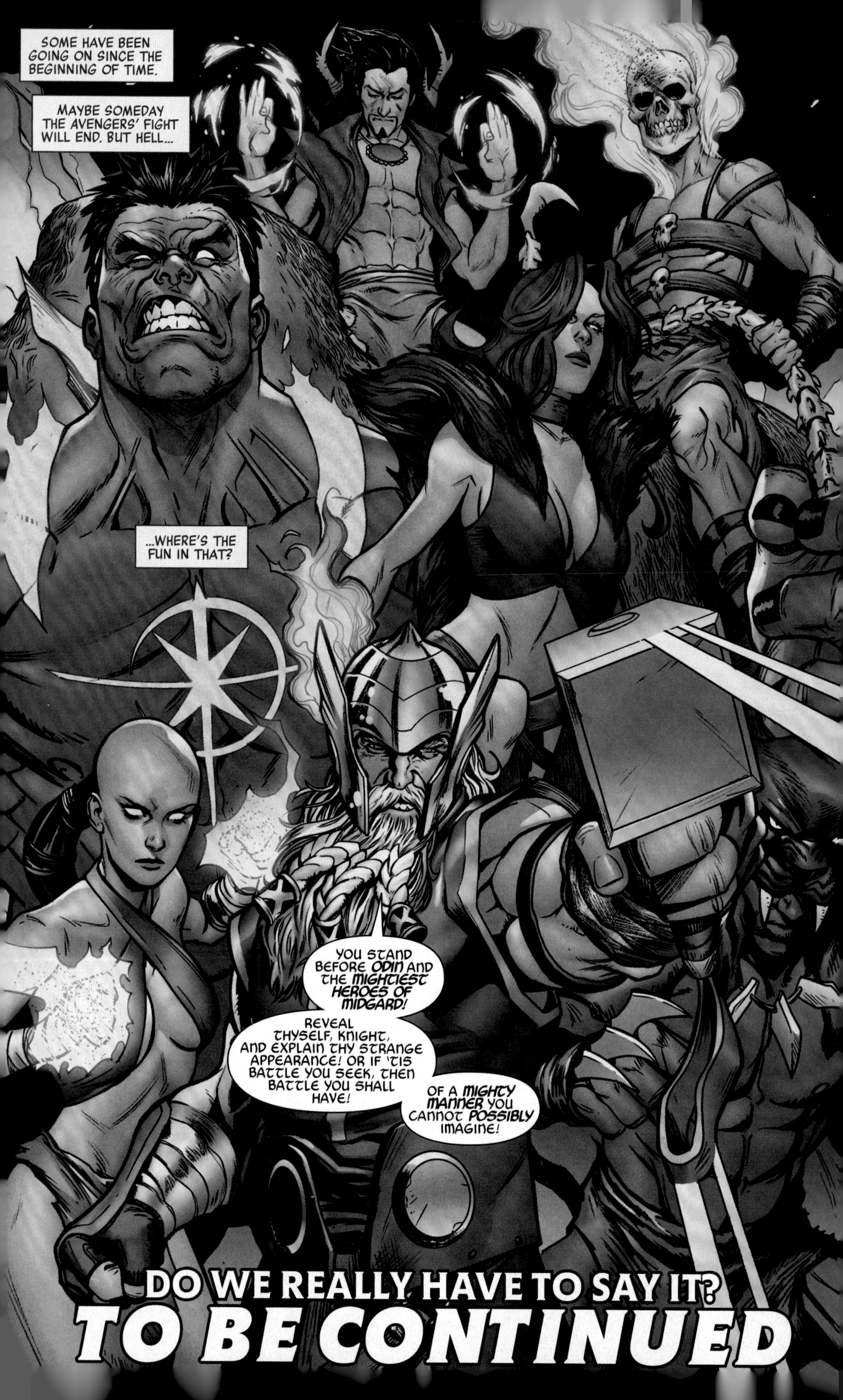
SOME HAVE BEEN GOING ON SINCE THE BEGINNING OF TIME.
MAYBE SOMEDAY THE AVENGERS' FIGHT WILL END. BUT HELL...
...WHERE'S THE FUN IN THAT?
YOU STAND BEFORE ODIN AND THE MIGHTIEST HEROES OF MIDGARD!
REVEAL THYSELF, KNIGHT, AND EXPLAIN THY STRANGE APPEARANCE! OR IF 'TIS BATTLE YOU SEEK, THEN BATTLE YOU SHALL HAVE!
OF A MIGHTY MANNER YOU CANNOT POSSIBLY IMAGINE!
DO WE REALLY HAVE TO SAY IT?
TO BE CONTINUED

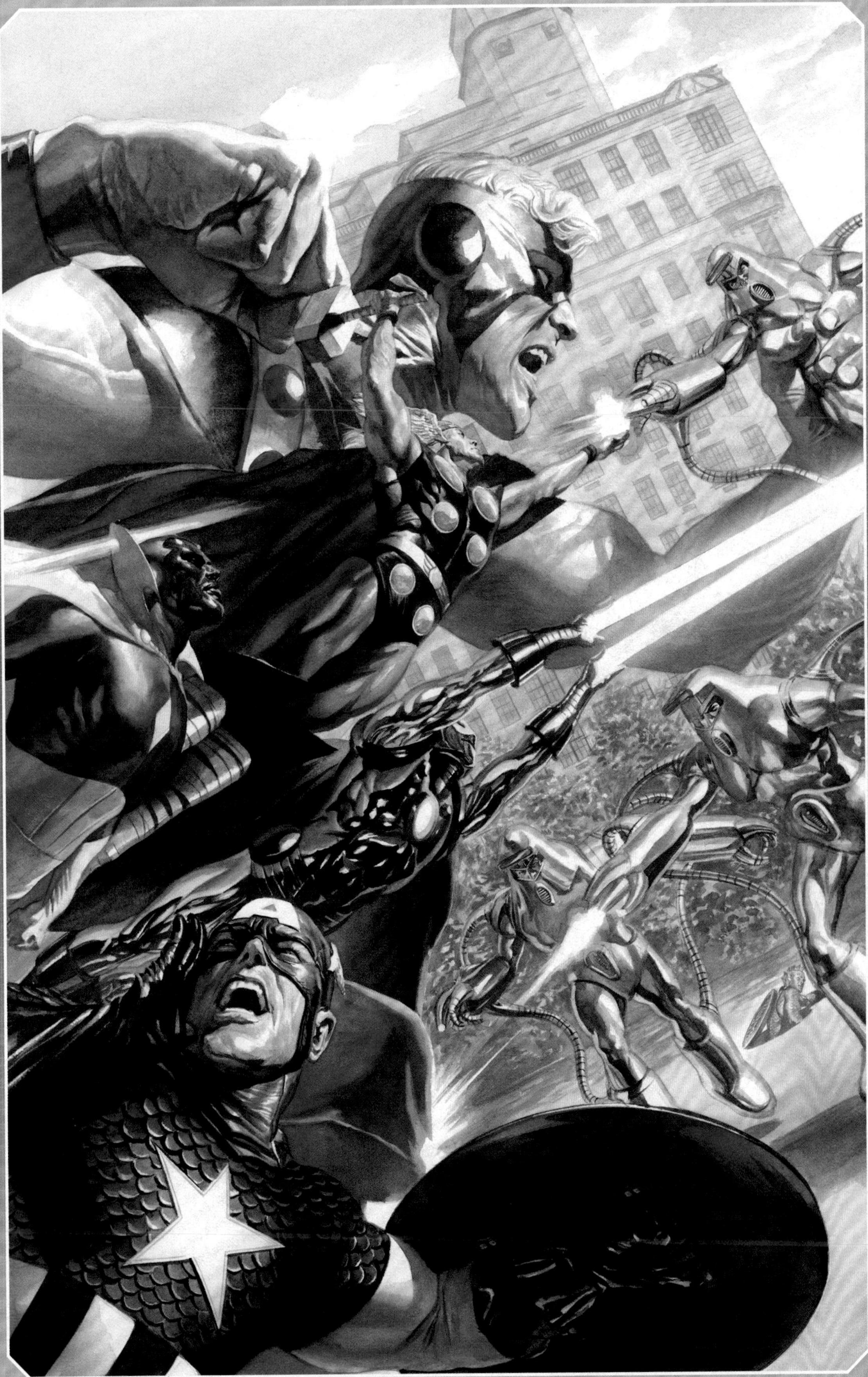

ALEX ROSS
18 MARVELS 25TH ANNIVERSARY VARIANT

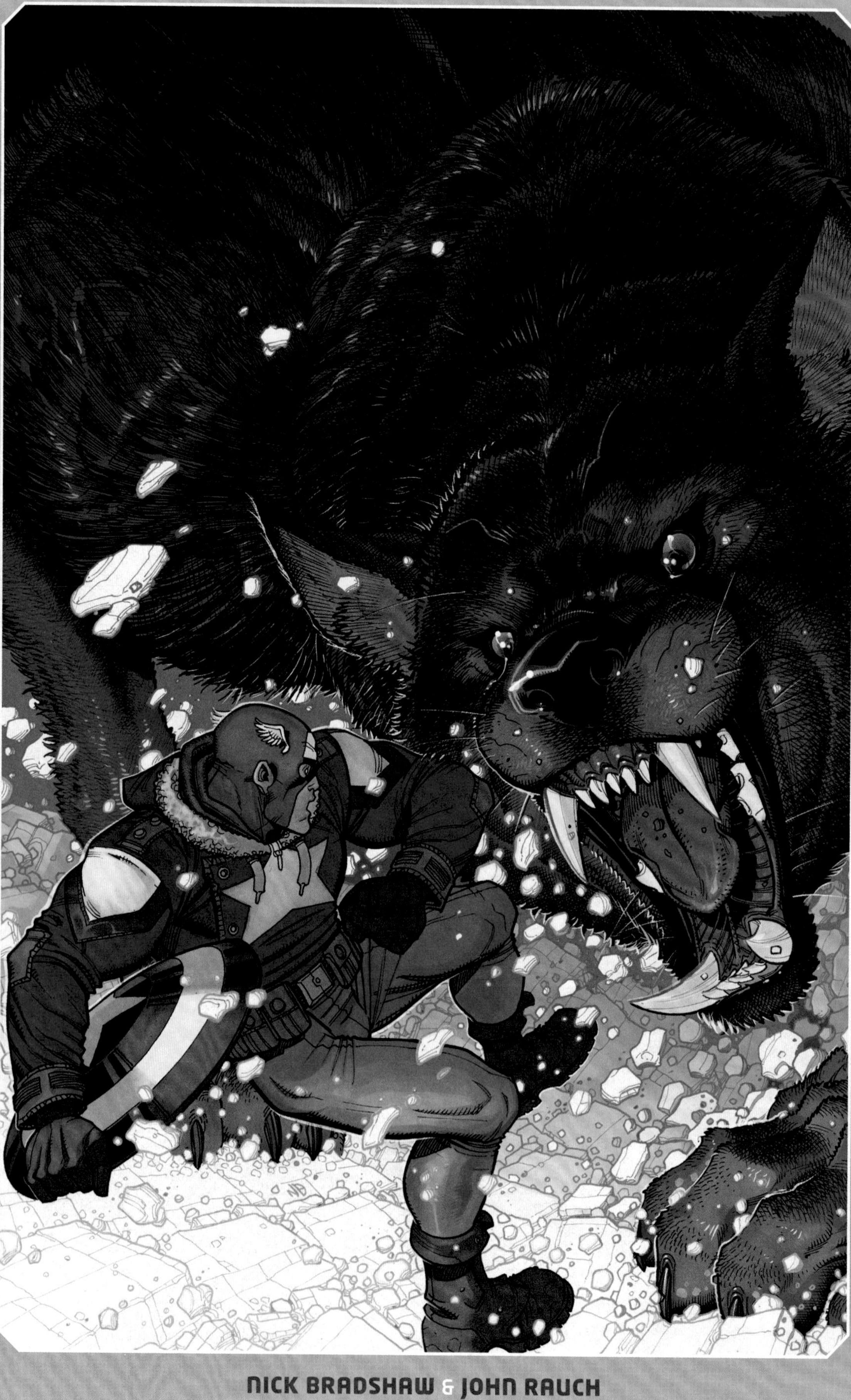

NICK BRADSHAW & JOHN RAUCH
19 VARIANT

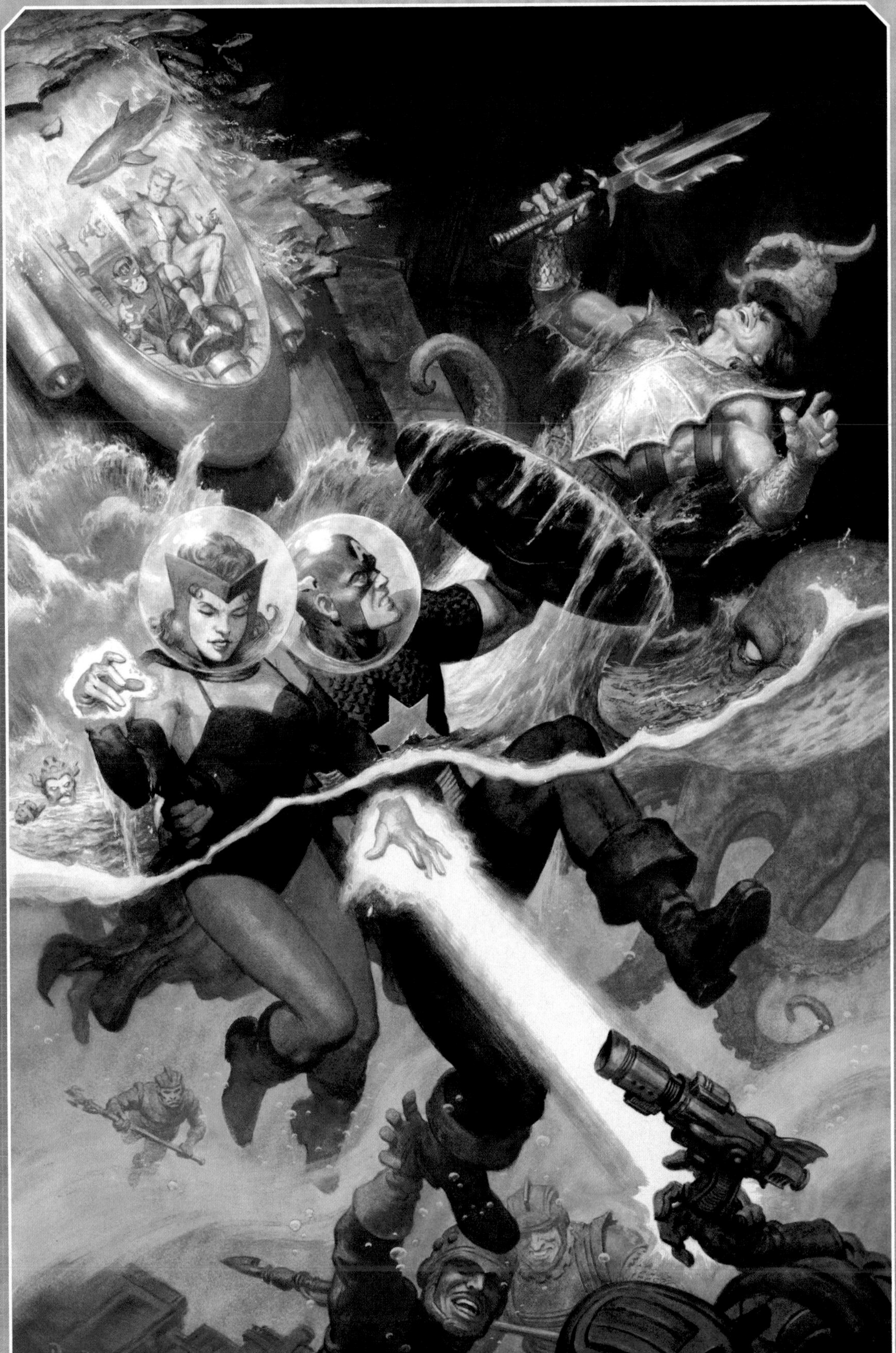
RIVERA

PAOLO RIVERA
20 VARIANT

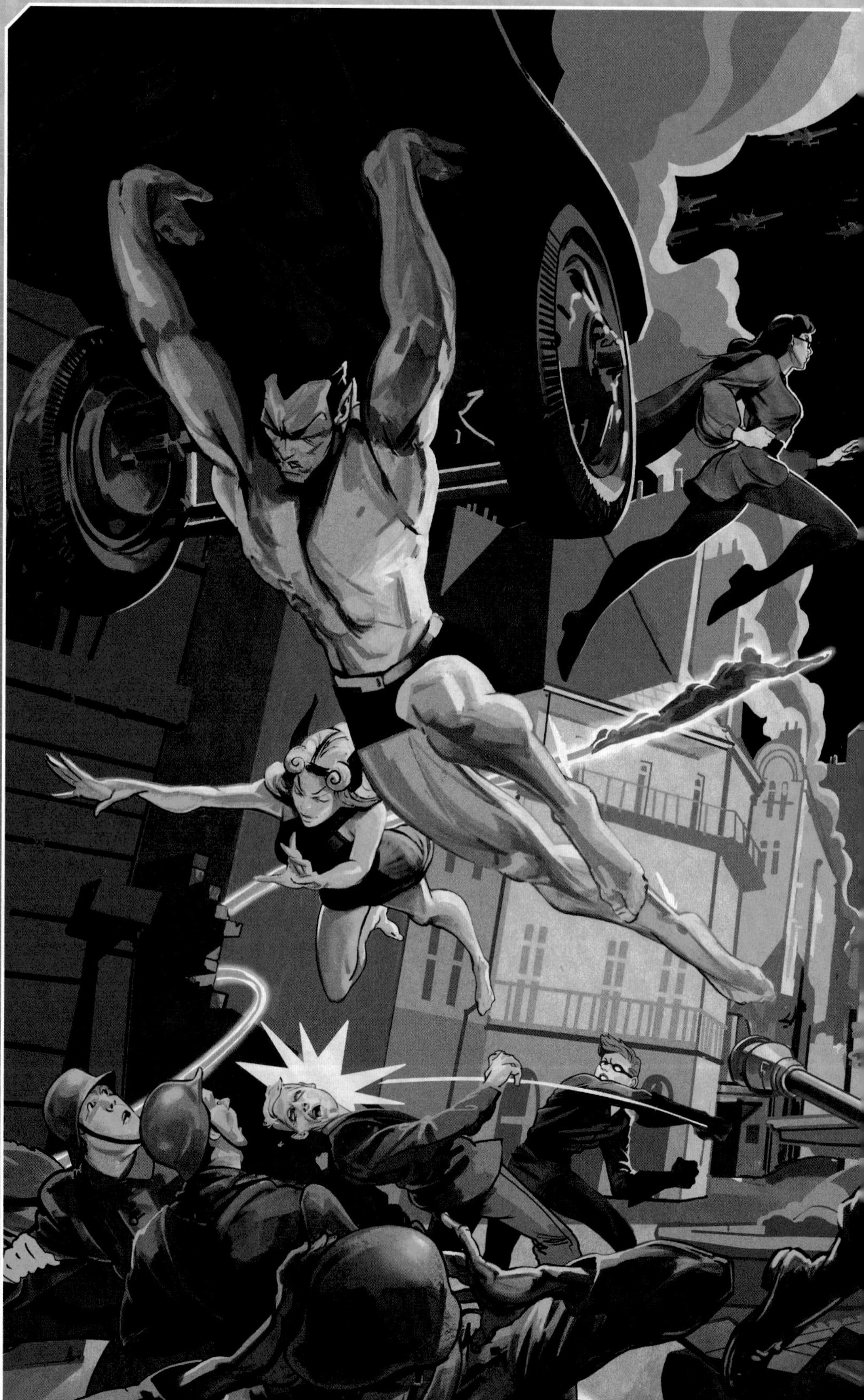

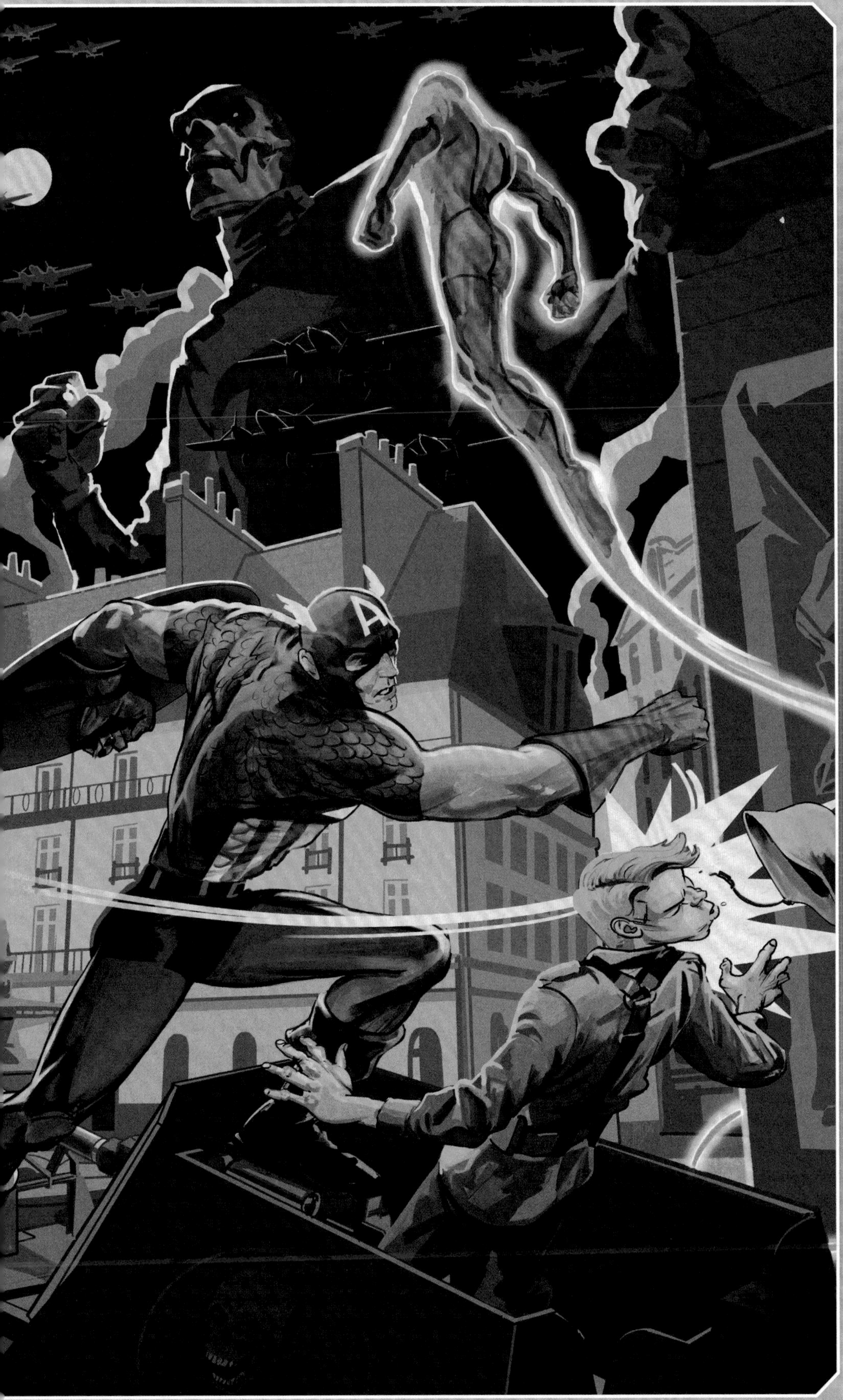

RICH KELLY
21 SDCC VARIANT

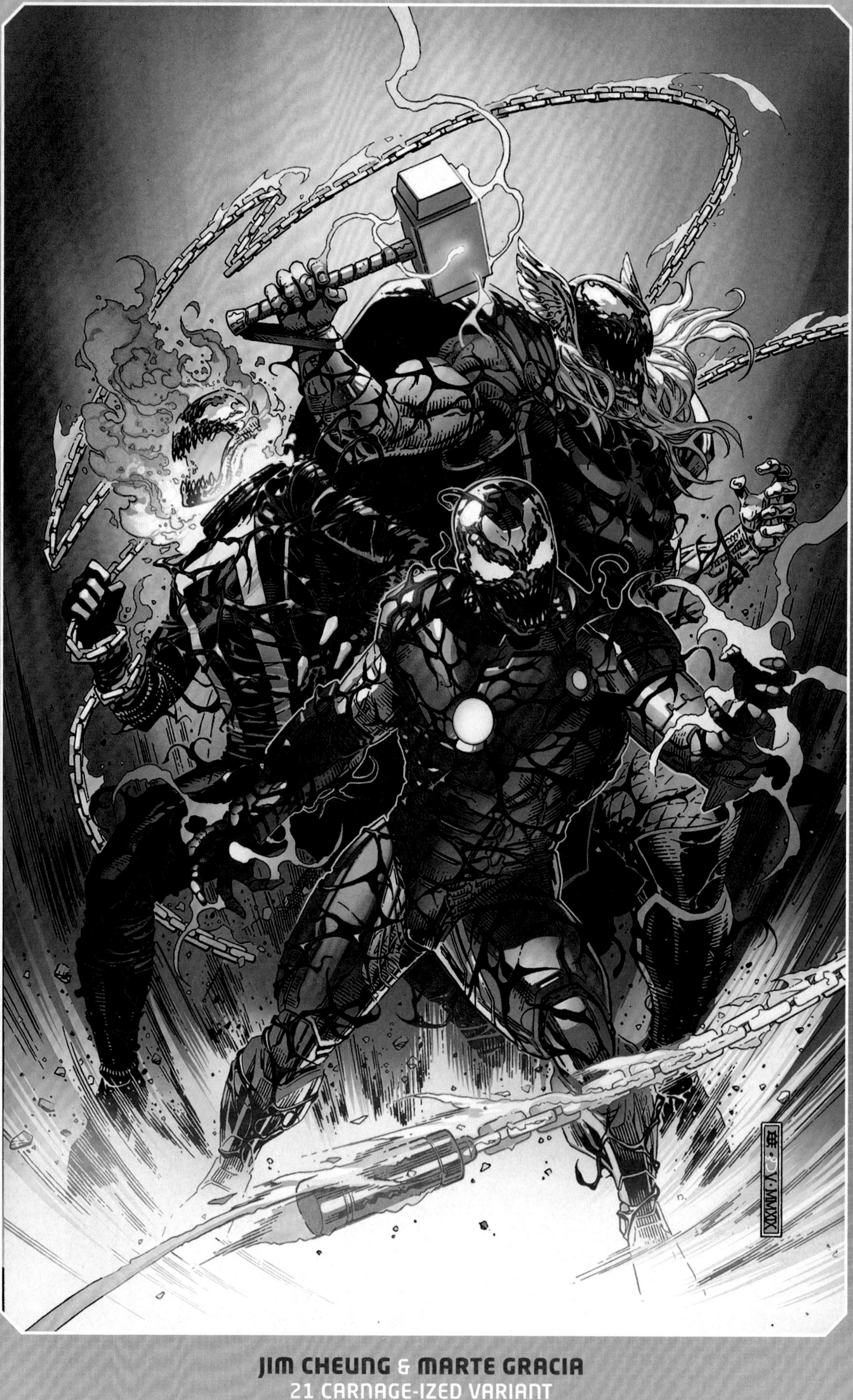

JIM CHEUNG & MARTE GRACIA
21 CARNAGE-IZED VARIANT

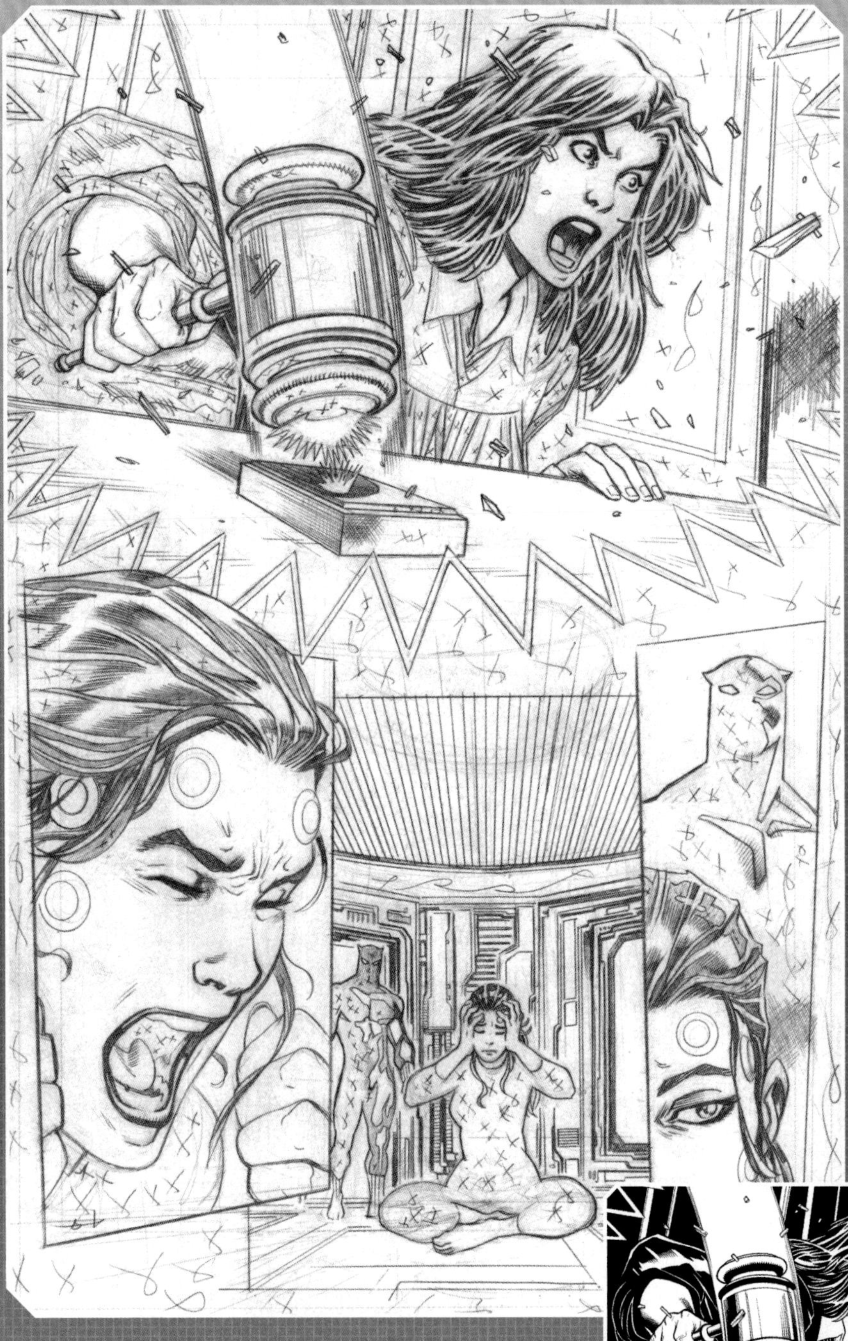

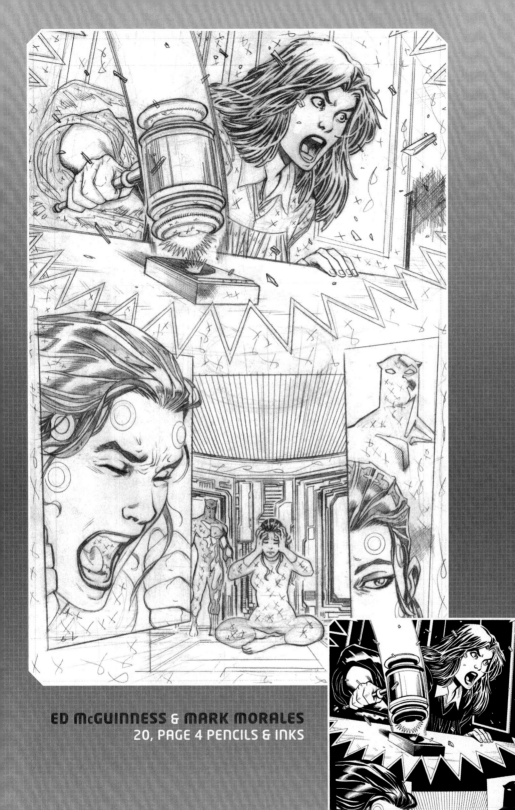

ED McGUINNESS & MARK MORALES
20, PAGE 4 PENCILS & INKS

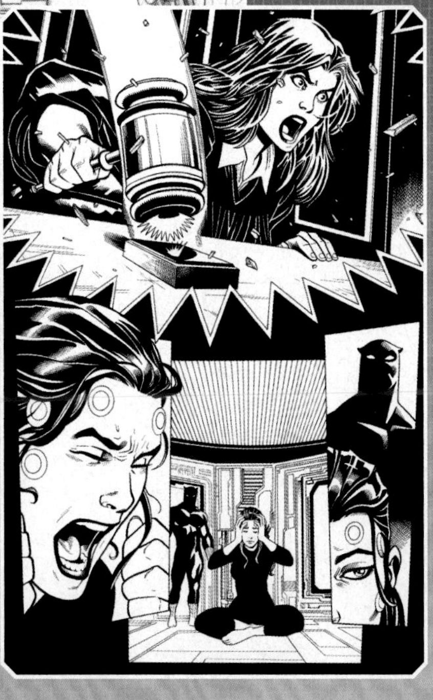

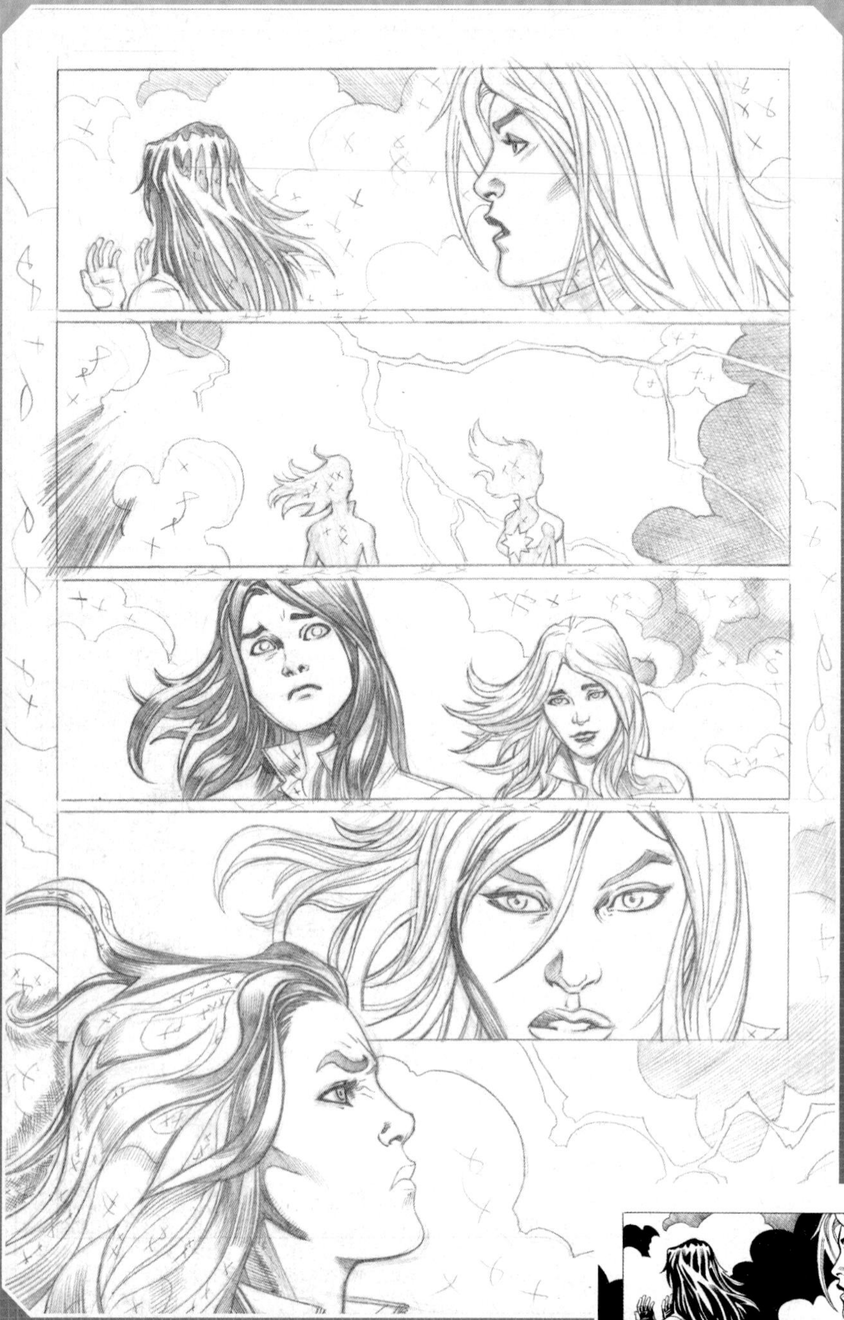

ED McGUINNESS & MARK MORALES
20, PAGE 9 PENCILS & INKS

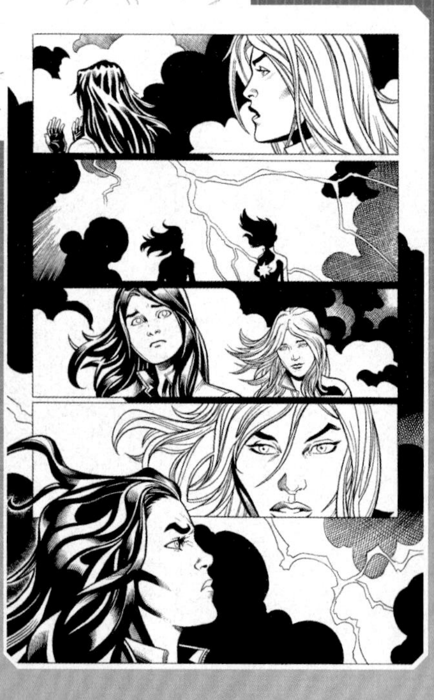

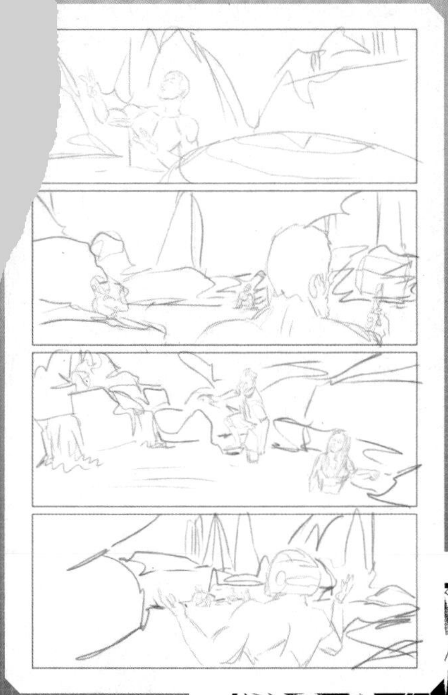

JASON MASTERS
21, PAGE 16 SKETCH & FINAL ART

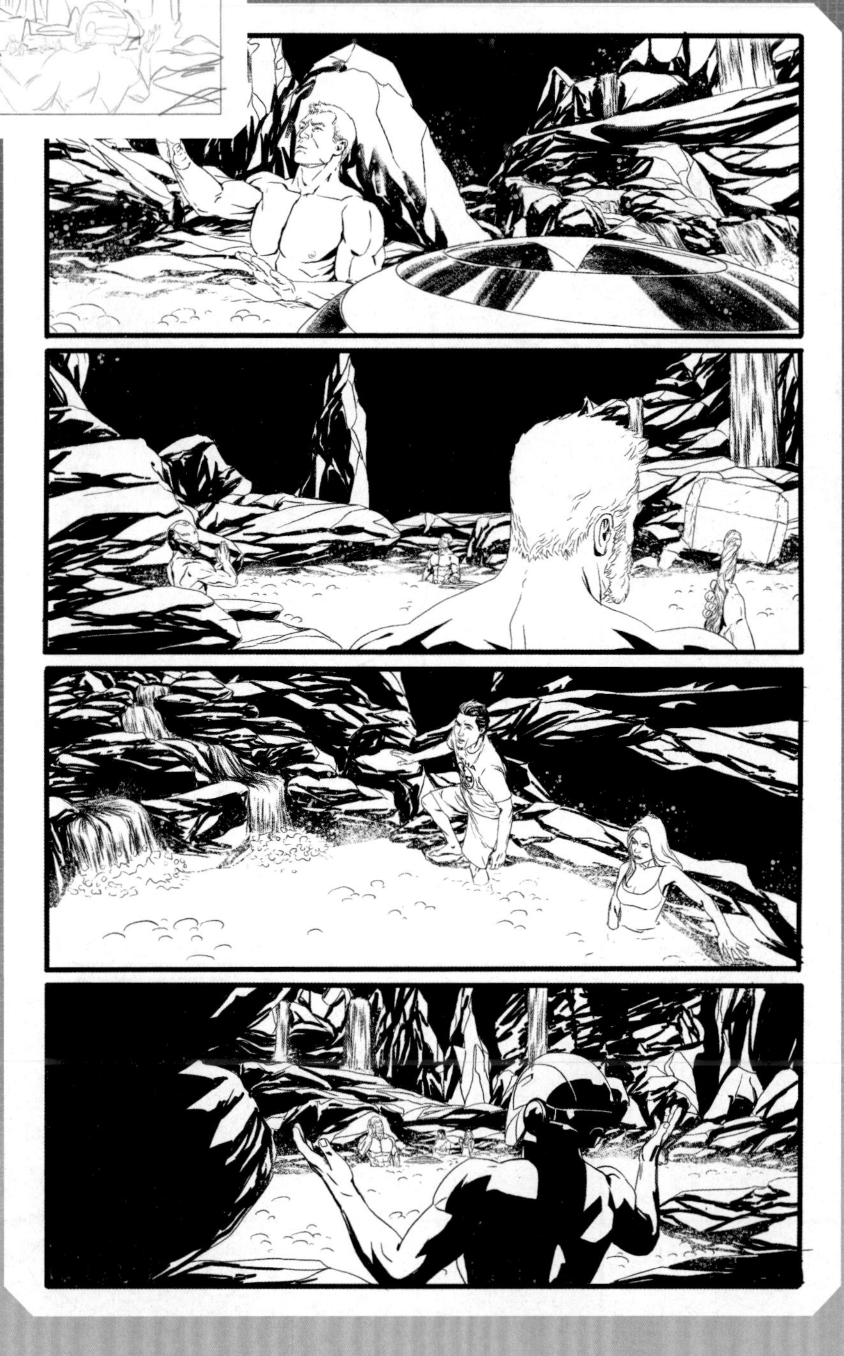

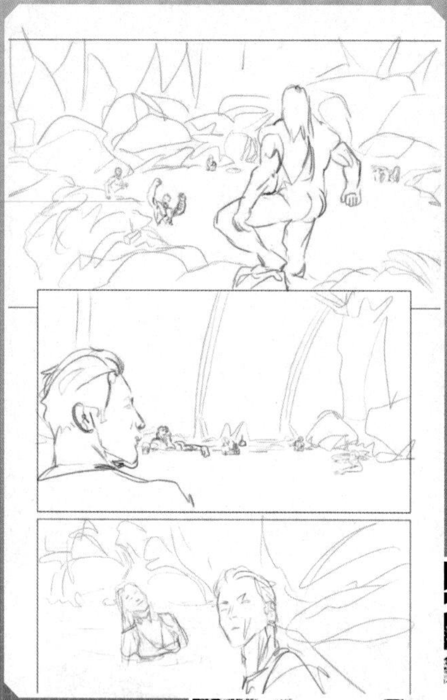

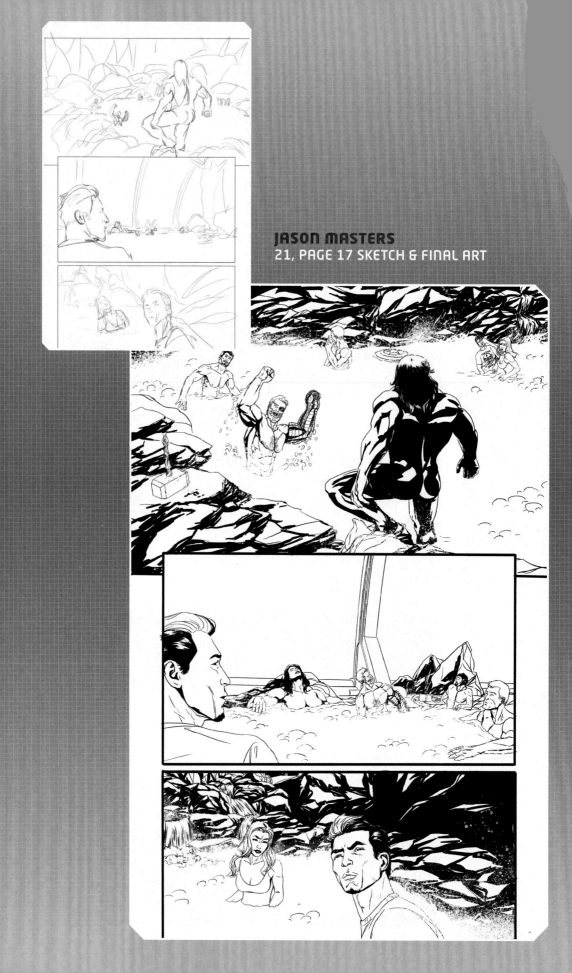

JASON MASTERS
21, PAGE 17 SKETCH & FINAL ART

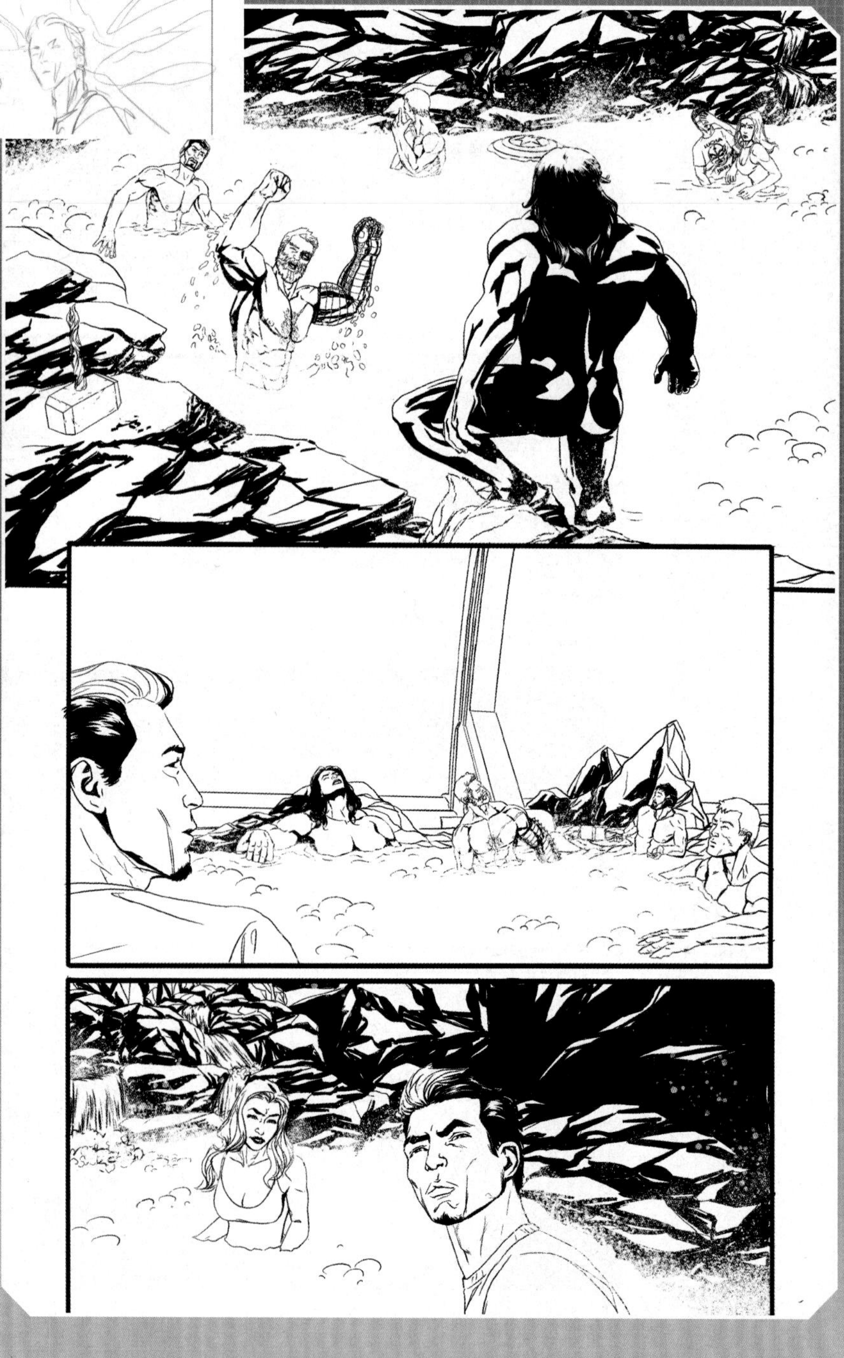

JASON MASTERS
21, PAGE 18 SKETCH & FINAL ART

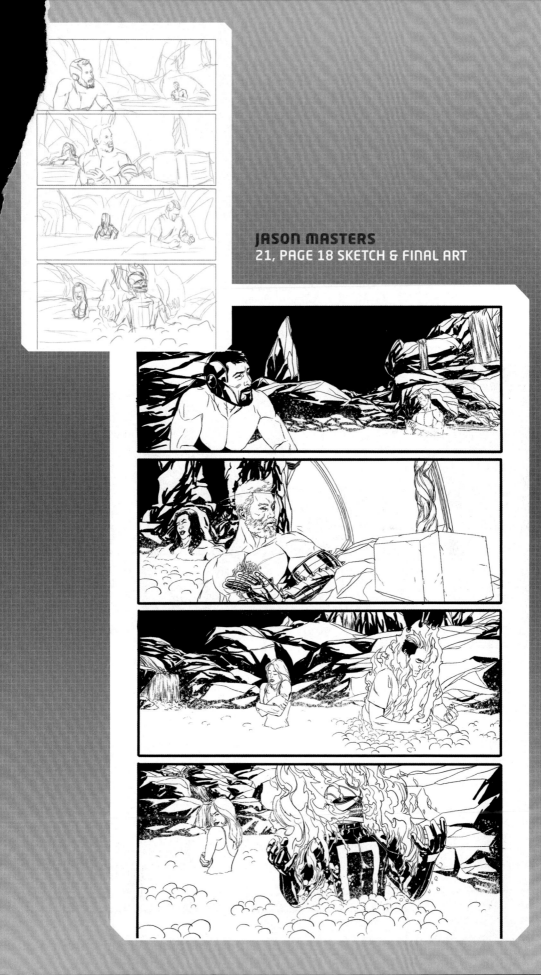

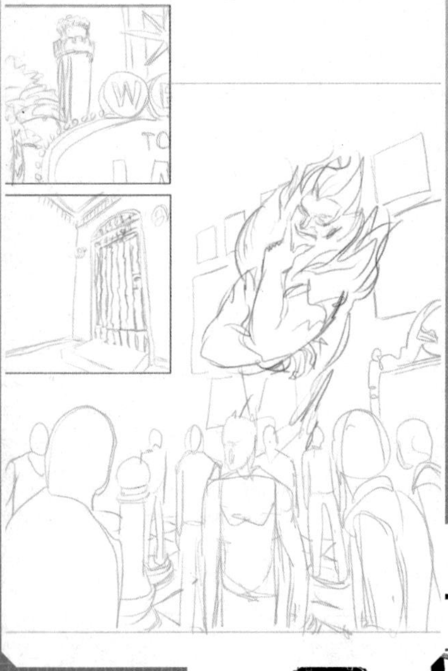

JASON MASTERS
21, PAGE 20 SKETCH & FINAL ART

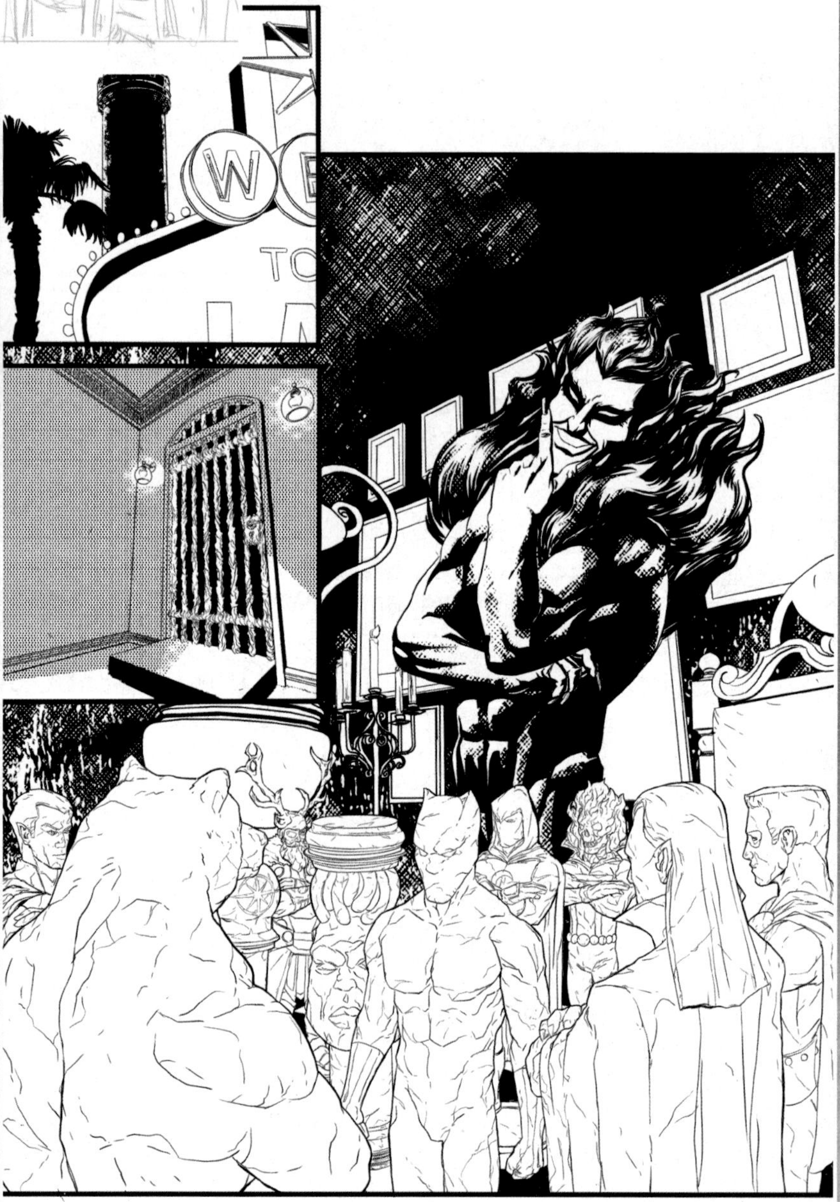